MIDLOTHIAN SPEECHES
1879

THE VICTORIAN LIBRARY

MIDLOTHIAN SPEECHES
1879

W. E. GLADSTONE

WITH AN INTRODUCTION BY
M. R. D. FOOT

LEICESTER UNIVERSITY PRESS
NEW YORK: HUMANITIES PRESS
1971

First published in 1879
Victorian Library edition published in 1971 by
Leicester University Press

Distributed in North America by
Humanities Press Inc., New York

Introduction copyright © Leicester University Press 1971

Printed in Great Britain by
Unwin Brothers Limited, Old Woking, Surrey
Introduction set in Monotype Modern Extended 7

ISBN 0 7185 5009 9

THE VICTORIAN LIBRARY

There is a growing demand for the classics of Victorian literature in many fields, in political and social history, architecture, topography, religion, education, and science. Hitherto this demand has been met, in the main, from the second-hand market. But the prices of second-hand books are rising sharply, and the supply of them is very uncertain. It is the object of this series, THE VICTORIAN LIBRARY, to make some of these classics available again at a reasonable cost. Since most of the volumes in it are reprinted photographically from the first edition, or another chosen because it has some special value, an accurate text is ensured. Each work carries a substantial introduction, written specially for this series by a well-known authority on the author or his subject, and a bibliographical note on the text.

The volumes necessarily vary in size. In planning the newly-set pages the designer, Arthur Lockwood, has maintained a consistent style for the principal features. The uniform design of binding and jacket provides for ready recognition of the various books in the series when shelved under different subject classifications.

Recommendation of titles for THE VICTORIAN LIBRARY and of scholars to contribute the introductions is made by a joint committee of the Board of the University Press and the Victorian Studies Centre of the University of Leicester.

INTRODUCTION

Most people get their idea of a nineteenth-century election from the uproarious contest at Eatanswill, in the *Pickwick Papers*. Moscow radio was still using Dickens to illustrate current British electoral practice as late as 1950, but was over a century behind the times. Even by the end of the 1870s, the way the British behaved at elections had changed a good deal, as the electorate had got larger and party organizations had grown; though there had lately been widespread treating by and for candidates. When the Liberal party suffered a sharp defeat in the general election of February 1874, Mr Gladstone wrote to his enormous brother Robertson that "We have been borne down in a torrent of gin and beer." Yet recent research has shown that the brewers' interest was by no means entirely devoted to the Conservative side and there were several other important reasons for the Liberals' defeat. They had been in power since December 1868; their great reforming measures – the disestablishing of the Irish church, the introduction of compulsory schooling for children and of the ballot for adult voters, the reorganizing of the army, of the old universities, of the trade unions – had made them enemies as well as friends. Their opponents had a new and much superior organization in the constituencies. And above all, enthusiasm had waned. People felt it was time for a change; Disraeli's hit about ministers lining the treasury bench like "a range of exhausted volcanoes" was shrewd. The Conservatives carried some 352 seats to the Liberals' 243; and there were 57 more or less independent Irish members, returned under the new protection of the ballot.

Mr Gladstone at once resigned the prime ministership, buried himself in a pamphlet war with the Roman Catholics, and, early in 1875, gave up also the Liberal leadership in the Commons. He had long "deeply desired an interval between parliament and the grave". He had never really enjoyed his profession of politics. His primary interests remained religious, and family tradition laid down that a man should spend his declining years – he was already sixty-five – in meditating quietly on his past and preparing to meet his Maker. He kept his seat in the Commons, as the junior member for Greenwich; but seldom appeared there. He spent most of his time at Hawarden Castle, his country place a few miles west of Chester, just across the Welsh border.

Thence he found himself summoned back into politics by the Balkan crisis of 1876. Popularly, he is still remembered as having led the agitation against the "Bulgarian Horrors" he denounced in a once famous pamphlet published that September. Dr Shannon, in an incisive recent study, has shown that the agitation originated elsewhere, from three men acting independently – Stead the journalist, Freeman the historian, and Canon Liddon – and that Gladstone only just joined in the tumult in time to make his great influence felt. In the short run, the Earl of Beaconsfield (as Disraeli became in 1876) had the better of the dispute about the eastern question. While the tireless Gladstone tried, time and time again, to get the Commons to condemn government policy, Beaconsfield held to his course of standing up to Russia; and of standing by Turkey, in return for a protectorate over Cyprus. London roughs broke the Gladstones' windows in Harley Street, and in the music-halls they sang

> We don't want to fight,
> But, by jingo, if we do,
> We've got the ships, we've got the men,
> We've got the money too.

Beaconsfield and Salisbury went to the Congress of Berlin in midsummer 1878, signed the treaty that was supposed to settle the eastern difficulty, and returned bringing, they said, "peace with honour".

During the following winter, and in the course of 1879, the Turks showed no alacrity in carrying out the provisions of the treaty of Berlin, while British forces became engaged in two unusually expensive small wars, one in Zululand and the other in Afghanistan. (People forget that the country was more often at war than at peace in Victoria's reign.) The harvest, which had been bad in 1878, was worse in 1879; British agriculture was hard hit, Irish agriculture was ruined. The trade depression which had been marked already in 1877 seemed to get worse still. In Parliament, the Conservative majority was powerless to enact much useful legislation, because a few of the Irish members exploited the forms of the Commons' procedure to obstruct business altogether.

Gladstone by now was firmly back in politics, for there was much he disapproved of in current government policy abroad; so much, in fact, that his indignation grew daily more hot. But in his retirement he had somewhat detached himself from his political base, the Liberal party, in which he no longer had any formal standing, though he was its most famous living member. (His formal accession to it was indeed recent. Not till 1871 had he altered the description of himself in Dod's *Parliamentary Companion* from "Liberal Conservative" to "Liberal".) Moreover, he had indicated in 1878 to the Greenwich Liberals that he would not stand there again.

Several constituencies were competing for his candidature: among them Manchester, where he had been bottom of the poll (as a Tory, run for the seat against his own wish) in 1837; the county division of south-west Lancashire, which he had carried "unmuzzled" in 1865 when Oxford University rejected him; Edinburgh city, a safe Liberal seat; and Leeds, another, which persisted in refusing to take no for an answer, and ran him anyhow in the forthcoming general election. This candidature at Leeds provided him with a safety net for his next leap on the political trapeze.

This leap was his decision to contest Midlothian, the metropolitan county seat of Scotland: the country district round

Edinburgh, which normally returned a Conservative. The sitting
member, Lord Dalkieth, was the eldest son of the Duke of
Buccleuch; Buccleuch had himself sat with Gladstone in the
forties in Peel's great Liberal Conservative cabinet. Why did
Gladstone decide to risk this contest?

He was assured that he had a good chance of winning it, from
two different but well informed sources: W. P. Adam, the chief
Liberal whip, who had had a careful canvass made; and James,
Lord Moncreiff, a friend of Gladstone's youth who was now a
Scottish judge. Adam's assurances, repeated at mid-winter
1878–9, are often quoted. Opposition chief whips have buoyant
hopes, as a rule, as distant general elections come nearer. Moncreiff's balanced judgement, that after a tough struggle Gladstone would just win, probably weighed far more with his old
friend. Certainly, a day or two after hearing from him, Gladstone
decided to let his name go forward.*

The news that Mr Gladstone was to stand for Midlothian made
an immediate sensation in January 1879; to understand why, we
must try to put ourselves back into the context of political life
ninety years and more ago. This was before the modern entertain-
ment industries had begun to grow; before photography and
broadcasting had transformed advertising from a minor into a
major aspect of the normal visual scene; before sport had replaced
politics and religion among the principal preoccupations of the
masses. All daily newspapers then published were primarily
political in content and in interest. Debates at Westminster were
reproduced almost verbatim in the press (Hansard indeed was
compiled by conflating newspaper reports), were widely studied,
and were still often read out loud in town and village inns.
Ordinary people followed the fortunes of the leading statesmen
of the day quite as ardently as they now follow the fortunes of

---

* Morley saw and even cited Moncreiff's principal letter (*Life of W. E.
Gladstone*, Vol. ii, p. 584); but does not seem to have appreciated its full
weight. He kept it by him, with a pile of other dubious papers, and never
returned it to Hawarden; it turned up, generations later, in a safe at his
publishers'.

football teams or race horses, of film stars or of pop group leaders. A smaller, more compact, socially more homogeneous ruling class was also primarily interested in politics; most of its members knew the principal contestants personally, or at least had been present at their parliamentary performances.

And of these principal contestants, two statesmen stood out above the rest, in sharp and visible rivalry: Gladstone and Disraeli. Each cordially detested the other, whom he regarded as the main source of the country's political ills. They were icily polite when they met; but Gladstone had once said (in private) that Disraeli "had generosity and temper, but was hopelessly *false*", while Beaconsfield had quite recently at a London banquet called Gladstone "a sophisticated rhetorician, intoxicated with the exuberance of his own verbosity". When it became known in the autumn of 1879 that Gladstone was about to visit his proposed constituency, to introduce himself to its electors in a series of public speeches, everyone could expect an explosion of oratorical fireworks from one of the foremost speakers of the age.

Such a thing had never been done before, and loud protests were raised by those who thought (if we may borrow a phrase from thirty years later) that "nothing should ever be done for the first time". But Gladstone was Gladstone, a man notoriously difficult to turn aside from a set purpose; and anything he did was interesting to his fellow citizens. In the days before aircraft, telephones or television, there was no flood of reporters from all the world over; but every newspaper of any size in the British Isles sent somebody, and so did one in New York. What happened in Midlothian was the principal news of the day. Every member of and candidate for Parliament, every senior civil servant, every clergyman – indeed every person – interested in politics; every local party chieftain, of course; read carefully what Mr Gladstone said there.

On first glancing at the pages that follow, the reader is bound to wonder quite what all the sensation was about; why such strong adjectives have been applied to such elaborate, and not always enthralling, prose. People have called the Midlothian campaign not merely exciting, but terrific, electric, epoch-making, revolutionary, seismic: where has all the magic gone?

Much of any orator's magic is personal: Gladstone's was no exception. Ordinary men who managed actually to hear him speak, at one of these meetings or a similar one, might find in next day's newspaper "but a miserable paraphrase of what was said – of what *we* said"; for Gladstone had the gift of getting his audience involved, with him, in enthusiasm or indignation, so that they felt they participated in his speech-making. In a large, tight-packed, mainly admiring crowd, ardour and excitement can spread fast; neither can easily be recaptured a day, let alone nine decades, later. (Anyone interested in examining the actual process of speech-construction can find the notes Gladstone used when preparing – jottings on slips of octavo paper, interspersed with newspaper cuttings and tables of figures – in the British Museum.)*

Yet the fact remains, beyond dispute. This campaign of half-a-dozen long speeches and nearly a score of shorter ones, delivered in a wintry fortnight, transformed the political scene, brought the next general election appreciably nearer, and laid the groundwork for the overthrow of the Conservative government and the Liberals' return to power. Gladstone himself seems not to have realised till quite late on that the effect of his own speech-making must be to bring himself back to the office of prime minister. He was loyally anxious to defer to Lord Granville and Lord Hartington, the Liberal leaders in Lords and Commons respectively; though when it came to the pinch he was not ready to serve under either, and neither dared form a ministry with him outside it. It was certainly not with any conscious idea of getting back to Downing Street that he went to Midlothian. He was impelled by a stronger, a simpler, and a more characteristic motive.

He thought that Lord Beaconsfield's policies were wrong, and that it was his own duty to say so. This is the real core of the

---

* Additional MS 44666, ff. 62–155.

Midlothian speeches; and from this derives the principal impact that they made, both on their audiences in Scotland and – to a lesser, but still to a marked, extent – on their readers next day. For Gladstone's strength of personality, and command of language, voice and gesture, were such that he could carry his hearers along with him in his proofs of how ministers had left undone those things which they ought to have done, and had done those things which they ought not to have done, so that there was no health in them. And he could go farther, and convince the men who heard him that it was their right, indeed their bounden duty, to send these ministers packing, and to put in their place men who understood right conduct better.

There was a high seriousness about this appeal to the electors' moral judgement, that gave the Midlothian campaign its importance at the time; and renders it today an occasion of almost suspicious interest. Politicians' motives have become more blown upon since then. The party machines that Gorst and Disraeli had prepared for one side in the early, and Joseph Chamberlain had launched for the other in the late, 1870s, have now become commonplace features of the unwritten constitution. "Ninepence for fourpence", the Liberal slogan of 1910, inaugurated electoral bribery as a national, one might almost say a nationalized, industry; and general elections are now regarded by all but political fanatics with some degree of detachment or even disdain. Electors no longer feel quite the weight of responsibility they felt in 1879.

In one way at least they are right: British power is much less. Great Britain then was *the* predominant world power, excelling all others in steel production, coal production, shipping tonnage, merchanting capacity; her navy ruled the seven seas unchallenged. Rival French power had broken at Sedan; the menaces of German, American, Russian, Chinese, African power lay hidden in the future. The great age of the expansion of European power over non-European territory, mainly in Africa and Asia – what people call the age of imperialism – had begun with the Russian drive

into central Asia; the British were about to embark on their main
share in it, in northern and southern Africa and in Burma.
Gladstone was seeking, as he had done for many years, to lay
down what the principles of British expansion ought to be.

He laid them down with a directness and a moral fervour that
impressed his hearers deeply, and set the tone for all that was
admirable in the British imperial spread. A great deal of empire
building was admirable, just as much was abominable; good
empire-builders, and good men, could look to Midlothian for a
view of the principles on which men ought to treat other men
(pp. 92–4, for example). All this of course was before the days of
air or nuclear warfare.

This is not the place to expound the complexities of Balkan
politics, the anti-Turkish revolts of 1875–6, the anti-Bulgarian
atrocities and the Russo-Turkish war that followed; nor the
Congress of Berlin and its aftermath, nor the current eccentricities
of British colonial and Indian frontier policy. (There is a note on
further reading on page ⟨17⟩.) But a word or two is needed on one
or two of the more domestic points that Gladstone raised. Finance,
as usual, he made perfectly clear, with that gift for lucid un-
ravelling of complex issues by which he fascinated the Commons
whenever he was chancellor of the exchequer. He treated his
Scottish audiences much as he treated his colleagues in Parliament – with deference, humour, respect, and an earnest desire to
explain. To figures, one of his private secretaries once said, he used
to turn for recreation, when he wanted a rest from policy; he had
got a mathematical as well as a classical first at Oxford, and
numbers fascinated him all his life. Some of this fascination he
could transmit.

The chancellor of the exchequer whom he assailed, Sir Stafford
Northcote, who had been his own private secretary at the Treasury nearly twenty years before, was about to have his political
career blasted by Lord Randolph Churchill's Fourth Party; but
no one could foresee that. No more could, or at any rate did,
anyone foresee that the main business of British politics for the

next dozen years was going to be the Irish question, to which only a few minutes of the campaign were devoted (pp. 86–8).

The purely electoral questions Gladstone raised are some of them perennially familiar – prime ministers and whips are used to juggling with election dates to suit their party advantage; but some by now are strange. Before ever he reached Midlothian, he raised the issue of faggot votes, one which had pestered him since (he believed) they had beaten his brother-in-law in Flintshire in 1841. These were votes manufactured by great landlords in county constituencies. This of course was a time when the franchise was still restricted; about one man in three (and no women) had a vote at all, even in towns, and in the countryside the proportion was much smaller: in Midlothian then, about one in seven. Under ancient acts, anyone holding some quite small properties had a vote for a knight of the shire, as a county member was formally called. A landlord would give his friends adequate properties; the friends would vote for the landlord's candidate, and after the election would give him the properties back. The Duke of Buccleuch was known to be prepared to do just this to secure his son's return.

John Reid, the Edinburgh advocate who was the main moving spirit of the Midlothian Liberal association (and who wrote the preface below), followed the duke's moves closely, and consulted about them with Lord Rosebery, the greatest Liberal landowner in the constituency. Rosebery, already Gladstone's friend, was to act as his host and indeed his impresario during the campaign; and was determined that the Tory dogs should not have the best of it. He secretly arranged with Reid that he would create a faggot voter on his own estates for every one made by Buccleuch; so that in the end the faggots cancelled each other out.* Needless to say, not a whisper of this reached Mr Gladstone's ears. This

---

* I am indebted for information on this point to Mr Alastair Cooke of the University of Belfast, who has a forthcoming article on the subject in the *Scottish Historical Review*, which dots the i's and crosses the t's of R. R. James's *Rosebery*.

is a considerable tribute to Rosebery's and to Reid's security. Rosebery's friendship with Gladstone deepened, in spite of occasional tiffs; when Gladstone, prime minister against all expectations for the fourth time, finally resigned in 1894 it was Rosebery whom the Queen chose to succeed him.

But we have run too far ahead of the winter of 1879–80. This first Midlothian campaign dislocated the political scene enough to bring on a general election in the spring. Gladstone conducted a second Midlothian campaign in March, and made even more speeches than in his first; his address to the electors is set out below (following p. 255), so that readers can see how fully he explained his policy on paper to his constituents. Its length and lavish detail provide a short proof of how much more seriously he and his age took politics than we do.

In the country as a whole, there were for the first time contests in as many as three-quarters of all the constituencies. The Liberals won some 351 seats, giving them a majority over both 239 Conservatives and 62 Irish Nationalists combined (precise figures cannot easily be arrived at, in an age when party lines had still not set quite firm). Gladstone described his own result in his diary: "At 7.20 Mr Reid brought the figures of the poll – Gladstone, 1579; Dalkieth, 1368; quite satisfactory . . . Home about 10. Wonderful & nothing less has been the disposing guiding hand of God in all the matter." He gave all praise to God, as he always did; but his niece, Lady Frederick Cavendish, who met him at Hawarden "as fresh as paint" the day after he came back from the first campaign, did note that "For the 1st time, I deliberately believe, in my recollection, he seems a little *personally* elated! It has always hitherto been the cause, or the moment, or the circumstances, or *something*, that he thinks he is the mere mouthpiece of; but this unheard-of enthusiasm for his name, in his own country (for he is a pure-bred Scotchman), and after the long time of abuse and loss of influence, has deeply moved him."

M. R. D. Foot

University of Manchester: August 1970

A note on further reading

J. Morley, *Life of W. E. Gladstone*, three volumes, Macmillan 1903

R. W. Seton-Watson, *Disraeli, Gladstone and the Eastern Question*, Macmillan 1935

R. C. K. Ensor, *England 1870–1914*, Oxford University Press 1936

Sir P. Magnus, *Gladstone*, Murray 1954

H. J. Hanham, *Elections and Party Management*, Longmans 1959

R. T. Shannon, *Gladstone and the Bulgarian Agitation 1876*, Nelson 1968

T. O. Lloyd, *The General Election of 1880*, Oxford University Press 1968

H. Gollwitzer, *Europe in the age of imperialism*, Thames and Hudson 1969

BIBLIOGRAPHICAL NOTE

This volume reprints the whole text of Gladstone's *Political Speeches in Scotland, November and December 1879*, published, with an appendix of non-political speeches, under the auspices of the Central Liberal Association in 1879. To this is added the text of two addresses to the electors of Midlothian which were included in the appendix to the succeeding volume of *Political Speeches in Scotland, March and April 1880*. Both this volume and a reprint of the 1879 volume were issued in 1880 as a "revised edition".

Cheap editions of both volumes, with some alterations and abridgements, were also published with the approval of the Central Liberal Association in 1879 and 1880. These were issued under the same titles as the longer volumes but were closely printed on poor-quality paper at a cost of sixpence each.

J. L. Madden

POLITICAL SPEECHES IN SCOTLAND.

SOLD ALSO BY

ANDREW ELLIOT,   .   17 PRINCES STREET, EDINBURGH.

JOHN HEYWOOD,   .   MANCHESTER.

JOHN MENZIES & CO.,   EDINBURGH AND GLASGOW.

CORNISH BROTHERS,   BIRMINGHAM.

POLITICAL SPEECHES
IN SCOTLAND,

NOVEMBER AND DECEMBER 1879.

BY

THE RIGHT HON. W. E. GLADSTONE, M.P.

WITH AN APPENDIX,

CONTAINING THE RECTORIAL ADDRESS IN GLASGOW, AND
OTHER NON-POLITICAL SPEECHES.

The Speeches revised by the Author.

LONDON: W. RIDGWAY, 169 PICCADILLY.
1879.

[*Reprinted from the 'Scotsman' Reports by the East and North of Scotland
Liberal Association*]

PREFACE.

ONE, and not the least useful, among the duties of a Central Liberal Association is that of affording to the general public and to its own members an opportunity of perusing in a convenient form the principal political speeches of eminent Liberal Statesmen. No fitter occasion could have been found for the exercise of this duty than Mr. Gladstone's recent visit to Midlothian, and indeed to Scotland, while no series of speeches could in their character more forcibly have called for publication and general distribution. Whether regard be had to the personal gifts and qualities of the right honourable gentleman himself, or to the spontaneous enthusiasm with which he was everywhere received, or to the wide range and engrossing interest of his addresses, we think all will agree in the benefit to be derived from their issue in a pamphlet shape.

J. J. R.

19 CASTLE STREET,
EDINBURGH, *December* 1879.

ITINERARY.

MONDAY, NOVEMBER 24.

Mr. Gladstone left Liverpool for Scotland. Addresses presented at Carlisle from the Langholm Working Men (Dumfriesshire), the Carlisle Liberal Association, the Newcastle-upon-Tyne Liberal Association, and the Gateshead Liberal Association; at Galashiels from the Galashiels Liberal Association and the Selkirk Liberal Association; and lastly, at Edinburgh, from the Executive Liberal Committee of Midlothian.

TUESDAY, NOVEMBER 25.

Speech to the Midlothian Electors (Edinburgh District) in the Music Hall. Address presented by the Corporation of Edinburgh.

WEDNESDAY, NOVEMBER 26.

Speech to the Midlothian Electors (Dalkeith District) in the Corn Exchange, Dalkeith. Speech to the Committee in the Foresters' Hall, Dalkeith, and Presentation.

THURSDAY, NOVEMBER 27.

Speech to the Midlothian Electors (West Calder District) at West Calder. Address by the West Calder Non-Electors' Association.

FRIDAY, NOVEMBER 28.

Reception at Dalmeny Park for the Members of the Midlothian Executive Committee. Address presented by the Corporation of Leith.

SATURDAY, NOVEMBER 29.

Speech to the Members of the East and North of Scotland Liberal Association, and Representatives of upwards of one hundred other local Associations, in the Corn Exchange, Edinburgh. Presentation of many Addresses in the Waverley Market, Edinburgh, in presence of a Mass Meeting of nearly 20,000 persons, and Speech in reply by Mr. Gladstone.

MONDAY, DECEMBER 1.

Mr. Gladstone left Dalmeny Park for Taymouth Castle. Addresses presented at Inverkeithing, at Dunfermline, at Perth by the County and City Associations, and at Aberfeldy from the Local Liberal Association, and Speeches in reply.

TUESDAY, DECEMBER 2.

Address presented at Taymouth by the Killin Breadalbane Liberal Association, and Speech in reply.

WEDNESDAY, DECEMBER 3.

THURSDAY, DECEMBER 4.

Mr. Gladstone left Taymouth Castle for Glasgow.

FRIDAY, DECEMBER 5.

Lord Rector's Address to the Students at the Kibble Palace, Glasgow. Speech to a Public Meeting in the St. Andrew's Hall, Glasgow. Presentation of an Address by the Corporation, and Speech in reply.

SATURDAY, DECEMBER 6.

Mr. Gladstone left Glasgow for Dalzell House, Motherwell. Presentation of Addresses at Motherwell Station, and Speech in reply. Presentation of the Freedom of the Burgh of Motherwell at Dalzell House.

MONDAY, DECEMBER 8.

Mr. Gladstone left Dalzell House for Hawarden Castle, Chester.

CONTENTS.

―◆―

INTRODUCTORY.

SPEECHES AT CARLISLE, HAWICK, AND GALASHIELS.

FIRST MIDLOTHIAN SPEECH.

SECOND MIDLOTHIAN SPEECH.

THIRD MIDLOTHIAN SPEECH.

WAVERLEY MARKET SPEECH.

CONTENTS.

DUNFERMLINE SPEECH.

PERTH SPEECH.

ABERFELDY SPEECH.

TAYMOUTH SPEECH.

CONTENTS.

SPEECH AT MOTHERWELL STATION.

APPENDIX.

ADVERTISEMENT.

I HAVE this day been favoured with a letter from the Chancellor of the Exchequer, containing explanations as to the reconstruction of the Civil Service Commission, and the appointment of Lord Hampton, which have not heretofore been made known to the world. They do not in any way affect my opinion of the proceedings in point of policy or of economy. But they satisfy me that the transaction need not, and therefore should not, be interpreted so as to carry the moral taint implied in the word 'job.' I therefore at once, and with pleasure, withdraw that word.

I observe with less satisfaction that a correspondent of the *Globe* newspaper, writing from Bath on the 9th, has been so unkind to Lord John Manners as to charge me with having wilfully misquoted him at Glasgow. I quoted him as having stated, in contradiction to Lord Cairns, that we made war upon the Ameer of Afghanistan because he refused to receive our Mission. The statement was, says the correspondent, that he refused it 'with insult and violence.' But that statement is grossly and absolutely untrue, as is now known from the Parliamentary papers. It was reserved for the champion of the Ministry, in his uninstructed eagerness, to exhibit him to the world as the author of such a statement, which, of course, greatly aggravates the case.

W. E. GLADSTONE.

HAWARDEN, *Dec.* 12, 1879.

I.

INTRODUCTORY.

THE Right Hon. W. E. Gladstone, M.P., left Liverpool on the morning of Monday, November 24, on his way to Scotland, and at the various points of the route through Lancashire, such as St. Helens, Wigan, and Preston, he was greeted with hearty cheers by the large crowds who had assembled to do him honour. On the arrival of the train at Carlisle, Mr. Gladstone was received on the platform by a number of leading Liberals, including Mr. George Howard, M.P. for East Cumberland; Sir Wilfrid Lawson, M.P.; Mr. W. H. James, M.P., Gateshead; Major Thomson, Melton Hall; Mr. Allison, Scaleby Hall; Mr. Jardine of Castlemilk, Liberal candidate for Dumfriesshire; and Mr. John M'Laren, advocate, Edinburgh, Vice-President of and representing the East and North of Scotland Liberal Association. The right hon. gentleman proceeded to the County Hotel, in the hall of which a representative gathering of Liberals, numbering some 500 or 600, had assembled, all of whom on his appearance, with one accord, rose and cheered with unmistakeable enthusiasm.

The addresses were then presented in the following order:— Langholm, Dumfriesshire, with a gift of cloth, introduced by Mr. Jardine of Castlemilk; Carlisle Liberal Association, introduced by Sir Wilfrid Lawson, M.P.; Newcastle-on-Tyne Liberal Association, with Newcastle Liberal Club and Gateshead Liberal Association, all introduced by Mr. James, M.P. Mr. Gladstone replied—

I am afraid the circumstances under which we meet here

to-day will scarcely enable me to give even the briefest acknowledgment of the extraordinary kindness with which I have been received. But I will say, in the first place, this, that the sentiment which is evidently bursting forth from every heart among those of our own political opinions in Carlisle, is in my opinion a good omen of that which we shall find elsewhere; not, I trust, in Scotland only, or in Cumberland only,—for if the whole country be like Scotland and like Cumberland, the whole matter is safe enough,—but also in every portion of the country. I accept with the greatest pleasure this gift of the working men who have been so good as to send a deputation for the purpose of presenting it. I shall wear it with a sense that a great honour has been conferred upon me. I believe that if I were to cause it to be immediately made up, and were beginning to wear it every day, Sundays included, the probability is that before this dress was worn out, the Government under which we at present live would be worn out. When it has been said from Newcastle that the address presented to me expresses the sentiments of the Liberals of Newcastle generally, I trust and believe that the meaning of that is, that it expresses the sentiments of the large majority of the inhabitants of the town.

This is an occasion, gentlemen, of an extraordinary character. I have had an opportunity of reading the address from Newcastle, and likewise the address from Carlisle, though I have not had yet the opportunity of reading the other addresses; and I observe that in both of those addresses a capital point, a salient point, if I may so speak, on which those who have

This is a crisis of an extraordinary character. signed them fix is this, that the crisis is one of an extraordinary character. It is, gentlemen, a crisis of an extraordinary character which brings you together necessarily at much inconvenience, many of you coming from considerable distances, to greet me for a moment on my way northwards; it is a crisis of an extraordinary character, and no other, that would induce me at my time of life, when every sentiment would dictate a desire for rest, to undertake what may be called an arduous contest. It is because I believe every circumstance marks this occasion that is now approaching,—whether it be a little nearer or a little farther, we do not know,—but every circumstance marks it as one of unequalled interest and importance. I say, gentlemen, of unequalled interest and importance, because already in eleven former dissolutions and elections it has been my fortune to take an active part; but in no one of those eleven, although they have extended over very nearly half a century, have I known the interests of the country to be so deeply and so vitally at stake as they are upon the dissolution that is now approaching. You are good enough to say in these addresses much that I cannot honestly appropriate to myself. Nevertheless I accept them with gratitude, because I know that many of the expressions that you have applied to me, and which perhaps, if rigidly examined, would not bear criticism as applied to me, are expressions which are symbols of your feeling upon the character of this crisis generally, and upon the interests that are engaged. And, gentlemen, let me say this before I close,—because I feel sure that the few minutes which are kindly allowed to us must by this time have reached their expiration,—depend upon it, though the leaders of the Liberal party may do all they can, and I am satisfied they will do all they can ; though I in my distinct position may do everything that depends upon me, and on me you may depend for that,—it is not upon what they can do, much less upon what I can do, that the final issue must ultimately hang; it is upon the individual exertions of you, as true Britons and true patriots, each in his own separate place, every man in his own office and function, to contribute that which he can contribute to the settlement of the great and tremendous question, and to place anew the fortunes of this country in hands more competent to guide them with honour and with safety than those to which they are now entrusted.

At Hawick a short stoppage took place, and Mr. Gladstone,

being pressed by the Provost and other leading Liberals, addressed a few words to a large crowd assembled around the station. After thanking those present for their cordial welcome, Mr. Gladstone proceeded to say:—

We are comrades in a common undertaking; we are fellow-soldiers in a common warfare; we have a very serious labour to perform. The people of this country, and you among them in your place, have to consider what is the system upon which such an Empire ought to be governed. It is a subject on which I for one have a strong opinion, known to you. We should endeavour to bring about a great and fundamental change in regard to those dangerous novelties which have of late been introduced into the policy of this country, which have disturbed the world at large, and which have certainly aggravated the distress of the nation at home. I believe that in our efforts to do away with that system, and to return to the sound Liberal and just principles that have commonly distinguished in our time British administration, we have in our charge a cause which is the cause of peace, which is the cause of justice, which is the cause of liberty, which is the cause of honour, and which, in the hands of the people of this country, by the blessing of God, will not fail.

Proceeding by St. Boswells and Melrose, where crowds had gathered to cheer him as he passed, Mr. Gladstone arrived at Galashiels, and was there received by the Provost. An enormous crowd had assembled around a platform prepared for the occasion, and the cheering was loud and hearty. Addresses were presented by Mr. Brown, Chairman of the Galashiels Liberal Committee, and by Mr. Anderson on behalf of the Selkirk Liberal Association; Mr. Frater also presented, on behalf of the work-people, gifts of tartan and tweed, the staple manufacture of the town of Galashiels. Mr. Gladstone said in reply:—

Ladies and gentlemen, I am afraid I can hardly hope to

convey to every member of this vast assemblage the few words that may proceed from my lips upon the present occasion ; but your kindness and evident interest, and the stillness with which you have gathered in this crowded mass, will give me a better opportunity than I should otherwise have had to assure you of the gratitude, and not only the gratitude, but the very lively pleasure, with which I accept the kind present you have made me. We are all of us, as human beings, apt to be influenced by signs; and you may have observed that I was covetous of getting hold in my hand, ay, and in both hands, of those two parcels. It was not only that I might test the quality—about that I felt perfectly sure ; but I wished to speak to you holding them in my grasp. I would do so now, were it not that I am afraid that my powers, my physical powers, of speech would be so affected by the weight that I should be less able to make you hear. However, ladies and gentlemen, I must not dwell upon these particulars. I must beg you to take for granted, and you, sir, likewise, who have been good enough to present to me the Selkirk address, I beg you to take for granted the personal feelings that I entertain upon an occasion like this.

It is not possible for any one to witness such a pouring out of the population of a district; it is not possible for any one to see you here, gathered as you are, and willing to listen to the words that may reach you, without asking himself whether there is or is not a serious cause for this extraordinary liveliness of feeling, and for so remarkable a manifestation from the population of this district. It ought to be understood, gentlemen, better than it is by some of the politicians of this country, that the people do not love to meddle in political demonstrations, *The people do* except when there is a strong cause. It is all very well for the *not love* *political* idle or the leisured part of the community, but you are working *demonstrations* men ; the great bulk of you are working men who have serious *save for a* *strong reason.* matters to attend to, and I well know that it is not your desire to leave them for any frivolous reason, but only when you think that the interests of your country are at stake. It is that same consideration, gentlemen, that has brought me down among you, and that is carrying me to the county of Midlothian.

Gentlemen, I certainly shall not stay among you. There is nothing to do here in amending the representation of the burghs. This is as satisfactory to me as it is to you, and I beg therefore that my friend Mr. Trevelyan may entertain no fears or apprehensions at all that I am going to run away with your hearts, if, indeed, it were in my power to do so. No, gentlemen, but I am come down here certainly for a most serious purpose—that is to say, for the purpose of doing all in my power to raise effectually before the people of this country the great question in what manner it is that they wish to be governed. Does the present method of Government please them, or does it not? If it pleases them, then they have nothing to do but to send us about our business and to continue it; but that is not what we believe, not what we expect, any more than it is what we desire. But what I beg to insist upon before you and before all is this—it is not now a question of this or that particular measure. We are all of us, or most of us here, I take it, of Liberal politics, and have a great interest in many particular measures. There are a great many things that we wish to be done, which we are not likely to see done by the present Government. Some of us are very anxious for one thing, and some for another, and some for all. But it is a great deal more than that. It is a system and a method of Government with which we have to deal. Look at the state of the world. Look at the disturbed and troubled condition of Europe, of Asia, in India, in Afghanistan, in Africa, in the remote South. Look at the engagements into which we are forced here, there, and everywhere. Look at the condition of the finances at home, which, depend upon it, is only the first-fruits, not the consummation, of all those strange and most unwise proceedings. It is, gentlemen, a new method of Government to which we are now subjected; and if you, instead of being Liberals, were an

Does the present method of Government please or not?

assembly of those who call themselves Conservatives, I would appeal to you, and say that of all Administrations which have been in power within the last half century, there never has been one which has ventured upon so many measures not only mischievous, but new-fangled, with the effect of vexing and alarming the people of the country, and compromising the interests of the Empire.

I have been reminded here in one address that there is also an important local question deeply interesting to you in Scotland. I am come here not only for the purpose of maintaining what we think a sound general policy, but for another purpose too, which is really not less important —the purpose of vindicating the freedom of election. It is *The freedom* idle to talk of freedom of election if the votes of gentlemen *of election.* who have nothing whatever to do with particular counties and places are to be brought in by legal chicanery for the purpose of setting aside the verdict given by the independent electors. You know what a faggot vote is ? In your part of the country you have had experience of it. In Midlothian a bold, daring attempt has been made to carry the apparent sense of the county by means of the faggot votes of gentlemen who have no *Faggot votes.* moral right or title to appear more than I have, and I have none, upon the electoral list of the county. I am come to assert in opposition to these—what shall I call them ?—these phantom voters ; but unfortunately the votes when recorded are no phantoms—I am come in contradiction of and in protesta-tion against a system of this kind. According to the law and the constitution of this country, the power of returning members is to be given to those who have a genuine, legitimate interest as inhabitants and as possessors of property in each circum-scription of the country ; and as for those who introduce these sham voters—I do not want to use harder words, but even harder words might be used—introduce these sham voters for the purpose of overbearing and overpowering the real voters, it is idle for them to call themselves friends of the Constitution.

They are no friends of the Constitution, they are defying the Constitution, they are trampling the Constitution under foot,

An attempt to nullify the franchise.

for they are endeavouring to nullify those franchises which are the most fundamental and most sacred part of the Constitution.

That is the cause, gentlemen, for which I came here, and I assure you I shall go forward to take the steps that that cause shall require in the county of Midlothian cheered by the encouragement and supported by this extraordinary manifestation with which to-day you have gratified me to the bottom of my heart.

At Edinburgh an immense crowd had assembled at the railway station, completely filling the building and its approaches, and extending in dense masses along the whole of Princes Street and Queensferry Street. The right honourable gentleman was received at the station by the Earl of Rosebery, President of the East and North of Scotland and of the Midlothian Liberal Associations ; the Right Hon. W. P. Adam, M.P.; Sir D. Wedderburn, Bart., M.P.; Mr. Cowan, M.P.; Mr. Pender, M.P.; Sir William Miller, Bart.; by nearly all the members of the Midlothian Executive Committee ; by a deputation from the Trades Council, and by a considerable number of the members of the Corporation. Mr. Gladstone, meeting with an enthusiastic greeting by the way, proceeded with Lord Rosebery in an open carriage to Dalmeny Park, an address from the Corporation of the ancient burgh of South Queensferry being presented at the Chapel Gate entrance.

II.

TUESDAY, NOVEMBER 25, 1879.

FIRST MIDLOTHIAN SPEECH.

Delivered in the Music Hall, George Street, Edinburgh, to the Electors of the Parishes of Liberton, Duddingston, South Leith, Canongate, St. Cuthberts, Cramond, Corstorphine, Currie, and Colinton.

Every Elector, irrespective of politics, was entitled to a ticket of admission to this or one of the other Midlothian meetings, and at the Music Hall upwards of one thousand availed themselves of the privilege. The character of the majority of the parishes embraced in the Edinburgh district of the county may rather be described as suburban than as rural.

EDINBURGH MUSIC HALL MEETING.

ON Tuesday, November 25, Mr. Gladstone addressed a meeting of Midlothian electors in the Music Hall, Edinburgh. On the platform there were, amongst other gentlemen, Viscount Dalrymple, Hon. Henry J. Moncreiff, Hon. J. W. Moncreiff, Sir Walter Simpson, Bart.; Sir George Campbell, M.P.; Sir George Balfour, M.P.; Sir W. H. Gibson Carmichael, Bart.; Sir David Wedderburn, Bart., M.P.; Messrs. James Cowan, M.P.; Andrew Grant, M.P.; W. Holms, M.P.; J. W. Barclay, M.P.; Charles Tennant, M.P.; Fortescue Harrison, M.P.; P. M'Lagan, M.P.; J. Ramsay, M.P.; Sir C. Farquhar Shand; Donald Currie, Liberal candidate for Perthshire; Edmund F. Davis, Liberal candidate for East Kent, etc. etc.

On the motion of Mr. Charles Cowan, seconded by Sir W. Miller, Bart., the chair was taken by Sir David Wedderburn, Bart., M.P., a member of the Executive Committee of the Midlothian Liberal Association. After apologizing for the absence from illness of Mr. John Cowan, Chairman of the Executive, Sir David introduced Mr. Gladstone, who was received with enthusiastic and prolonged cheering, the whole audience rising. When the commotion had subsided, he proceeded as follows:—

The occasion no ordinary one.

My Lords and Gentlemen,—All will feel who are present, and all who, being absent, give any heed to the proceedings of to-day will feel that this is not an ordinary occasion. It is not an ordinary occasion which brings you and me together—me as a candidate for your Parliamentary suffrages, and you, I will not say as solicited by me, for by me you have not been solicited—but you as the spontaneous and gracious offerers to me of a trust which I deem it a high duty under these circumstances to seek, and which I shall deem it the highest honour to receive. It is not an ordinary occasion, gentlemen, because, as we all know, the ordinary rule is that in county representation it is customary, though not invariably the rule—it is customary to choose some one who, by residence, by property, by constant intercourse, is identified with the county that he is asked to represent. In these respects I come among you as a stranger. It is not the first time that such a combination has been known. On the contrary, it has been, I may say, not unfrequent for important counties, and especially for metropolitan counties, to select those who, in that sense, are strangers to their immediate locality to be their candidates or to be their representatives in Parliament, but always with a special purpose in view, and that purpose has been the rendering of some emphatic testimony to some important public principle. It is not, gentlemen, for the purpose of gratuitously disturbing your county that I am come among you, for before I could think it my duty to entertain the wishes so kindly pressed upon me, I used the very best exertions in my own power, and called in the very

best and most experienced advice at my command, in order
that I might be assured that I was not guilty of creating that
wanton disturbance—in truth, that I was to come among you
not as an intruder, not as a voluntary provoker of unnecessary
strife, but as the person who, according to every reasonable
principle of evidence, was designated by the desires of the
decided majority of electors as their future representative.

Then, my lords and gentlemen, neither am I here, as I can *A tribute to*
truly and cheerfully say, for the purpose of any personal con- *the personal worth of his*
flict. I will begin this campaign, if so it is to be called,—and a *opponents.*
campaign, and an earnest campaign I trust it will be,—I will
begin by avowing my personal respect for my noble opponent,
and for the distinguished family to which he belongs. Gentlemen, I have had the honour—for an honour I consider it—to
sit as a colleague with the Duke of Buccleuch in the Cabinet
of Sir Robert Peel. This is now nearly forty years ago. Since
that time I frankly avow that I have changed various opinions;
I should say that I have learned various lessons. But I must
say, and express it as my distinct and decided conviction, that
that noble Duke, who was then my colleague under Sir Robert
Peel, has changed like myself, but in an opposite direction, and
I believe that on this great occasion he is farther from his old
position than I am. Let me, gentlemen, in the face of you who
are Liberals, and determined Liberals, let me render this tribute
to the memory of Sir Robert Peel. I never knew a more conscientious public man; I never knew — in far the greater
portion of questions that concerned the public interest —
a more enlightened statesman. And this opinion I give with
confidence, in the face of the world, founded upon many years
of intimate communication with him upon every subject of
public interest; that, could his valuable life have been prolonged to this moment, could he have been called upon to take
part, as we are now called upon to take part, in the great
struggle which is commencing in this country, Sir Robert Peel
would have been found contending along with you against the

principles which now specially place you in determined opposition to the Government of the day. I render to the Duke of Buccleuch as freely as to Lord Dalkeith this tribute, that he—given and presupposed the misfortune of his false political opinions—is in all respects what a British nobleman ought to be, and sets to us all an example in the active and conscientious discharge of duty, such as he believes duty to be, which we shall do well, from our very different point of view, to follow.

The manufacture of faggot votes.

And now I hope I have spoken intelligibly upon that subject, and I will pass on to another which is far less agreeable. I thought when the invitation of the electors of Midlothian was sent to me, that the matter in controversy was one of sufficient breadth and complication, and I then was not aware that it would become still more enhanced and still more entangled by a question which, in its first aspect, was local, but which, in its ulterior aspect, is of the deepest importance, embraces in its scope the whole country, and descends to the very roots of our institutions. I thought that in one thing at least my noble opponent and myself were agreed—that is to say, that we were agreed in making a common appeal to the true and legitimate electors of Midlothian. I am grieved to find that that is not to be the case; that, mistrusting the body to whom the constitution and the law had given the power of choice between candidates for Midlothian, an attempt has been made to import into the county a body of strangers, having no natural interest in the county, gifted with colourable qualifications invented by the chicanery of law, and that it is on this body that reliance is placed, in order, perchance, to realize some faint hope of overbearing the true majority of the constituency. I won't dilate, gentlemen, upon that subject—I won't now expatiate upon it,—but this I must say, that if anything was wanting to make me feel it more than ever a duty to endeavour to fight the battle with energy and determination, this most unfortunate act was

Its imprudence.

the very thing destined for that purpose. Why, gentlemen, quite apart from every question of principle, nothing, I venture to say, can be so grossly imprudent as that which is familiarly known in homely but most accurate phrase as the manufacture of faggot votes. Those who manufacture faggot votes provoke investigation into the whole state of the law, and of those provisions of the law which at the present moment are framed with such liberality towards the possessors of property.

Why, sir, is it not enough that the man who happens to have *Multiplication of qualifications.* property in six or ten counties can give a vote in respect of that property, in conformity with the rules of the Constitution, in every one of those counties? Is it not enough that he who, after all, has only the interests of a citizen in the wellbeing of the country, shall be permitted, by the free assent of all parties, without dishonour, without evasion, to multiply his own individual existence, and to contribute to the issue of six or ten electioneering contests, instead of one? Is not this enough? Is not this sufficiently liberal to the rich man as compared with the poor man, who hardly ever, though he may be a voter, can by possibility have more than a single vote? Ought not the Duke of Buccleuch and his friends to be satisfied with that state of law? Is it not the fact that in this country, although the law refuses to give a double vote in respect of a larger qualification, yet is it not the fact that it is the rarest thing in the world to meet a poor voter who has more than one vote, whereas it is the rarest thing in the world to meet a gentleman voter, as he is called, who has not got more than one vote? Why are they not content with that state of things? Why do they determine upon adding to that lawful multiplication of power, which, I must say, is based upon a remarkable liberality towards the possessors of property? why, in addition to that, are they determined to aim at an unlawful multiplication of power, and to bring in upon you, the genuine voters of Midlothian, those guests, those foreigners—for foreigners they are— foreigners they are in respect of the concerns of this county— its political concerns — for the purpose of overbearing the genuine and true sense of the constituency? Gentlemen, my anticipation is that this extraordinary manœuvre will utterly, certainly, and miserably fail of its purpose. I have not been surprised to be assured by those among you who have interested themselves specially in the affairs of the coming election, that we stand quite as well as we did, or better than we did, before the introduction of these faggot votes. We are divided into parties in this country, and the division is a healthy one. But there is always, at the same time, a certain margin of gentlemen who will have regard to other than party considerations, where they think that some great public principle is at stake ; and my belief is that there will be, and must be, many in Midlothian who will not consent to compromise a principle more sacred and more important than any of the ordinary differences of party, namely this, that the representative of each county shall be chosen by the county itself, and shall not be chosen by importations of gentlemen from abroad, brought in to overbear its true and native sense.

Is a dissolution imminent?

Well, gentlemen, I pass on from that subject, which you are very capable of handling, and which, I daresay, you will find a good deal to say upon before we have brought this business to a conclusion—I pass on to other matters, and I wish to say a word upon the subject—having thus far spoken of my own personal appearance and its grounds—upon the subject of the time at which I appear before you. Why do I come here to trouble you at this time ? Are we going to have a dissolution ? There is a question of great interest. I won't pretend, gentlemen, to answer it. My belief is that there has been a good deal of consultation in high quarters upon that subject; and observe the reason why there should be, and why there must have been

The invariable practice is not to transact the business of more than six sessions.

consultation. The reason is plain. It is this : we have arrived at the time wherein, according to the fixed and invariable practice, I think, of the entire century, nay, even of more than the entire century, there ought to be a dissolution. The rule, and the wise rule, of our governors in other times has been, that although the law allows a duration of seven years to

Parliament, it should not sit to transact more than the regular business of six sessions. And you will see, gentlemen, the good sense, I think, of such a rule. It appears to be founded upon *The good sense of this* this, that the operations of the seventh session would be likely *practice.* to descend as to their moral level below the standard of the earlier portions of a Parliament; that the interests of the country would be more liable to be compromised by personal inducements, and personal inducements not in relation to the country at large, but in relation to particular groups and cliques of persons—in relation to what are sometimes called harassed interests. And matters of that kind would be likely to bring about a bartering and trafficking in public interests for personal ends if it were made absolutely certain that in so many weeks, or in two or three months, the Parliament must be dissolved. Now, out of this has grown a rule; I am far *A departure* from saying that rule is a rule mathematical or inflexible; *from it justi-* *fied only by* for some great public or national reason it is perfectly justi- *national* fiable to depart from it—but what is the public or national *reasons.* reason for departing from it now? None at all. I defy the most ingenious man to suggest to me any reason whatever for departing from this rule, which has been in use through the whole of our lifetime—I believe even through the lifetime of your fathers and grandfathers. I don't believe the wit of man can give a reason for departing from it except this, that it is thought to be upon the whole for the interests of Her Majesty's Government. That, I say at once, is not a legitimate reason for departing from the constitutional rule. They have no right to take into view the interests of the Government in respect to a question whether a Parliament shall be prolonged beyond the period fixed by long and unbroken usage. They are bound to decide that question upon national and imperial considera- tions, and if no national or imperial consideration dictates a departure from the rule, they are bound to adhere to the rule. Well, now we are told they mean to break the rule. I can't say I shall be surprised at their breaking the rule of usage, for this Government, which delights in the title of Conservative, or rather which was not satisfied with the title of Conservative, but has always fallen back upon the title of Tory—this Tory Government, from which we have the right to expect—I would almost say to exact—an extraordinary reverence for everything that was fixed—reverence which has been paid in many instances whether it is good or bad—yet this Tory Government has undoubtedly created a greater number of innovations, broken away from a greater number of precedents, set a greater number of new-fangled examples to mislead and bewilder future generations, than any Government which has existed in my time. Therefore I am not at all surprised that they should have broken away from a rule of this kind so far as regards the respect due to an established and, on the whole, a reasonable and a useful custom ; but at the same time they would not break away without some reason—an illegitimate reason, because one connected with their interests ; a strange reason, because one would have thought that a Government whose proceedings, as will be admitted on all hands, have been of so marked a character, ought to have been anxious at the earliest period permitted by usage to obtain the judgment of the country.

Reasons why the Government are not anxious to dissolve. And why, gentlemen, are they not anxious to obtain the judgment of the country? It is surely plain that they are not anxious. If they were anxious, they would follow the rule, and dissolve the Parliament. It is plain, therefore, that they are not anxious. Why are they not anxious ? Have they not told us all along that they possess the confidence of the people ? Have they not boasted right and left that vast majorities of the nation are in the same sense with themselves ? Oh, gentlemen, these are idle pretexts ! It is an instinct lying far deeper than those professions that teaches them that the country is against them. And it is because they know that the country is against them that they are unwilling to appeal to the country. Why, gentlemen, a dissolution, an appeal to the public judgment, when there is a knowledge beforehand on the part of those who make the appeal that the answer will be favourable, gives additional strength to those who make the appeal. If it be true, as they still say, that the country is in their favour, I say that after the favourable reply that they would receive to their appeal, they would come back to Parliament far stronger for the purpose of giving effect to the principles that they hold to be true, than they are at this moment. They know perfectly well that a favourable appeal would strengthen their hands; they know perfectly well that an unfavourable answer will be the end of their ministerial existence; and it therefore requires no great wit on our part to judge why, when they have reached the usual, and what I may almost call constitutional period, they don't choose to make an appeal at all.

There are some reasons, gentlemen, why they ought to make that appeal which bear on their own party interests. They will not have a very pleasant operation to perform when they produce their next Budget. I am not going to enter into that subject now. You must excuse me if I do not attempt on this occasion to cover the whole of the enormously wide field that is open before me; but I promise, especially as the Chancellor *A promise to* of the Exchequer says it is most agreeable to him that the *discuss finance.* question of finance should be discussed, and, in fact, he has chosen the most extraordinary opportunity, for the first time that I can recollect, for discussing it—namely, at the Lord Mayor's dinner—but as he is so desirous it should be discussed, I, having every disposition to comply with his wishes as far as I can, will certainly endeavour to enter into that matter, and set out the main facts of the case as well as I am able. I do not think there is a great anxiety to produce that Budget; and this of itself would recommend a dissolution.

I tell you, gentlemen, what I think, and that is what has led me to dwell at length on the subject of dissolution. It is because it is not a theoretical, but a practical consideration. It is this: we are told by 'whippers-in,' and gentlemen who probably have an inspiration that sometimes flows from the higher quarters into those peculiar and favoured channels—we are told that they think there will not be a dissolution for twelve months. Twelve months, gentlemen! There is what is called a 'chapter of accidents,' and by postponing the dissolution for twelve months you get your twelve months of the exercise of power. Now, I am not going to impute to this Government, or any Government, sordid motives for the desire to retain power. In my opinion, imputations of that kind, which are incessantly made upon me, and incessantly made upon the Liberal party generally, and especially upon the leaders of the Liberal party—in my opinion, imputations of that kind are disgraceful only to those who make them.

Reliance on the chapter of accidents.

I pass on. The love of power is something much higher. It is the love, of course, of doing what they think good by means of power. Twelve months would be secured in that sense—something more would be secured. There would be the chance of striking some new theatrical stroke. There would be the chance of sending up some new rocket into the sky—the chance of taking some measure which again would carry misgiving and dismay to the hearts of the sober-minded portion of the nation—as I believe, at this time the great majority of the nation—but which, appealing to pride and passion, would always in this, as in every country, find some loud-voiced minority ready to echo back its ill-omened sounds, and again to disturb the world, to destroy confidence, to unsettle business and the employments of life, to hold out false promises of greatness, but really to alienate from this country the sympathies of the civilised world, and to prepare for us the day of misfortune and of dishonour.

'Some new theatrical stroke.'

Now, gentlemen, I am not saying that which is peculiar to persons of my political creed. It was only upon the 10th of November that the Prime Minister gave to the world the assurance that he thought peace might be maintained. I thought that matter had been settled eighteen months ago,

Peace assurances of the Premier.

when he came back from Berlin and said he had got 'peace with honour.' Now he says, 'I think peace may be maintained, and I think it is much more likely now than it was twelve months ago'—more likely than it was five months or four months after he had come back from Berlin and announced 'peace with honour.' That is what he says—he thinks it may be maintained. But on the very next morning, I read what I consider by far the cleverest of all the journals that have been used to support the foreign policy of the Ministry in the metropolis, viz. the *Pall Mall Gazette*. In it I read a passage to *Uneasiness* this effect: 'We have before us ample evidence, in the tone of *abroad as to* the foreign press, of the alarm which is felt upon the Continent *projects.* at the supposed projects of the English Government.' Rely upon it, gentlemen, there are more of these projects in the air. For the last two years their whole existence has been a succession of these projects. As long as Lord Derby and Lord Carnarvon were among them there was an important obstacle placed in their way in the character of these men. But since that time we have had nothing but new projects, one more alarming and more dangerous than another.

They began with sending their fleet to the Dardanelles with- *Causes for* out the consent of the Sultan, and in violation of the Treaty of *alarm among* Paris, which gave them no right to send it. After that they *foreign Powers.* went on by bringing their Indian troops into Europe against the law of the country. After that they proceeded to make their Anglo-Turkish Convention, without the knowledge of Europe, when for six months they had been contending, I may say, at the point of the sword, that it was Europe, and Europe alone, that had a right to manage the concerns of the Turkish Empire. It is difficult, gentlemen, human memory will hardly avail, to bring up all these cases. I have got now as far as the Anglo-Turkish Convention. What is the next? The next is Afghan-istan. A war was made in Afghanistan to the surprise and astonishment—I might almost say to the horror—of this country, upon which I shall have occasion, either to-day or on another day, to enlarge more than I can do at the present moment. I am now only illustrating to you the manner in which a series of surprises, a series of theatrical expedients, calculated to excite, calculated to alarm, calculated to stir pride and passion, and calculated to divide the world, have been the daily employment and subsistence, the established dietary of the present Government. Afghanistan, gentlemen, was not the last. Having had a diversion of that kind in Asia, the next turn was to be in Africa. But there a different course was adopted. The practice which in other circles is well known by the name of ' hedging ' was brought into play, and Sir Bartle Frere was exhorted and instructed as to affairs in Africa with infinite skill, and in terms most accurately constructed in such a way that if they turned out well, the honour and the glory would redound to this patriotic Government; but if they turned out ill, the responsibility and the burden would fall on the shoulders of Sir Bartle Frere.

Movements of the Mediterranean Fleet. Well, these came one after another, gentlemen, and now we have not done. We end where we began, and again it is a question of sending the fleet to the Dardanelles. Whether it is on its way there we do not know at this moment. We know that the officers—at least that is the last account I have seen— that the officers are only allowed to be within call at two hours' notice. When the catalogue of expedients is exhausted, it is just like a manager with his stock of theatrical pieces—after he has presented them all he must begin again—and so we are again excited, and I must say alarmed, and I believe that Europe is greatly disquieted and disturbed, by not knowing what is to be the next quasi-military operation of the Government.

These are not subjects, gentlemen, upon which I will dilate at the present moment, but this I will say, that in my opinion, and in the opinion which I have derived from the great statesmen of the period of my youth, without any distinction of party, but, if there was any distinction of party, which I have learned more from Conservative statesmen than from Liberal statesmen, the great duty of a Government, especially in foreign affairs, is to soothe and tranquillize the minds of the people, not to set up false phantoms of glory which are to delude them into calamity, *'False phantoms of glory which delude into calamity.'* not to flatter their infirmities by leading them to believe that they are better than the rest of the world, and so to encourage the baleful spirit of domination; but to proceed upon a principle that recognises the sisterhood and equality of nations, the absolute equality of public right among them; above all, to endeavour to produce and to maintain a temper so calm and so deliberate in the public opinion of the country, that none shall be able to disturb it. The maxim of a Government ought, gentlemen, to be that which was known in ancient history as the appeal from Philip drunk to Philip sober. But the conduct of the present Government, and their resort one after another to these needless, alarming, and too frequently most discreditable measures, has been exactly the reverse. Their business has been to appeal to pride and to passion, to stir up those very feelings which every wise man ought to endeavour to allay, and, in fact, constantly to appeal from Philip sober to Philip drunk.

Gentlemen, I have come into this county to repeat, with your permission, the indictment which I have to the best of *The indictment against the Government.* my ability endeavoured to make many times elsewhere against Her Majesty's Government. It is a very serious indictment. It is well in these things that men should be held to the words that they utter, should be made to feel that they are responsible for them, and therefore you will perhaps allow me to read a sentence which I embodied in the letter written in reply to your most flattering and most obliging invitation. My sentence was this: 'The management of finance, the scale of expenditure, the constantly growing arrears of legislation, serious as they are, only lead up to still greater questions. I hold before you, as I have held in the House of Commons, that the faith and honour of the country have been gravely compromised in the

foreign policy of the Ministry; that by the disturbance of confidence, and lately even of peace, which they have brought
about, they have prolonged and aggravated the public distress;
that they have augmented the power and influence of the
Russian Empire, even while estranging the feelings of its
population; that they have embarked the Crown and people in
an unjust war (the Afghan war), full of mischief if not of
positive danger to India; and that by their use of the treaty-
making and war-making powers of the Crown they have
abridged the just rights of Parliament and have presented
prerogative to the nation under an unconstitutional aspect
which tends to make it insecure.' Not from one phrase, not
from one syllable of that indictment do I recede. If, gentlemen, in addressing this constituency there be any part of it
upon which at the close I shall not seem to have made good
the original statement, most glad shall I be to attend to the
legitimate appeal of those who may think fit to challenge me
upon the point, and to bring forward the matter—alas! only too
abundant—by which every one of them can be substantiated
before the world. Those, certainly, gentlemen, are charges of
the utmost gravity.

Alleged facti-
ous opposition
by the Liberal
party.

But we are met with preliminary objections, and we are
told, we are incessantly told, that there is no fault in the
Government, that this is all a spirit of faction on the part of the
Liberal party. I need not quote what you know very well; that
that is the stock and standing material of invective against us
—it is all our faction. The Government is perfectly innocent,
but we are determined to blacken them because of the selfish and
unjust motives by which we are prompted. Now that charge,
standing as it usually does stand, in the stead of argument
upon the acts of the Government themselves, and being found
far more convenient by our opponents than the justification of
those acts upon the merits, I wish to try that charge. I will
not try it by retorting imputations of evil motive. I have
already said what I think of them. And to no man will I, for

one, impute a want of patriotism in his public policy. It is a
charge continually made against us. So far as I am concerned,
it never shall be made against our opponents. But I am going
to examine very shortly this charge of a spirit of faction on the
part of the Liberal party. I do not condescend to deal with it
by a mere counter-assertion, by a mere statement that we are
innocent of it, nor will I endeavour to excite you—as probably
a Tory speaker would excite you—as a thousand Tory speakers
have excited their hearers, by drawing forth their uninformed
cheers through assertions of that kind. But I will come to
facts, and I will ask whether the facts of the case bear out, or
whether they do not absolutely confute that assertion.

Now, the great question of dispute between the two parties, and
the question out of which almost every other question has grown
collaterally, has been what is known as the Eastern Question.

And what I want to point out to you is this—the date at
which the Eastern Question, and the action of the Government
upon the Eastern Question, began, and the date at which the
action of the Liberal party, as a party, upon the Eastern
Question began. The Eastern Question began, that is, its recent
phase and development began, in the summer of 1875, and it
immediately assumed great importance. In the winter of 1875
the Powers of Europe endeavoured to arrange for concerted action
on the Eastern Question by what was called the Andrassy Note. *The commencement of the Government action in the Eastern Question in 1875.*

They had first endeavoured to arrange for concerted action by
their consuls. The British Government stated that they
objected on principle to any interference between the Sultan
and his subjects. Nevertheless, they were willing to allow
their consuls to act, provided it were done in such a way that
no interference should be contemplated. Of course this failed.
Then came the Andrassy Note. The Government objected on
principle to the Andrassy Note, but they finally agreed to it,
because the Turk wished them to agree to it—that is to say,
that the Turk, who has very considerable astuteness, saw that
he had better have in the councils of Europe some Power on *The Andrassy Note, 1875.*

which he could rely to prevent these councils from coming to practical effect, rather than to leave the Continental Powers of Europe to act alone.

The Berlin Memorandum, 1876. In the spring of 1876, the Andrassy Note having been frustrated of its effect, not owing to the Government, who finally concurred in it, but owing to circumstances in Turkey, the Powers of Europe again endeavoured more seriously to arrange for concerted action, and produced what they called the Berlin Memorandum. The British Government absolutely and flatly refused to support the Berlin Memorandum. We have now arrived, gentlemen, at the end of the session of 1876. Now, mind, the charge is that the Liberal party has been cavilling at the foreign policy of the Government in the East from a spirit of faction. What I point out to you is this—that down to the end of the session 1876, although the Government had been adopting measures of the utmost importance in direct contradiction to the spirit and action of the rest of the Powers of Europe, there was not one word of hostile comment from the Liberal party.

On the 31st July 1876, at the very end of the session, there was a debate in the House of Commons. In that debate I *Mr. Gladstone first censured the Government 31st July 1876.* took part. I did censure the conduct of the Government in refusing the Berlin Memorandum without suggesting some alternative to maintain the concert of Europe, and Lord Beaconsfield—I am now going to show you the evidence upon *Lord Beaconsfield said he was the only assailant of the Ministry.* which I speak — Lord Beaconsfield, in reply to me on the debate, said that the right honourable gentleman, meaning myself, was the only person who has assailed the policy of the Government. Now I ask you, was it faction in the Liberal party to remain silent during all these important acts, and to extend their confidence to the Government in the affairs of the Turkish Empire, even when that Government was acting in contradiction to the whole spirit, I may say, of civilised mankind—certainly in contradiction to the united proposals of the five Great Powers of the continent of Europe ?

Far more difficult is it to justify the Liberal party upon the *The Liberal* *party were not* other side. Why did we allow the East to be thrown into con- *factious, rather* fusion? Why did we allow the concert of Europe to be broken *they were too* *long silent.* up? Why did we allow the Berlin Memorandum to be thrown behind the fire, and no other measure substituted in its place? Why did we allow that fatal progression of events to advance, unchecked by us, so far, even after the fields of Bulgaria had flowed with blood, and the cry of every horror known and unknown had ascended to heaven from that country? Why did we remain silent for such a length of time? Gentlemen, that is not all.

It is quite true that there was, soon after, a refusal of the great human heart of this country, not in Parliament, but outside of Parliament, to acquiesce in what was going on, and to maintain the ignominious silence which we had maintained on the subject of the Bulgarian massacres.

In August and September 1876 there was an outburst, an *The outburst* *in August* 1876 involuntary outburst, for the strain could no longer be borne, *denouncing the* from the people of this country, in every quarter of the *massacres.* country, denouncing those massacres. But that, gentlemen, was not by the action of the Liberal party. It was admitted by the Government themselves to be the expression of the country —misled, as they said, but still the expression of the country. It is true that it was said with reference to me that any man who made use of the susceptibilities of the country for the purpose of bringing himself back to office was worse than those who had perpetrated the Bulgarian massacres. But that was only a remark which hit one insignificant individual, nor was he very deeply wounded by it. But the Liberal party was not, as a party, in the field. Nay, more; that national feeling *This was the* *action of* produced its effects. It produced the Conference at Constan- *national feel-* tinople. That was eighteen months after the Eastern Question *ing.* had been opened. Down to the date of that Conference, the Liberal party had taken no step for any purpose prejudicial to the action of the Government; and when Lord Salisbury went to the Conference at Constantinople, he went, I say it without fear of contradiction, carrying with him the goodwill, carrying with him the favourable auspices, carrying with him, I will even say, the confidence of the Liberal party as to the result and the tendency of his exertions.   And it was not till after nearly

The Liberal party began to act in 1877.

two years—viz. late in the spring, or during the spring of 1877 —it was not until nearly two years after the Government had been busy with the Eastern Question that the Liberal party first began somewhat feebly to raise its voice in the House of Commons, and to protest against the course that had been adopted, which was evidently, as we thought, a course tending to bring about war, bloodshed, and disturbance, that might very easily have been avoided.

Where is the factious spirit?

Now, gentlemen, I think I have shown you that it requires some audacity to charge with faction in this matter a party which maintained such a silence for nearly two years; which was even willing to acquiesce in the rejection of the Berlin Memorandum, and which heartily accompanied with its goodwill and confidence Lord Salisbury when he went to the Conference at Constantinople.   I do not hesitate to say this, gentlemen, that when Lord Salisbury went to Constantinople—I believe with a perfectly upright and honourable intention—he carried with him a great deal more confidence from the Liberal party than he carried with him from some among his own colleagues.

But now, gentlemen, I can only say that if the Liberal party are governed by a factious spirit, they are great fools for their

The alleged desire of the Liberals to get into office.

pains.   What means a factious spirit but the action of an ungovernable desire to get into office?   And it is alleged that the Liberal party are under the influence of such a desire. Well, gentlemen, if they are, all I can say is that there is no disputing about tastes; but men must be men of a very extraordinary taste who desire to take such a succession as will be left by the present Government.

I hope the verdict of the country will give to Lord Granville and Lord Hartington the responsible charge of its affairs.

But I must say I think them much to be pitied on the day

when that charge is committed to their hands. Never, gentlemen, never in the recollection of living man has such an *The inherit-*
entangled web been given over to any set of men to unravel. *by the Tories.*
Did they receive a similar inheritance from us when we went
out of power? Did we give over to them that which will be
given over by them to their successors? Gentlemen, I make
no boast. We simply gave over to them what every Government has usually given over to its successors. Let us do them
justice. Do not let us allow party feelings to lead us to suppose that there never has been prudence and discretion and
right principle on the part of a Conservative Government, at
least so far as to make sure that any evils for which they were
responsible would be tolerable evils, and would not greatly
disturb the general stability of the country. We did, merely
to the best of our ability, what others had done before us.

But still, when we shall have so largely to consider the state
of things to which the action of the present Government has
brought the affairs of this country, it is absolutely necessary
that I should briefly recall to your minds the nature of the
starting-point from which they set out. What was their *The financial*
starting-place, gentlemen, in finance? The starting-point in *of this Govern-*
finance was this, that we handed over to them a surplus which, *ment was a*
in our hands, I will venture to say, would have been a surplus *surplus.*
closely approaching six millions of money. Now, I have
spoken of the manner in which they carry on this warfare, and
you will believe that their scribes, with a pertinacious activity,
feeling the difficulties of their case, have been very very hard
driven to know how to deal with this question of the surplus.
It has been necessary for them to get rid of it in some way or
other, and some of them have actually had the cool audacity to
say—I have read it in various newspapers; I have read it in a
Sheffield newspaper, which, however, I won't name; it would
not be delicate in reference to the feelings of the high-minded
gentleman who wrote it—but they have asserted that we left to
them £3,000,000 of Alabama payment, which we ought to have

made, but which we handed over to them to pay. The only objection to this is that, if you consult the accounts, you will find that that £3,000,000 was paid by us in the year before we left office.

Then it is said this surplus was not a 'realized surplus.' *What is a 'realized surplus.'* What is meant by a realized surplus? According to them, there never has been such a thing in this country as a realized surplus. The law of this country provides, and most wisely provides, that when for the current year there is a certain surplus of revenue over expenditure, the money shall, in fixed proportions, be then and there applied to the reduction of debt. That, of course, was done in the last year of our Government. But what we left was the prospect of the incoming revenue for the following year. That was the prospect, which distinctly showed that there would be a surplus of £5,000,000 to £6,000,000, and that was the prospect we handed over to them; and if they choose to say it was not a realized surplus—undoubtedly it was no more realized than the Duke of Buccleuch's rents for next year are realized; but if, as is not likely, the Duke of Buccleuch has occasion to borrow on the security of his rents for next year, I suspect he will find many people quite ready to lend to him. Well, gentlemen, that is the only explanation I need give you. But I do assure you that such has been the amount of Tory assertion on this subject of the surplus, that I have been pestered for the last two or three years of my life with letters from puzzled Liberals, who wrote to say they had believed there was a surplus of £5,000,000 or £6,000,000, but the Tories would not admit it, and they begged me, for their own individual enlightenment, to explain to them how it was. Our surplus was like every other real and *bona fide* surplus, which the law of this country contemplates or permits, and the effect of it was that the Tories, who have since done nothing but add to the burdens of the people, were able to commence their career with a large remission of taxation. That was the case with finance.

How did we leave the army? because one of the favourite

assertions of their scribes is that we ruined the army. Well, *The state of the army when the* gentlemen, undoubtedly we put the country to very heavy *Liberals left* expense on account of the army; but we put them to heavy *office.* expense for objects which we thought important. We found that the army, through the system of purchase, was the property of the rich. We abolished purchase, and we tried to make it, *Abolition of* and in some degree, I hope, have made it, the property of the *purchase.* nation. But we have been told that we weakened and reduced the army. Weakened and reduced the army! Why, we for the first time founded a real military reserve—that reserve *A real reserve* under which, in 1878, there happened an event previously quite *founded.* unknown to our history—namely, that, upon the stroke of a pen sent forth by the Minister to the country, almost in a day five-and-thirty thousand trained men were added to the ranks of the army. That was the result of the system of reserve; and the system of reserve, along with many other great and valuable reforms, the country owes to Lord Cardwell, the Secretary of War under the late Government.

Well, gentlemen, you know—I need not enter into details— what was the general state of our foreign relations. The topic of our foreign relations can be disposed of in one minute. It is constantly said, indeed, by the scribes of the Government, and it was intimated by Lord Salisbury,—to whom I will return in greater detail at a future time,—that the foreign policy of the late Government was discreditable. Well, but here I have got a witness on the other side. I have got the witness of Lord *State of our* Beaconsfield's Foreign Secretary at the time when he took office. *foreign rela-* *tions in 1874.* At the time when he took office in the House of Lords, Lord Derby, then enjoying the full undivided confidence of the Conservative party, used these words on the 19th March 1874: 'At the present moment the condition of the country in regard to our foreign relations is most satisfactory. There is no State whatever with which our relations are not most cordial.' Now, our unfortunate friends and fellow-citizens, the Tories, are constantly called upon to believe that at the time they took office the state of the country, in regard to foreign relations, was most unsatisfactory, and that with no State were our relations most cordial, because by every State we were undervalued and despised. Gentlemen, there was not a cloud upon the horizon at the time when the charge of foreign affairs was handed over to Her Majesty's present Government. Does that imply that there was nothing serious to be done? Oh no, gentlemen, depend upon it, and you will find it to your cost before you are five years older, you will know it better than you do to-day; depend upon it that this Empire is an Empire, the daily calls of whose immense responsibilities, the daily inevitable calls of whose responsibilities, task and overtask the energies of the best and ablest of her sons. Why, gentlemen, there is not a country in the history of the world that has undertaken what we have undertaken; and when I say ' what we have undertaken,' I don't mean what the present Government have undertaken—that I will come to by and by—but what England in its traditional established policy and position has undertaken.

The anomalous constitution of the British Empire. There is no precedent in human history for a formation like the British Empire. A small island at one extremity of the globe peoples the whole earth with its colonies. Not satisfied with that, it goes among the ancient races of Asia and subjects two hundred and forty millions of men to its rule. Along with all this it disseminates over the world a commerce such as no imagination ever conceived in former times, and such as no poet ever painted. And all this it has to do with the strength that lies within the narrow limits of these shores. Not a strength that I disparage; on the contrary, I wish to dissipate, if I can, the idle dreams of those who are always telling you that the strength of England depends, sometimes they say upon its prestige, sometimes they say upon its extending its Empire, *Our true strength is within the United Kingdom.* or upon what it possesses beyond these shores. Rely upon it the strength of Great Britain and Ireland is within the United Kingdom. Whatever is to be done in defending and governing these vast colonies with their teeming millions; in protecting that unmeasured commerce; in relation to the enormous responsibilities of India—whatever is to be done, must be done by the force derived from you and from your children, derived from you and from your fellow-electors, throughout the land, and from you and from the citizens and people of this country. And who are they? They are, perhaps, some three-and-thirty millions of persons,—a population less than the population of France; less than the population of Austria; less than the population of Germany; and much less than the population of Russia. But the populations of Austria, of Russia, of Germany, and of France find it quite hard enough to settle their own matters within their own limits. We have undertaken to settle the affairs of about a fourth of the entire human race scattered over all the world. Is not that enough for the ambition of Lord Beaconsfield? It satisfied the Duke of Wellington and Mr. Canning, Lord Grey and Sir Robert Peel; it satisfied Lord Palmerston and Lord Russell, ay, and the late Lord Derby. And why cannot it satisfy—I do not want to draw any invidious distinction between Lord Beaconsfield and his colleagues; it seems to me that they are all now very much of one mind, that they all move with harmony amongst themselves; but I say, why is it not to satisfy the ambition of the members of the present Government? I affirm that, on the contrary, strive and labour as you will in office—I speak after the experience of a lifetime, of which a fair portion has been spent in office—I say that strive and labour as you will in Parliament and in office, human strength and human thought are not equal to the ordinary discharge of the calls and duties appertaining to Government in this great, wonderful, and world-wide Empire. And therefore, gentlemen, I say it is indeed deplorable that in addition to these calls, of which we have evidence in a thousand forms, and of our insufficiency to meet which we have evidence in a thousand forms—when, in addition to these calls, all manner of gratuitous, dangerous, ambiguous, impracticable, and impossible engagements are contracted for us in all parts of the world.

Prudential considerations against the Government's policy abroad.

And that is what has lately been happening. I am not now going to discuss this question upon the highest grounds. I assail the policy of the Government on the highest grounds of principle. But I am now for a few moments only about to test it on the grounds of prudence. I appeal to you as practical men, I appeal to you as agriculturists, I appeal to you as tradesmen —I appeal to you in whatever class or profession you may be, and ask whether it is not wise to have some regard to the relation between means and ends, some regard to the relation between the work to be done and the strength you possess in order to perform it. I point to the state of our legislation, our accumulated and accumulating arrears constantly growing upon us; I point to the multitude of unsolved problems of our Government, to the multitude of unsolved problems connected with the administration of our Indian Empire—enough, God knows, to call forth the deepest and most anxious reflection of the most sober-minded; and even the most sanguine man, I say, might be satisfied with those tasks.

Our annexations of territory since 1874.

But what has been the course of things for the last three years? I will run them over almost in as many words. We have got an annexation of territory—I put it down merely that I might not be incomplete—an annexation of territory in the

Fiji Islands.

Fiji Islands, of which I won't speak, because I don't consider the Government is censurable for that act, whether it were a wise act or not. Nobody could say that that was their spontaneous act. But now let us look at what have been their

The Transvaal.

spontaneous acts. They have annexed in Africa the Transvaal territory, inhabited by a free European, Christian, republican community, which they have thought proper to bring within the limits of a monarchy, although out of 8000 persons in that republic qualified to vote upon the subject, we are told, and I have never seen the statement officially contradicted, that 6500 protested against it. These are the circumstances under which

we undertake to transform republicans into subjects of a *Zululand.*
monarchy. We have made war upon the Zulus. We have
thereby become responsible for their territory; and not only
this, but we are now, as it appears from the latest advices, about
to make war upon a chief lying to the northward of the Zulus;
and Sir Bartle Frere, who was the great authority for the proceedings of the Government in Afghanistan, has announced in
South Africa that it will be necessary for us to extend our
dominions until we reach the Portuguese frontier to the north.
So much for Africa.

I come to Europe. In Europe we have annexed the island *Cyprus.*
of Cyprus, of which I will say more at another time. We have
assumed jointly with France the virtual government of Egypt; *The Protector-*
and possibly, as we are to extend, says Sir Bartle Frere, our *ate of Egypt.*
southern dominions in Africa till we meet the southern frontier
of the Portuguese—possibly one of these days we may extend
our northern dominions in Africa till we meet the northern
frontier of the Portuguese. We then, gentlemen, have undertaken to make ourselves responsible for the good government
of Turkey in Asia—not of Asia Minor, as you are sometimes *The Protector-*
told, exclusively, but of the whole of that great space upon the *ate of Asia*
map, including the principal part of Arabia, which is known *Minor.*
geographically as Turkey in Asia. Besides governing it well,
we have undertaken to defend the Armenian frontier of Turkey
against Russia, a country which we cannot possibly get at
except either by travelling over several hundreds of miles by
land, including mountain-chains never adapted to be traversed
by armies, or else some thousands of miles of sea, ending at
the extremity of the Black Sea, and then having to effect a
landing. That is another of our engagements.

Well, and as if all that were not enough, we have, by the
most wanton invasion of Afghanistan, broken that country into *Afghanistan.*
pieces, made it a miserable ruin, destroyed whatever there was
in it of peace and order, caused it to be added to the anarchies
of the Eastern world, and we have become responsible for the

management of the millions of warlike but very partially civilised people whom it contains, under circumstances where the application of military power, and we have nothing but military power to go by, is attended at every foot with enormous difficulties.

This is not a question of party, but of a system of Government.

Now, gentlemen, these are proceedings which I present to you at the present moment in the view of political prudence only. I really have but one great anxiety. This is a self-governing country. Let us bring home to the minds of the people the state of the facts they have to deal with, and in Heaven's name let them determine whether or not this is the way in which they like to be governed. Do not let us suppose this is like the old question between Whig and Tory. It is nothing of the kind. It is not now as if we were disputing about some secondary matter—it is not even as if we were disputing about the Irish Church, which no doubt was a very important affair. What we are disputing about is a whole system of Government, and to make good that proposition that it is a whole system of Government will be my great object in any addresses that I may deliver in this country. If it is acceptable, if it is liked by the people—they are the masters— it is for them to have it. It is not particularly pleasant for any man, I suppose, to spend the closing years of his life in vain and unavailing protest; but as long as he thinks his protest may avail, as long as he feels that the people have not yet had their fair chance and opportunity, it is his duty to pro-test, and it is to perform that duty, gentlemen, that I come here.

I have spoken, gentlemen, of the inheritance given over to the present Government by their predecessors, and of the inheritance that they will give over to those who succeed them. Now, our condition is not only, in my judgment, a condition of embarrassment, but it is one of embarrassment we have made

Why did the Liberals quarrel with the Government about Turkey?

for ourselves; and before I close, although I have already detained you too long, I must give a single illustration of the manner in which we have been making our own embarrassments. Why did we quarrel with the present Government about Turkey ? I have shown that we were extremely slow in doing it. I believe we were too slow, and that, perhaps, if we had begun sooner our exertions might have availed more ; but it was from a good motive. Why did we quarrel ? What was the point upon which we quarrelled ?

The point upon which we quarrelled was this : Whether coercion was under any circumstances to be applied to Turkey to bring about the better government of that country. Now that will not be disputed, or if it is disputed, and in order that it may not be disputed, for it is very difficult to say what won't be disputed—in order that it may not be disputed I will read from two conclusive authorities. That is my point. The foundation of the policy of the present Government was that *The founda-* coercion was not to be applied to Turkey. Here is what Lord *Turkish policy* Cranbrook, who stated the case of the Government in the *was no coer-* House of Commons, said : ' We have proclaimed, and I proclaim again, in the strongest language, that we should be wrong in every sense of the word if we were to endeavour to apply material coercion against Turkey;' that was what Lord Cranbrook said on the 15th February 1877, nor had he repented in April, for in April he said : ' Above all, we feel that we, who have engaged ourselves by treaty, at least in former times, who have had no personal wrong done to us, have no right and no com- mission, either as a country, or, as I may say, from Heaven, to take upon ourselves the vindication by violence of the rights of the Christian subjects of the Porte, however much we may feel for them.' Higher authority, of course, still than Lord Cran- brook, but in perfect conformity with him, was Lord Beaconsfield himself, who, on the 20th February 1877, after a speech of Lord Granville's, said this : ' The noble Lord and his friends are of opinion that we should have coerced the Porte into the acceptation of the policy which we recommended. That is not a course which we can conscientiously profess or promote, and I think, therefore, when an issue so broad is brought before the

House, it really is the duty of noble Lords to give us an opportunity to clear the mind of the country by letting it know what
is the opinion of Parliament upon policies so distinct, and which
in their consequences must be so different.'   Now, you see
plainly that coercion in the extreme case that had arisen was
recommended by the Liberal party.   Coercion was objected to
on the highest grounds by the Tory party ; and Lord Beaconsfield
virtually said, 'Such is the profound difference between these
policies that I challenge you to make a motion in Parliament,
and to take the opinion of Parliament in order that we may
know which way we are to move.'   That was not all, for after
the English Government had disclaimed coercion, and after that
terribly calamitous Russo-Turkish war had been begun and
ended, Lord Beaconsfield declared that if the Government had
been entirely consistent, they would not have rested satisfied with
protesting against the action of Russia, so sacred was this principle of non-coercion in their eyes, but that they ought to have
warned Russia that if she acted she must be prepared to encounter the opposition of England.   I will read a very short
passage from a letter of Sir Henry Layard which refers to that
declaration.   Sir Henry Layard, on the 18th April 1879, wrote
or spoke as follows, I am not quite sure which ; I quote it from
an unexceptionable authority, the *Daily Telegraph* of April 19 :
'I agree with the remark of Lord Beaconsfield when he returned
from the Berlin Congress, that if England had shown firmness in
the first instance the late war might have been avoided.   That is
my conviction, and everything I have seen tends to confirm it.'
If England had shown firmness—that is to say, if she had
threatened Russia.   There is no other meaning applicable to
the words.   I have shown you, therefore, gentlemen, what it is
upon which we went to issue — whether Turkey should be
coerced, or whether she should not.

But there is an important limitation.   We had never given
countenance to single-handed attempts to coerce Turkey.   We
felt that single-handed attempts to coerce Turkey would pro-

bably lead to immediate bloodshed and calamity, with great *The Liberal party desired coercion by united Europe.* uncertainty as to the issue. The coercion we recommended was coercion by the united authority of Europe, and we always contended that in the case where the united authority of Europe was brought into action, there was no fear of having to proceed to actual coercion. The Turk knew very well how to measure strength on one side and the other, and he would have yielded to that authority. But no, there must be no coercion under any circumstances. Such was the issue, gentlemen. Well, where do we stand now? We know what has taken place in the interval. We know that a great work of liberation has been done, in which we have had no part whatever. With the traditions of liberty which we think we cherish, with the recollection that you Scotchmen entertain of the struggles in which you have engaged to establish your own liberties here, a great work of emancipation has been going on in the world, and you have been prevented by your Government from any share in it whatever. But bitter as is the mortification with which I for one reflect upon that exclusion, I thank God that the work has been done. It has been done in one sense, perhaps, by the most inappropriate of instruments; but I rejoice in the result, that six or seven millions of people who were in partial subjection have been brought into total independence, and many millions more who were in absolute subjection to the Ottoman rule have been brought into a state which, if not one of total independence, yet is one of practical liberation actually attained, or very shortly to be realized— practical liberation from the worst of the evils which they suffered.

But what happens now? Why, it appears the Turk is going *The sudden change by the Government to a coercion policy.* to be coerced after all. But is not it a most astounding fact that the Government, who said they would on no consideration coerce the Turk, and who said that if Europe attempted to coerce the Turk nothing but misery could result, now expects to coerce the Turk by sending an order to Admiral Hornby at

Malta, and desiring him to sail with his fleet into the east of
the Mediterranean ? Now, gentlemen, neither you nor I are
acquainted with the whole of the circumstances attendant upon
these measures. We don't know the reasons of State that have
brought about this extraordinary result. But what I have
pointed out to you is this, that Her Majesty's Government
have in matter of fact come round to the very principle upon
which they compelled the Liberals to join issue with them two
or three years ago — the very principle which they then
declared to be totally inadmissible, and for urging which upon
them, their agents and organs through the country have been
incessantly maintaining that nothing but the spirit of faction
could have induced us to do anything so monstrous. That
which nothing but the spirit of faction could have induced us
It is an at- to do, is embraced in principle by Her Majesty's Government.
tempt at single- But is it embraced in the same form ? No. We said : Let
handed coer-
cion. coercion be applied by the united authority of Europe—that is
to say, for it is not an exaggeration so to put it, by the united
authority of the civilised world applicable to this case. Our
American friends have too remote an interest in it to take part.
God forbid I should exclude them from the civilised world ;
but it was by the united authority of Europe that we demanded
it. It is now attempted by the single authority and by the
Its dangers. single hand of England. Will it succeed ? All I can say is
this, if it be directed to good and honest ends, to practical
improvement, with all my heart I hope it may ; but it may
not, and then where is the responsibility ? Where is the
responsibility of those who refused to allow all Europe to act
in unison, and who then took upon themselves this single-
handed action ? If it fails, they incur an immense responsibility. If it succeeds, it only becomes the more plain that had
they but acceded to the advice which was at first so humbly
tendered by the Liberal party, and which only after a long
time was vigorously pressed—had they then acceded to the
view of the Liberal party, and allowed Turkey to be dealt with

as she ought to have been dealt with at the close of the Constantinople Conference, Turkey would have given way at once. The Power which yields to one State would still more readily have yielded to the united voice of the six great States. The concessions to be made by her would then have been made, and the horrors and the bloodshed, the loss of life and treasure, the heartburnings, the difficulties, the confusion, and the anarchy that have followed, would all of them have been saved.

Therefore, gentlemen, I say that our present embarrassments are of our own creation. It would be a very cruel thing to hold the present Government responsible for the existence of an Eastern Question that from time to time troubles Europe. I have not held them so responsible. I hold them responsible *The present* for having interrupted that concerted action which, it is as *Government is* evident as considerations of sense and policy can make it— *responsible for* which could not have failed to attain its effect; and for now *the interruption of con-* being driven to make the same effort, with diminished *certed action.* resources, in greater difficulties, and after the terrible penalties of an almost immeasurable bloodshed had been paid.

Now, gentlemen, all this, and a great deal more than this, has to be said, which cannot be said now. Neither your patience nor my strength could enable me to say it. I have detained you at great length. I have only opened, as it were, these questions. I have not even touched the great number of important subjects in which you naturally, as men of Scotland and men of Midlothian, feel very special interest. I will, however, gentlemen, for this day bid you farewell. But I shall say one word in closing, and it is this. It is constantly said by the Government, and it is a fair claim on their part, that they have been supported by large majorities in the House of *The majority* Commons. It is a very fair claim, indeed, for a certain purpose. *in the House of* I should, indeed, have something to say upon the other side— *Commons.* viz. this, that you will find in no instance that I am aware of in history, neither in the American War nor in the great Revolutionary War, nor at any period known to me, has objec-

tion been taken, persistently and increasingly taken, by such
large fractions of the House of Commons—not less, at any rate,
than two-fifths of the House, sometimes more—to the foreign
policy of the Government, as during this great controversy.
The fact is, gentlemen, that in matters of foreign policy it does
require, and it ought to require, very great errors and very
great misdeeds on the part of the Government to drive a large
portion of Parliament into opposition.   It is most important to
maintain our national unity in the face of the world.   I, for my
part, have always admitted, and admit now, that our responsibility in opposing the Government has been immense, but their
responsibility in refusing to do right has been still greater.   Still
they are right in alleging that they have been supported by large
majorities.   Pray, consider what that means.   That is a most
important proposition ; it is a proposition that ought to come
home to the mind of every one here.   It means this, that
though I have been obliged all through this discourse to attack
the Government, I am really attacking the majority of the
House of Commons.   Please to consider that you might, if
you like, strike out of my speech all reference to the Government, all reference to any name, all reference to the body.

It is no longer the Government with which you have to deal.
You have to deal with the majority of the House of Commons.
Has always The majority of the House of Commons has completely
steadily sup- acquitted the Government.   Upon every occasion when the
ported the Government has appealed to it, the majority of the House
Government. of Commons has been ready to answer to the call.   Hardly
a man has ever hesitated to grant the confidence that was
desired, however outrageous in our view the nature of the
demand might be.   Completely and bodily, the majority of
the House of Commons has taken on itself the responsibility
of the Government—and not only the collective majority of
the House of Commons, gentlemen.   If you had got to deal
' They must be with them by a vote of censure on that majority in the lump,
dealt with that would be a very ineffective method of dealing.   They must
individually.'

be dealt with individually. That majority is made up of units. It is the unit with which you have got to deal. And let me tell you that the occasion is a solemn one; for as I am the first to aver that now fully and bodily the majority of the House of Commons has, in the face of the country, by a multitude of repeated and deliberate acts, made itself wholly and absolutely responsible in the whole of these transactions that I have been commenting upon, and in many more; and as the House of Commons has done that, so upon the coming general election will it have to be determined whether that responsibility, so shifted from an Administration to a Parliament, shall again be shifted from a Parliament to a nation. As yet the nation has had no opportunity. Nay, as I pointed out early in these remarks, the Government do not seem disposed to give them the opportunity. To the last moment, so far as we are informed by the best authorities, they intend to withhold it. The nation, therefore, is not yet responsible. If faith has *The nation is* been broken, if blood has been needlessly shed, if the name of *not yet respon-* *sible.* England has been discredited and lowered from that lofty standard which it ought to exhibit to the whole world, if the country has been needlessly distressed, if finance has been thrown into confusion, if the foundations of the Indian Empire have been impaired, all these things as yet are the work of an Administration and a Parliament; but the day is coming, and *The issue we* is near at hand, when that event will take place which will *have to try.* lead the historian to declare whether or not they are the work, not of an Administration and not of a Parliament, but the work of a great and a free people. If this great and free and powerful people is disposed to associate itself with such transactions, if it is disposed to assume upon itself what some of us would call the guilt, and many of us must declare to be the heavy burden, of all those events that have been passing before our eyes, it rests with them to do it. But, gentlemen, let every one of us resolve in his inner conscience, before God and before man—let him resolve that he at least will have no share in such a proceeding; that he will do his best to exempt himself; that he will exempt himself from every participation in what he believes to be mischievous and ruinous misdeeds; that, so far as his exertions can avail, no trifling, no secondary consideration shall stand in the way of them, or abate them; that he will do what in him lies to dissuade his countrymen from arriving at a resolution so full of mischief, of peril, and of shame.

Gentlemen, this is the issue which the people of this country will have to try. Our minds are made up. You and they have got to speak. I for my part have done and will do the little that rests with me to make clear the nature of the great controversy that is to be decided; and I say from the bottom of my soul, 'God speed the right.'

On the motion of Mr. John M'Laren, seconded by Mr. Usher of Woodhall, a vote of thanks was enthusiastically accorded to Mr. Gladstone.

Mr. Gladstone, after the meeting, was presented with an address from the Corporation of Edinburgh.

III.

WEDNESDAY, NOVEMBER 26, 1879.

SECOND MIDLOTHIAN SPEECH.

Delivered in the Corn Exchange, Dalkeith, to the Electors
of the Parishes of Stow, Heriot, Temple, Borthwick,
Crichton, Fala, Carrington, Dalkeith, Cockpen, New-
battle, Cranstoun, Newton, Inveresk, Lasswade, Glen-
corse, and Penicuik.

*The population in these parishes is to a great extent agricul-
tural, with a considerable manufacturing interest in such
places as Penicuik, Lasswade, and Stow.*

DALKEITH MEETING.

On Wednesday, November 26, Mr. Gladstone proceeded by
special train from Dalmeny to Dalkeith, where he addressed
a second meeting of Midlothian electors in the Corn Exchange.
On the platform there were, amongst other gentlemen, Lord
Dalrymple, Sir William Johnston, Sir David Wedderburn,
M.P.; James Cowan, M.P.; Peter Maclagan, M.P.; G. O.
Trevelyan, M.P.; Charles Tennant, M.P.; Provost Mitchell;
John J. Reid, advocate; Ralph Richardson, W.S., etc. etc.

On the motion of Viscount Dalrymple, the chair was taken
by the Chief Magistrate of Dalkeith, Alexander Mitchell,
Esq., who briefly introduced the right honourable gentleman.

Mr. Gladstone, who was received with a perfect storm of
applause, said :—

Mr. Provost of Dalkeith and Gentlemen,—I ask the attention of this crowded and immense audience in the capacity

not of a leader of the Liberal party, but of one of its most convinced and not least loyal members, happy to follow those who in two Houses of Parliament have ably discharged the duties of the leadership under unfavourable circumstances, and most anxious to contribute my part, such as it may be, towards giving the right direction to the national wishes and convictions at what I think to be, and what I know to be, the most important crisis in our national history that has occurred during the last half-century.

The principles to be observed during the contest. Gentlemen, in conducting that portion of this contest which falls to my special care, I will endeavour to observe fair play. I will not willingly wound the feelings of any man. I shall be compelled to use strong language in speaking of measures which seem to me incapable of just description by any language which is weak. But to the authors of these measures I shall give, as I am bound to give—there is no merit in according it—I shall give all along the same implicit credit for honourable and patriotic motives which I claim on behalf of the great political party in whose ranks I have the honour to stand. Yesterday, gentlemen, it was my duty to commence a detailed exposition of what appears to me necessary to be laid before you. It is not an easy task, for it involves a survey of a long series of complicated transactions. These are not the transactions with which you are familiar from youth upwards in the scene and upon the stage of domestic affairs, but transactions largely concerned with the most distant quarters of the globe, and likewise involving that complicated subject of the foreign relations of the country with almost every one of the States of the civilised world. It is a very difficult task, gentlemen; it is only with your help, with the assistance of your kind attention, that I can hope to be useful in addressing myself to its performance. Yet with such assistance I have that hope, and I will venture to point out to you now the ground that we have already made, in order that both to friends and opponents I may be perfectly clear—that there may be no

mistake as to the issue which is raised before the county of
Midlothian.

We have arrived, in my judgment, gentlemen, at the time *The issue raised before Midlothian.*
when it is necessary frankly to avow that we so widely and
fundamentally differ from the course pursued by Her Majesty's
Government in affairs of vital moment to the country, that
we cannot contemplate with satisfaction the longer continuance
of that Government in office.   Some public writer has said
within a few days that there ought not to be a dissolution
of Parliament, for that it is most desirable that the Government should have time to finish those foreign affairs which
they have begun.   I won't enter at this moment, gentlemen,
into the logic of that argument, but I will make a frank and,
I think, liberal admission.   If I believed, if I could possibly
hope, that those gentlemen now in office would, as it is called,
finish those foreign affairs, I should be inclined to say, ' In
Heaven's name let them finish them !'   They have begun them ;
they have created them ; they have staked their reputation
upon them; they have desired to be remembered, and they
will be remembered, in connection with them ; and I would
not grudge them for a moment the satisfaction of finishing
them, nay, I should share that satisfaction.   There is nothing I
should delight in, nothing I desire so much, as to see them
finished.   But I am afraid, gentlemen, the case stands far
otherwise.   Yet that is a matter on which I at once admit
that broad assertions are not to be taken for granted.   I ask
you not to look to my assertions, but to look to my proofs
and my arguments.   And having stated that, I hope to observe
fair play.   I will say this, that when I attack the foreign
policy of the Government I will not confine myself to the
comparatively easy duty of objecting to decisions taken in difficult circumstances, but I will endeavour to place before you
in a clear and intelligible light those which I conceive to be
the true principles of our foreign policy, that you may have
an opportunity of comparing them with the false.

Now, gentlemen, I wish here, in Dalkeith, to say one word as to local questions. The particular feature of this crisis is, that *Local and* it is a crisis at which local affairs are most unhappily swal-*domestic ques-* *tions are swal-* lowed up in general questions, and domestic questions are to *lowed up.* a great extent absorbed in foreign questions, and therefore I must, before I proceed to touch upon these local and domestic matters, I must remind you how far I conceive myself to have carried the discussion upon the great, the vital question, how the foreign affairs of this country, and its affairs beyond the sea, are to be administered, and how we are to deal with the consequences of that administration in our domestic sphere. I have endeavoured to point out, gentlemen, that as the affairs of this country stood before the present Government acceded to office, the calls of the business of so vast an Empire afforded much more than ample occupation for the very best and very ablest men that could be called to the administration of affairs. A certain progress had been made down to the year 1874 in dealing with some of those calls, but the business of the country still remained confronting us in great mass at the time when the majority of the constituency, in the exercise of its undoubted right, dismissed us from our offices.

The country Since that time I make the complaint that the shoulders, *has been loaded* *by mischievous* so to speak, of this nation have been loaded by a multitude *engagements* of gratuitous, mischievous, and dangerous engagements. I *abroad.* point to Africa, I point to India, I point to Afghanistan, to Syria, to Asia Minor, to the whole of Turkey in Asia; I point to our assumption practically, and in an alliance with France most critical in its nature, our assumption of the virtual government of Egypt; I point to our practical annexation of the island of Cyprus, to all the military dangers and responsibilities of undertaking the defence of the Turkish frontier in Armenia; in fact, I point to enormous increase of difficulty and labour all over the world,—and I challenge it, in the first instance, upon the most modest and lowest ground, I challenge it on the ground of its prudence. Common sense, after all, gentlemen, is the rule as of private so of public life, and it is a rule of common sense which every one of you would observe in his private concerns, that you would not undertake new engagements when your hands were full.

My contention is that our hands were full; that we had *The hands of* no business to go into South Africa, into Afghanistan, into *the Govern-* *ment were* Turkey in Asia, into Cyprus, into Egypt, into so many of *quite full* *enough at* those various countries that one can hardly give a complete *home.* and accurate catalogue of them all. We had no business to go there with these gratuitous and unnecessary difficulties, disturbing confidence, perplexing business, unsettling the fabric of civilised society through the world. We had no business to take those engagements when our hands were full. But I contend, also, that the engagements were bad; and that being bad, we ought not to have undertaken them, even if our hands, instead of being full, had been perfectly empty. But now, how can I illustrate my meaning? The country has been appealed to repeatedly upon the ground that this Government was determined that there should be no diminution of the Empire, but was not at all indisposed to increase the Empire.

Well, now, what does increasing the Empire mean for us? *The true* *meaning of* What does possessing Cyprus mean for us? Pray observe that '*increasing the* *Empire.*' when we occupied Cyprus we became bound in honour to its maintenance and defence, we became bound in honour to have troops there, we became bound in honour to raise fortifications if they be required, and to uphold the flag of England which has been there erected. Now, we had done much the same thing in the Transvaal, a country where we have chosen, most unwisely, I am tempted to say insanely, to place ourselves in the strange predicament of the free subjects of a monarchy going to coerce the free subjects of a republic, and to compel them to accept a citizenship which they decline and refuse. But if that is to be done, it must be done by force. If we pass into Afghanistan and occupy Cabul and Candahar, and, as some say we are

The expenditure of money and men.

going to do, occupy Herat—and I can see no limit to these operations—everything of that kind means a necessity for more money, and means a necessity for more men.

From whence are the money and the men to come ? What do you mean by this sort of strengthening the Empire ? It is simply loading the Empire. It is not strengthening the Empire. I can understand some extensions of territory. I have no doubt that when the Germans were unfortunately led to annex Alsace and Lorraine they reckoned that Alsace and Lorraine would contribute in men and money to the purposes of the Empire, just like the rest of Germany. But that is not the case with our annexations ; that is not the case with our undertaking the government of Egypt, and the government of Asia Minor, and the government of Syria, and making ourselves responsible for those countries. The meaning of it is this, that with that limited store of men and of funds which these islands can supply, we are continually to go on enlarging our responsibilities and our dangers all over the surface of the earth. Why, gentlemen, many of you are agriculturists. What would you think of the man who, having a farm of 100 acres, takes another farm of a couple of hundred acres, and makes no increase of his farming stock ? That is an illustration—a partial illustration—of the sort of proceeding that has been going on, but it is a very feeble illustration. What would you think of the landlord who, having a great avidity for land, and being possessed of a splendid estate—for a splendid estate these islands with this Empire are—purchased another estate next to his own, or if at a distance from his own, so much the worse—but purchased another estate, whether near or far from his own, on this condition, that he should pay the tithe —or teinds, as you call them—that he should pay the rates and taxes, and the charges of every kind, but somebody else should receive the rents.

The extension of the Empire does not add strength.

Morally, these illustrations are utterly barren and feeble— they don't touch the essence of the case—but economically they are sound and true. There is no strength to be added

to your country by governing the Transvaal, by overrunning
Zululand, by undertaking to be responsible for Egypt, or for
the vast mass of mountains in Central Asia, and for keeping
in order their wild and warlike tribes. It is sheer and pure
burden imposed upon you; and I appeal to you, the Liberals
of Midlothian,—ay, I appeal to the Conservatives or Tories of
Midlothian,—whether their creed of prudence is such a creed
as to admit of the perpetration of follies of this kind. But,
gentlemen, I will endeavour to give you another illustration.
I have no doubt they will say, ' Oh, this country is very
strong.' Thank God, it is, notwithstanding the proceedings
of the Beaconsfield Administration. This country is very
strong, but that is no reason why it should load itself with a
multitude of needless and mischievous engagements. Multitude of engagements may enchain even a great strength. If
our strength was great before the Beaconsfield Government
came in, so were our duties great. There was not a disturbance that could happen in Europe that did not touch us.
There were many calls which the people of this country
thought involved their honour. You may recollect that under
the late Government—though I hope it was not deficient in a
pacific spirit—when an attempt, which I must call a wicked
attempt, was by somebody or other suggested between two
great Powers against the freedom and integrity of Belgium—
you may recollect that the people of this country almost as
one man cried out for measures to be taken in order to show
their sympathy with that freedom, and their determination,
within limits of reason, to do their best to preserve it. Gentlemen, it is idle to talk of our strength ; whatever it was, we
had no strength to spare for mischievous and idle purposes.

We had strength enough for every duty, and our duties
were weighty and numerous enough ; we had none to misapply
or to throw away. But now what have they done ? I will tell
you what they have done, gentlemen. They have placed upon
us those engagements, which remind me of a little incident

in a book which is both a great ornament of our literature
as a work of fancy, and at the same time full of the most
profound good sense—I mean the *Travels of Gulliver.* Yes;
under the veil of allegory is there conveyed, with infinite fun
and humour, a lesson of profound political wisdom. When
Gulliver lands among the Lilliputians he is a man of six feet,
landing among men of six inches. He goes to sleep, and the
Lilliputians, you would say, would have no chance of dealing
with such a man; but they tie him down with their greatest
cables, which are about the thickness of pack-thread, and by
using an enormous number of those cables, which are pack-
threads in our sense, and fastening them into the ground by
the most powerful rivets they could get—which were nearly
as large as the smallest of our pins upon a lady's toilette—
they contrived through the multitude of those ties to fasten him
down to the ground by the arms and legs and the locks of the
hair, so that it was only with the utmost effort that he could
liberate one of his arms, and as to the other limbs and the hair,

The country is he thought it best not to try to liberate them at all. Well,
tied down by now, that is the way in which we are being tied down,
needless
covenants. gentlemen, by all sorts of covenants of this kind, to do this
and to do that, north, south, east, and west, when we had
enough to do before with all the strength we possess. We
are gradually being drawn into a position at once ridiculous
and dangerous in consequence of these needless engagements,
contemplating no public good, lying wholly beyond the line of
our duty and our responsibility—hardly one of them, perhaps,
in itself of an enormous magnitude, but in their combination
most fatal to our freedom of action, most injurious to our
power of disposing of our resources freely, as occasion shall
arise, for objects which may seem to be worthy objects.
Gentlemen, I challenge on that ground the prudence of the
foreign policy which has thus involved us at almost every
point of the compass in those new and strange engagements.

Now, gentlemen, for the present I would turn from the

subject of foreign policy in order to touch upon some of those subjects which it is quite necessary that I should notice— namely, the local and special questions in which you feel a special interest. But I cannot do this without offering you, in the first place, what I may call a warning. Gentlemen, do not be deceived as to our position. Do not suppose that when you get quit of the present Administration you will get quit of the consequences of its deeds. The present Adminis- tration, whether it dies intestate or not, will undoubtedly leave an inheritance—an inheritance of financial confusion at home ; financial confusion in India ; treaties of the strangest and most entangling kind, to be dealt with subject to the honourable engagements under which they will have brought the country ; a state of things where the troops of Her Majesty —her gallant forces—are at various points, in Asia and in Africa, engaged in wars from which they must heartily wish to be relieved, and from which it must be the first desire, I think, of every right-minded man to relieve them. All these things, gentlemen, will be handed on to the future, and it is an utter mistake to suppose that you will find things as they were in 1874 ; that you have got nothing to do but to forget the six years of Tory administration, and to proceed peacefully and quietly with the work of improving the laws and main- taining the interests of the country. On the contrary, any men who are so unfortunate as to succeed to this inheritance will find all their best energies tasked in dealing with the direct consequences of Tory administration, in replacing the finances in something like order, in removing the confusion into which the affairs of India have been brought, in bringing within some tolerable limits the territorial responsibilities and the treaty obligations which we have undertaken. All these things are matters of the greatest difficulty and anxiety ; for you know, gentlemen, it is not difficult for a madman to burn York Minster, but it is not an easy task even for a man of sense to build it. That is all I will say on the general

Local ques- tions.

The difficulty of dealing with them while so much may require to be done elsewhere.

position of your domestic affairs ; but do not conceal from yourselves the fact that we have not merely lost the six years
during which the present Government has been in office ; we
have lost to a great degree those other years during which it
must be the main and the most sacred duty of a succeeding
Government to endeavour to deal with the perplexing and
almost portentous consequences of the unfortunate errors of
the existing Administration.

Now, gentlemen, I have considered in my own mind what
are the subjects most likely to have a special interest for you.
I will take, first, a subject that I feel must have a hold upon
your feelings. At any rate, I myself have an opinion on it
that I am desirous of laying before you. I do not think you
will disapprove of it, although it is a subject which has not of
The inade- late been much discussed in Scotland. It is my opinion that
quate represen- Scotland is not represented in the Imperial Parliament up to
tation of Scot-
land. the full measure which justice demands. [A voice—Whose
According to fault is it ?   Mr. Gladstone—I will tell you in a moment.]
population. If Scotland were represented according to population, it would,
According to instead of sixty members, possess seventy members. If Scot-
revenue. land were represented according to the share of revenue which
it contributes, it would, instead of sixty members, possess
seventy-eight members. I am sorry that my friend asked me
whose fault it was, for I had no intention of making any charge
against the members of the present Government in connection
with this subject. But as he asks me whose fault it is, I must
tell him that it is the fault of those who framed and carried
the Reform Bills of 1867 and 1868 in such a manner as not
to accord to Scotland a fairer share of the representation.

Now, gentlemen, besides the consideration of population,
which I think to be the main one, and besides the consideration of revenue, which also has some importance, there is
The distance another element that enters into the equitable examination of
from the seat
of Government the question, and that is the element of distance. A small num-
is an element
in the question. ber of representatives are more effective when they are close to

the seat of government, than when they are far from the seat
of government. On that account it is that London and the
metropolitan district, with their vast population of four
millions, or one-sixth of the whole population of England and
Wales, do not influence the return of more than between
thirty and forty members, which would only be about one-
twelfth or one-thirteenth of the population of England and
Wales. It is thus recognised that nearness is a reason for having
a more limited number of members, and consequently that distance constitutes a claim for a larger number of members than
the population would warrant. I hope, gentlemen, that you
will bear this subject in mind, because we are given to understand that Her Majesty's Government have a great anxiety to
dispose, by Act of Parliament, before the dissolution, of five
or six seats. I think six is the number that are now vacant.
I have no doubt that in the disposal of these seats they may
innocently have a certain regard to the probable use of the
franchise by those whom they may seek not to endow with
the franchise, for that they already have, but those to whom
they may seek to give an increased share, or a new form of
representation. My fear is, gentlemen, that they will not be
very anxious, from that point of view, to entertain the claims
of Scotland. I very much doubt whether Edinburgh or Glasgow, or whether any of your great counties, are likely to fare
favourably at the hands of the Government in regard to that
subject, and I recommend it to your careful and watchful
observance to see that whenever there are seats to be disposed
of Scotland should receive a fair measure of justice.

I pass on from that matter, gentlemen, to another matter
which is of great interest in two points of view, and that is
the old subject, well known to you by the name of Hypothec. *Hypothec.*
I am not, gentlemen, going to discuss the merits of the question in itself. Happily it is unnecessary, because opinion has
reached a stage and a condition in Scotland in which all
parties, it may be said, are agreed that the law of hypothec

ought to be done away with. That being so, I accept the
conclusion, and I do not waste your time in the discussion.
But I do occupy, and I hope not altogether waste your time, in
calling your attention to the way in which that question has
been worked. A political Catechism has been sent to me in
print, which, I suppose, is to be administered to me on some
convenient opportunity ; but at any rate it is complained in this
Catechism that when the Liberal Government was in office it
did not abolish the Law of Hypothec. Now, gentlemen, I am
bound to say that there was a great deal of legislative work
which it was quite impossible for us to achieve ; and the question which, as reasonable men, you will put to us and to
yourselves, is not whether we did everything that it was
desirable to do, but it is whether we manfully and seriously
employed our time and spent our energies in doing as much
as we could. But I must say it is rather hard that this
reproach should come from the opposite side, when I consider
that at the last election, when we were dismissed from office
by the verdict of the constituencies, in the address of Lord
Beaconsfield, then Mr. Disraeli, which was the manifesto of the
party, it was distinctly complained of us that we had neglected
foreign affairs, and had been too active in home legislation.

Well, now, gentlemen, I want to know whether you are
satisfied with the manner in which this question of hypothec
is worked in Scotland. How is it worked ? Why, all your
The conduct of Tory members, with one or two exceptions, vote for abolition.
the Tories in Is not that very delightful ? Does not that give you entire
regard to this satisfaction ? What complaint can you make when you find
question. them so rational as this ? Let me call your attention to a
closer examination of the subject, which I will endeavour to
make by the help of the political microscope. When I look
into it, I find that Mr. Vans Agnew, a stout Conservative,
moved a bill for the abolition of hypothec. Nay, more, he
has moved it for several years, and, as far as I see, if the
present Government and present Parliament could happily

for the Tories continue without limit, he would regularly go on moving it from year to year for your satisfaction, until old age should break down his energies, or death should remove him from this mortal scene. He moved the bill on some day in April—early in the session—or in March; and he carried the second reading of the bill by 204 ayes to 77 noes, and sent, no doubt, a throb of pleasure through the minds and hearts of all the farmers of Scotland, who are pretty much united on this subject. But his bill, though read a second time on some day in March or April, was never more heard of. The Government had the control of the business of the House—the session was very little advanced, but no attempt was made to carry forward the measure. That is not all. Let us examine the division. Most interesting documents these division lists sometimes are. The Lord Advocate warmly supported the bill. He supported it with such warmth that he convinced five of his colleagues, and five of his colleagues voted with him in the division for the bill abolishing the Law of Hypothec; but he also unfortunately convinced eleven of them the other way. We were told that the Government had become favourable to the abolition of the Law of Hypothec, but if we had depended on the votes of the members of the Government, there would have been ayes, 6; noes, 11; the bill condemned and turned out of the House of Commons by a majority of five. So much for the Government. But how, gentlemen, for your Tory members, who vote so steadily for the abolition of the Law of Hypothec? I make a further examination of the division lists and I find this, that every Tory member from Scotland except two voted for the abolition of hypothec, and I really have rather a respect for these two gentlemen—Lord Elcho was one of them—because I feel that their vote must have been a very sincere and conscientious vote under the circumstances. But the Tory members from Scotland voted for the abolition of the law; and it is supposed you can ask nothing more. Thirteen of them voted for the bill; and when I examine the position of the Tory party I find it to be as follows : For the abolition of the law in March last, after all your Scottish Tories had been converted—for the abolition of the law in March last there voted fifty-six Tories, and for maintaining the law there voted seventy-seven Tories, constituting the whole minority on the occasion. Consequently, if that law had been dealt with by the Tory party, what does it signify to you that your Conservative members voted for the abolition of the law, when they can trust to the votes of the majority of their colleagues from England, Wales, and Ireland to nullify their votes altogether, and to maintain the law you want to get rid of?

Gentlemen, this is a most curious system, thoroughly understood in the Tory party. You have no idea how tolerant that party is, under certain circumstances. When the profession of a particular opinion on a given measure in a particular constituency is necessary for gaining a seat, there are no bounds to the toleration of the Tories. For that reason, members favourable to the abolition of hypothec are allowed to stand as Tories, and are accepted as good and sound Tories if they come from Scotland. Members favourable to Home Rule are allowed as good and sound Tories if they come from Ireland—exactly on the same principle. And I remember in days before the ballot became law, when a Tory was accepted as a good and sound Tory, though he voted for the ballot in order that he might get a seat for the town of Stockport. Now, gentlemen, you are good enough arithmeticians, and good enough observers, to see how all this works. A certain number of Tories are returned as adverse to hypothec from Scotland, knowing that their brother Tories in the other two countries will destroy the effect of their votes. A certain number of Tories are, and may be, returned as Home Rulers from Ireland, because it is known that the votes of England and Scotland, including all your Tory opponents of hypothec from Scotland, will neutralize the vote of the Home Rulers from Ireland on the question of Home Rule, exactly as in all likelihood you will find on making the reference the Home Rulers from Ireland contribute to neutralize on the question of hypothec the vote of your Tories from Scotland. And with the ballot it is just the same. The Tory majority in the House of Commons is that which carries on the affairs of the country, and you, if you are as wise, will look to the general conduct of that majority, and will not be satisfied with the individual concession of the individual member in regard to the particular question, knowing that his individual vote will be neutralized, and is meant to be neutralized, by the votes of that majority of his friends elsewhere, who, where no local interest is felt, will join in maintaining the law you disapprove of.

But now, gentlemen, I must say this. My noble friend Lord Rosebery, speaking to me of the Law of Hypothec, said, and I thought with great force, of Mr. Vans Agnew's bill, ' It *Hypothec is a* is a Tulchan bill.' You know, gentlemen, better than I do *' Tulchan.'* what a Tulchan bishop was. Lord Rosebery, departing from the figure of the Tulchan bishop, speaks of a Tulchan bill. I think we can understand that. A Tulchan, as I understand it, was the figure of a calf stuffed with straw, and the practice, an old Scotch practice, I don't know whether it still prevails —the practice was to place this calf stuffed with straw under the cow, in order to induce the cow to give milk. Lord Rosebery's idea is that the bill of Mr. Vans Agnew is the Tulchan calf, that the cow is the Liberal party or the Scotch farmer, and that the Tulchan bill is put to the Scotch farmer in order to induce him to give milk, meaning his vote, to the Tory party. Now, I do believe that that illustration is a perfectly just and plain illustration. In the same way Home Rule is used as a Tulchan in Ireland, because that is meant to induce the Irish to give their milk—that is to say, their votes—to men who will vote for Home Rule, being in other respects Tories, and working with the Tory party on everything but that particular question. Well, gentlemen, there is so much to say that I won't dwell longer on that subject, except that I really do think that a very curious illustration is shown of the working of party organization by this toleration of Liberal votes on isolated questions, shown in the case of your Scotch Conservative members, with a view to securing seats, which on all other questions are to be used for the promotion of an anti-Liberal policy and an anti-Liberal administration.

The Liquor Laws.

But I have promised, gentlemen, to say a word during this course of addresses on a subject of very great importance—namely, the subject of the liquor laws of this country. I confess that the state of this country with regard to intemperance, we must all painfully feel it, is a national vice and scandal. I read with the greatest pain a very able work lately published by Mr. Saunders, a gentleman connected with the newspaper press in London—a very able work on the United States of America. It contains a statement of the comparative consumption of alcoholic liquors by the population there and the population of this country. The population of America, as a rule, have larger means, higher wages, than are current among the mass of the people here, and they have access to spirituous drinks at a lower price, for the tax is not so high; but, notwithstanding that, if I remember right, the statement of Mr. Saunders is to this effect, that the consumption in America is about one-half of the consumption of this country. Every one admits the seriousness of the case. But we come to great differences of opinion as to the mode of dealing with it. Now, gentlemen, I am not here to give what is called a pledge either upon this or upon any other subject. For I feel that, after a man has served his country in Parliament for nearly half a century, and after he has been called upon to take an active part, or at the very least to give a vote upon almost every imaginable subject that has been under discussion in that long period of years, if you cannot with such a man find evidence of his future course in that which he has already said and done, all I can say is this, you ought not to ask him

The relative consumption of alcohol in America and here.

for pledges, you ought politely to decline to have anything to do with him.

But my opinion is this, that the three principles which ought *The principles to be recognised* to guide the consideration of this difficult question are as *in dealing with* follows : Serious efforts ought to be made to abate this terrible *this question.* mischief. These efforts should be made just as the remarkable effort that was successfully made in past sessions to close the public-houses of Ireland on Sunday. They should be *Regard to* made with a due and a careful regard for the state of public *public* *opinion.* opinion. You cannot, gentlemen, judge in the abstract what law ought or ought not to be passed at a given time in a country like this. Shakespeare, who is as full of social and political wisdom as he is of flashing genius at every point, tells us—

> ' There is a tide in the affairs of men,
> Which, taken at the flood, leads on to fortune.'

And so it is with questions of this kind ; you must have regard to the ripeness or unripeness of public opinion, and to the favourable or unfavourable conjuncture of circumstances. But I must also add that I think that if it be necessary, if Parliament shall think it wise to introduce radical change into the working of the liquor law in such a way as to break down the fair expectations of persons who have grown up—whether rightly or wrongly is not the question, it is not their fault, it is our fault—under the shadow of these laws, their fair claim to compensation ought, if they can make good their case, to *Compensation.* be considered, as all such claims have been considered, by the wisdom and the liberality of the British Parliament.

It is said, gentlemen, that we are to be asked to vote for a principle which is called Local Option. Now, the form *Local Option.* of that principle, the mode of its application, the conditions of its application, as I understand, are reserved for the future. In that principle I do not see myself anything that is justly to be condemned. I do not think it is unfair to say that, within the limits of justice and fairness, the local opinion of a particular district may be considered in the particular conditions of those police laws which are to regulate the sale of alcoholic liquors. I may say so, because I have acted upon that principle. I supported, many years ago, a bill which unhappily failed in Parliament, through a combination of parties, under the Government of Lord Palmerston, but which that Government seriously endeavoured to pass, where the local opinion of Liverpool advising the adoption of a particular system was embodied in a private measure, and where, as I said, I myself was among the active supporters of that measure. During the late Government we introduced a bill which again embodied the principles of local option. It was not in our power to carry that bill. I do not dwell upon its provisions particularly. I do not ask now whether they were the wisest and the best, or the most unwise and the worst. I speak only of its principle, and I say that, so far as I am able to judge, there is no reason why upon the threshold a proposition for allowing the operation of local option in regard to the liquor laws should be rejected and condemned.

Now there is another question of great importance on which I must say a few words, but I hope I shall be able to dispose of it without very great difficulty. It is the question

Disestablish-
ment.

of the Disestablishment of the Church. I, gentlemen, have very little to say upon it at this moment, because you are substantially in possession of my opinions. I have no second thoughts kept in reserve in regard to this matter. The opinion I have indicated is perfectly transparent. I do not think it is a question for me to determine, so much as it is for the people of Scotland. It is not part of my duty to keep it backward. It is not part of my duty to endeavour to thrust it forward. It is our friends of the other way of thinking that are endeavouring to stir this question. They are endeavouring, gentlemen, to use it as a weapon against us, to sow dissension and division in our ranks. There are, happily, a considerable number of members of the Established Church of Scotland

who are good and sound Liberals.   And if it is their less happy
fortune to be associated in that Church with a great number of
other excellent persons who are not good and sound Liberals,
why that, instead of being a reason why we should value the
good and sound Liberals of the Established Church the less, is
a reason we should feel for them and value them all the more.

Now, gentlemen, in my opinion the Liberal party can stand
with a clear conscience in the face of the Established Church
of Scotland and say, ' We, at least, have done it no harm.'
When we were in office we raised no question that tended to
disturb its position.   Looking to the great religious divisions
in the country, we conscientiously believed that quietude was
the best policy for the Established Church to follow.   Those
who came after us, gentlemen, did not like a policy of
quietude.   They liked a policy such as they have been
applying to their foreign affairs.   They liked a policy of dis- *The Govern-*
quietude, and they succeeded, in one way or other, in con- *ment policy of*
triving to force the subject of Disestablishment into a certain *disquietude.*
amount of prominence, and making it one of the real factors
of political discussion.   We did not do it; but they did it.
I make no imputation upon them.   All I say is, it is not for
them, it does not lie in their mouths to call us agitators and
disturbers upon this question.

But I am going to make another criticism upon them,—I
shall have a great many to make before I have done,—and it
is this.   We had a debate on the affairs of the Scotch
Established Church last year in the House of Commons.   I
do not know if you read the speeches that were then made by
the gentlemen who call themselves the friends of the Church.
But if you do, you will be astonished to see how poor and
meagre is the colour of those speeches.   Instead of saying,
' This is a great and sacred connection; the Government is
prepared to stand or fall; or, the member is prepared to devote
the years of his life to maintaining it '—all that high romantic
and chivalrous style of policy seems to be, by the Tories of
the present day, thought quite inapplicable to the Established

The weak defence of the Church by the Tories themselves. Church of Scotland. Mr. Dalrymple made one of the strongest speeches for it; and what said he? I had the curiosity to consult Hansard. He said he would leave the defence of the Establishment to some future time. Mr. Cross, on the part of the Government, said when it was attacked they would be quite ready to defend it. But it had been attacked. The `Free Kirk had petitioned. The United Presbyterians were up in arms. Important bodies were discussing the matter. And if I may give a recommendation to the friends and members of the Establishment, it would be, not to look so much at this moment at the attitude of the Liberal party, who are disturbing nothing in regard to the matter, but to look to the attitude of their own friends, and see if they cannot inspire a little more pith into their opinions and intentions in regard to this matter.

Gentlemen, on this subject I have got a practical remark to make, as I understand there is a real anxiety, and, I think, a just and fair anxiety, prevailing among the members of the *The desire by Churchmen that the question be fairly and fully tried.* Established Church of Scotland; and it is this, that their cause should be fairly tried; that if the Established Church, so much respected, and so justly, for long services, for the character of its ministers and for the good they do, and for the suitableness of its institutions in many respects to the habits of the people,—if it is to be put upon its trial, it shall have a fair, full, and open trial, that it shall not be condemned without having been thus fairly tried. They hope, if I understand them rightly, that no Parliament will dispose finally of the case of the Church of Scotland unless that Parliament has been elected under circumstances when the people of Scotland had the whole case put before them. I think that hope, gentlemen, is a reasonable hope. I refer to it now, because it is the object of the opposite party to insinuate the belief that my purpose is, or that the purposes of other men more wicked than myself—if such there can be—is to smuggle the Established Church of Scotland out of existence. Lord Salisbury has been about the country, and he raises the question thus. I take the question as he has raised it. He wishes to inspire great distrust of me in this matter, and he does it by pointing back to what happened in the case of the Irish Church. Gentlemen, I have never said that the case of the Irish Church was like the case of the Established Church of Scotland. And I do not think that any of those—Free Churchmen, or United Presbyterians, or others who may be friendly to Disestablishment—would ever put the two cases on the same footing.

But the question directly raised is this—May the members and ministers of the Established Church of Scotland trust, make themselves assured, that, so far as there can be certainty of what is future in human affairs, there will be a full consideration of this matter by the people before the Parliament which may have to deal with it proceeds to deal with it? Lord Salisbury says, No—see what happened in the case of the Irish Church. I will go with him to the case of the Irish Church, and I say it proves directly the fact he wants. What happened in the case of the Irish Church? That down to the year 1865 and the dissolution of that year the whole question of the Irish Church was dead; nobody cared for it; nobody paid attention to it in England. Circumstances occurred which drew the attention of the people to the Irish Church. I said myself in 1865, and I believed, that it was out of the range of practical politics, that is to say, the politics of the coming election. When it came to this—that a great jail in the heart of the metropolis was broken open under circumstances which drew the attention of the English people to the state of Ireland, and when in Manchester policemen were murdered in the execution of their duty, at once the whole country became alive to Irish questions, and the question of the Irish Church revived. It came within the range of practical politics. I myself took it up, and proposed Resolutions to the House of Commons, declaring the view of the House that the Irish Church ought no longer to exist as an Establishment. But those Resolutions, though passed, did not bring about the destruction of the Irish Church, nor did any

The case of the Irish Church in 1868.

one expect that they would.　They raised the question in the face of the country; the Parliament was dissolved upon the question; the country, from one end of it to the other, considered it fully, made up its mind, and returned a Parliament with a vast majority empowered to speak and act for them on the matter.　So that the very chain of facts which is chosen by the Government in order to inspire suspicion in the minds of Liberals who are Established Churchmen—that very chain of facts shows that even in the case of the Irish Church, which was far weaker than that of the Scottish Church— even in that case there was, after the subject had been raised in Parliament, a dissolution expressly upon the case.　The verdict of the country was given only after a full trial and consideration; and this is what the Established Church of Scotland fairly and justly asks.

Gentlemen, I must say that those Liberal Churchmen run a risk of being placed in exactly the same condition with regard to the question of the Established Church, as the *The conclusion to be drawn from the action of the Tories.* Scotch farmer is in regard to hypothec.　The Established Church is attempted to be made into a tulchan question, to draw the milk of the Liberal Churchman—of all Churchmen who are Liberals—to persuade them that there is a danger, which I do not believe those very people conceive to exist —a danger of the destruction of that Church, venerated upon so many grounds, without a fair or full trial and consideration of the case by the people of Scotland.

Now, gentlemen, there is one question yet upon which I think it is quite necessary that I should still detain you, though time passes rapidly, and there is no reason why I should occupy much more time.　It is the great and important question of the *The Land Laws.* condition of the land in this country; and I propose now to consider it for a few moments in concluding the address I have had the honour to make to you.　I shall look at it for a few moments in connection with the various points of law or practice which touch the interests of the cultivators of the soil—the responsible cultivators of the land.　I mean the tenant-farmers of the country.

I will not dwell further, gentlemen, upon hypothec, because on that we seem, I think, to be all agreed, as far as the merits of the measure are concerned. I will not dwell upon the subject of game, which deeply interests the Scotch farmer in many portions of the country, because upon that subject, through the able exertions of Mr. M'Lagan, a bill has been passed, which, I believe, has, at all events, done very considerable good, and which perhaps renders it unnecessary, at any rate for the present moment, to enter further, under the present pressure of so many subjects, into the consideration of the matter. Neither will I dwell, gentlemen, upon what is commonly called security of tenure, because happily in Scotland the education of the country is so far advanced, both among landlords and tenants, that to a certain extent that security is attained by the system of leases, and no desire exists to disturb that system, either on the part of the landlord or on the part of the tenant.

There are other matters, however, upon which it may be well to say a few words. One of them is the practice of inserting in leases a number of covenants, which direct parti- *Restrictions* cular modes of cultivation, and by directing particular modes *upon the mode of cultivation.* do much to restrain its freedom. A good tenant, a good farmer, feels that after all he is the best judge of the mode of conducting what is his own business. Every one will agree with that. On the other hand, there is something, I think, of equity in the statement of the landlord, that during the closing years of a lease, if a tenant means to remove, it is difficult for him, without covenants of that kind, to prevent the wasteful use of the farm. Now it is not for me, gentlemen, to offer instruction, perhaps not even to offer a suggestion to you ; but there is a method in use with some landlords in England who have leases that I confess appears to me to be not without wisdom. I will just take a supposititious length of a lease, because that is not material. It will only serve to enable me clearly to explain the nature of the expedient by which it is endeavoured to do full justice to the interests of both the landlord and the tenant,—that is to say, to leave the tenant

entirely free in the prosecution of his business, but at the same
time to secure the landlord against the particular, though,
perhaps, rare instances—certainly I should think very rare in
Scotland—the rare instances in which a tenant intending to
leave, might leave the farm behind him in a state greatly
worse than that in which he had received it.   The method is
this : We will say the landlord gives his tenant a lease of
twenty-one years.   In that lease are included a number of
provisions directing, and therefore restraining, cultivation ; but
there is also a clause directing that those provisions shall not
operate during the first seventeen years of the lease.   At the
end of seventeen years, the tenant is to declare whether he
wishes to renew his lease or not.   If he exercises his option
to renew his lease, he receives at once, both parties being
willing, another lease, which immediately comes into operation
with similar provisions.   If he says, I mean to leave, then the
provisions directing and restraining the method of cultivation
come into operation for the last four years of the lease only,
so that the landlord is secured against the deterioration of the
farm.   Now I know that that method of proceeding is approved
by many men of good judgment.   It is not for me to pro-
nounce upon it ; I confess there appears to be much equity in
it.   I hold, as strongly as any of you can hold, that it is most
important to rid the tenantry of the country of all unnecessary
fetters upon the freedom of their action.   They are engaged
in a great struggle.   Time forbids me at this moment to enter
upon the particular character of this struggle.   I shall endeavour to do it elsewhere, if I am unable to do it to-day ; but I
wish you to believe that I am heartily and cordially associated
with you, not less in my own capacity as a landlord than in my
own capacity as a candidate before you, in the desire, not only for
the sake of gaining your suffrages, but upon higher and upon
national grounds, to give all possible freedom to the cultivation
of the soil, in order that the agriculture of England may have
full and fair play in competition with the agriculture of the world.

That is a point, gentlemen, from which I will pass on to

another subject of great importance —the law of entail and *Entail and settlement.*
settlement.   I believe that you view that law with disapproval
as being itself one of the most serious restraints upon the effective
prosecution of the agriculture of the country.   Gentlemen, I
need not dwell upon the matter.   I heartily agree with you on
the point at issue.   I am for the alteration of that law.   I
disapprove of it on economic grounds.   I disapprove of it on
social and moral grounds.   I disapprove of the relation which
it creates between the father and the eldest son.   I disapprove
of the manner in which it makes provision for the interests
of children to be born.   Was there ever in the history of
legislation a stranger expedient ?   Let us consider what takes
place in England habitually, and I believe habitually in Scotland also, but I am less conversant with the actual daily practice
of this country.   A possessor of an estate in England, having
sons, or having an eldest son, is in this condition : If he dies
intestate, his estate goes bodily to his son.   That law, gentlemen, is not just, and it ought to be altered, the law of intestacy.   But setting aside the question of intestacy, let us take
the ordinary case.   The ordinary case is this.   The son is
going to marry.   When he marries—because under the law,
supposing he does not marry, and his father dies, he becomes
absolute owner—when he marries his father gives him an
income for life, and he, in consideration of that income, re-
settles the estate upon his issue to be thereafter born.   Now,
what is the meaning of that process ?   It is this—that the
actual owner of the estate induces the son to make provision
for his own children by giving him an income for his life.
The provision for the children is not made by the freewill of
the father, but by the freewill of the grandfather, and it is
made by the freewill of the grandfather in order to secure the
future and further tying up of the estate.   Why, gentlemen,
it appears to me that if there is one law written more distinctly than another upon the constitution of human society
by the finger of the Almighty it is this, that the parent is
responsible for making sufficient provision on behalf of the

child. But the law of England is wiser than the Almighty; it improves upon Divine Providence. It won't trust the father to make provision for his son. It calls in the aid of the grand-father, commits to him the function of the parent, introduces a false and, in my opinion, a rather unnatural relation even into the constitution of that primary element of society, the sacred constitution of the family. Not only, then, to liberate agriculture, gentlemen, but upon other grounds—and I will say upon what I think still higher grounds—I am for doing away with the present law of settlement and entail.

Now, gentlemen, I have gone through, I think, all the questions, except one, that greatly affect the interests of occupiers of the soil—I mean all the questions capable of being dealt with by legislation. I am not speaking now of that great question of competition with foreign countries, to which I must revert elsewhere. But there is one that yet remains, *Local govern-* and that is the subject of our local and county government. *ment.* It is a strange anomaly that in this most important matter of local government, we who have representative institutions everywhere else have been content down to this time to remain without them. This is one of the greatest subjects that awaits the consideration of a future Parliament, and that, I hope, will receive that consideration so soon as those imme-diate and pressing impediments to which I have already referred can be taken, by care and skill, out of the way. Gentlemen, there was no question upon which the last Government was more severely criticised than its treatment of the subject of local government. Now, what did we do with regard to it? We avowed from the beginning that the state of our county government was wholly unsatisfactory, and must be radically reformed. We thought the law of liability in England, which threw the whole responsibility for the rates upon the tenant, was an unjust law, and we proposed to divide it, as it is divided in Scotland. We knew that there was a great desire in the country to relieve the ratepayer from the Consolidated Fund. We saw in that desire, and in the power to relieve the ratepayer from the Consolidated Fund, a strong leverage placed in the hand of the Executive Government to induce all the local interests to go freely into the changes that must be made in order to establish a sound system of county government, and to give you, gentlemen, a free and thorough control over the disposal of your own local taxes, as you have over the disposal of Imperial taxes. We therefore said, We will not give this money away until we are able to make it the means of bringing all parties to cope with the difficulties of establishing a new system of government, and so to lead to the enjoyment of whatever aid it may be right to give from the Imperial Treasury on behalf of the ratepayer. That, gentlemen, was our position. We were severely censured for it; but we were not willing to depart from it. Before it was in our power to deal thoroughly and effectively with the subject on this basis, we were removed from office. Our successors took an entirely opposite view. In their view the only thing material was to relieve the ratepayers, so they handed over year by year large sums from the Consolidated Fund, made no other change whatever, except, indeed, certain centralizing changes, left the present irresponsible authorities in possession, continued some five years in office before they produced even the phantom of a Local Government Bill; and when they produced one, contrived to frame it in such a way that no party and no section of a party in the House of Commons showed the smallest desire to have it. The consequence is that your local government remains in the unsatisfactory position in which it formerly stood. Whereas the Imperial Government, which is the only propelling power that can cause legislation of that kind to move onwards, has gratuitously and prematurely parted with the great inducement they held in their hands to bring all parties into a reasonable settlement, to induce magistrates to give in, to induce all constituted authorities to give in, and to abate of their respective pretensions; they have given up the lever by which they ought to have propelled the question on behalf of the public interest, and the question remains in that neglected and abandoned state in which they have left almost every other subject of that kind, or, rather, it is in a condition of greater difficulty and of less hope than ever it was before.

But, gentlemen, I have detained you long enough. I have endeavoured to be practical and intelligible in my remarks. I have endeavoured to show you that subjects of local and domestic interest do not escape my attention. I have warned you of the immense Imperial difficulties we have to contend with. I have not held out to you too sanguine expectations. I have told you that when you succeed in returning a more— what shall I say ?—a more enlightened Parliament—and in obtaining an Administration better qualified to give effect to your convictions, there will be much yet to do, much cause for patience and forbearance, before we can see the peaceful course of legislation which has been the practice of former Administrations—in many cases that I could name, and certainly in at least one Conservative Administration—I mean the Administration of Sir Robert Peel—before that course of peaceful and useful legislation can be resumed. Let me say that in my opinion these two great subjects of local government and the land laws ought now to occupy a foremost place in the thoughts of every man who aspires to be a legislator.

In the matter of local government, there may lie a solution of some national and even Imperial difficulties. It will not be in my power to enter largely while I am in the county upon the important question of the condition of Ireland ; but you know well how unhappily the action of Parliament has been impeded and disorganized, from considerations no doubt conscientiously entertained by a part of the Irish representa-

Home Rule. tives, and from their desire to establish what they term Home Rule. If you ask me what I think of Home Rule, I must tell you that I will only answer you when you tell me how Home Rule is related to local government. I am friendly to local government. I am friendly to large local privileges and powers. I desire, I may almost say I intensely desire, to see Parliament relieved of some portion of its duties. I see the efficiency of Parliament interfered with not only by obstruction from Irish members, but even more gravely by the enormous weight that is placed upon the time and the minds of those whom you send to represent you. We have got an over-weighted Parliament; and if Ireland or any other portion of the country is desirous and able so to arrange its affairs, that by taking the local part or some local part of its transactions off the hands of Parliament, it can liberate and strengthen Parliament for Imperial concerns, I say I will not only accord a reluctant assent, but I will give a zealous support to any such scheme.

One limit, gentlemen, one limit only, I know to the extension of local government. It is this. Nothing can be done, in my opinion, by any wise statesman or right-minded Briton to weaken or compromise the authority of the Imperial Parliament, because the Imperial Parliament must be supreme in these three Kingdoms. And nothing that creates a doubt upon that supremacy can be tolerated by any intelligent and patriotic man. But subject to that limitation, if we can make arrangements under which Ireland, Scotland, Wales, portions of England, can deal with questions of local and special interest to themselves more efficiently than Parliament now can, that, I say, will be the attainment of a great national good. The Scotch members, who always show in Parliament—I must say, speaking of them as an average, and perhaps it is all the more true because the majority of them are always Liberal—who always show in the transaction of Scotch business remarkable shrewdness and efficiency, yet all find cause to complain, and complain seriously and gravely, that they cannot get the Scotch business properly transacted.

The Parliament is overweighted. The Parliament is almost overwhelmed. If we can take off its shoulders that superfluous weight by the constitution of secondary and subordinate

The only limit to local government.

The relief to be afforded to Parliament.

authorities, I am not going to be frightened out of a wise measure of that kind by being told that in that I am condescending to the prejudices of Home Rulers. I will condescend to no such prejudices. I will consent to give to Ireland no principle, nothing that is not upon equal terms offered to Scotland and to the different portions of the United Kingdom. But I say that the man who shall devise a machinery by which some portion of the excessive and impossible task now laid upon the House of Commons shall be shifted to the more free and therefore more efficient hands of secondary and local authorities, will confer a blessing upon his country that will entitle him to be reckoned among the prominent benefactors of the land.

After the outburst of applause had subsided, a vote of thanks to Mr. Gladstone was proposed by Mr. Riddell, farmer, Corsehope, and carried amid loud cheers.

The right hon. gentleman proceeded from the Corn Exchange, after a short interval of rest spent at the house of Provost Mitchell, to the Foresters' Hall, where a presentation was made to Mrs. Gladstone. Mr. Gladstone, in acknowledging the gift, said :—

Provost Mitchell, Mr. Tod, Ladies and Gentlemen,—I rise to perform the duty of returning thanks on behalf of my wife and myself, at the same time that I feel that I can really add very little by expatiating upon the subject to the simple words that she has used, and which express a sentiment that comes with perfect sincerity from the very root of her feelings and of my own. You referred, sir, to the relations, the family relations in which I have had the happiness to stand ; to the inestimable blessing—not through my deserving—that has been permitted me through a long life, for these family relations have been the source of unequalled and unfailing consolations, without a break, without a shadow, without a doubt, without a change. I would, Mr. Tod, as far as I may presume to do so, venture so far to re-echo the words of that eloquent and beautiful eulogy, which I must in justice say to you, you have so admirably pronounced, even if its terms be warmer than a strict justice would warrant towards us who have been the subjects of the eulogy. Well, sir, you have spoken to me on a subject which always commands and stirs my feelings—the subject of Scotland. It is but two days since I re-entered it; and how many tokens, how unquestionable proofs, have I had presented to me at every turn of every road, at every hour of each of these days, and at every moment of each hour, that I am come back not only to the land of beautiful natural characteristics, not only to the

'Land of brown heath and shaggy wood,
Land of the mountain and the flood'—

but I come back to that which is better still, to the land which has a prerogative, to describe which I will borrow the terms used in a higher sense by one of the latest, and certainly not the least, of your writers of beautiful songs—I mean Lady Nairne. I hope Scotland may always itself deserve to be called, down to the latest posterity, 'The land of the leal.' And, sir, with regard to the special occasion which has brought us here to-night, I understand it to be your wish that I should use some words addressed to the particular share that ladies, and that women, may be thought to have in the crisis of to-day. I use the expression women with greater satisfaction than the former one which I uttered, the name of ladies; because it is to them, not only in virtue of a particular station, not only by reason of their possessing a greater portion of the goods of life than may have been granted to the humbler classes of society, that I appeal. I appeal to them in virtue of the common nature which runs through us all. And I am very glad, sir, that you have introduced to us with a special notice the factory girls of the place, who on this occasion have been desirous to testify their kindly feelings. I hope you will convey to them the assurance that their particular act is not forgotten, and that the gift they offer is accepted with as lively thankfulness and as profound gratification as the most splendid offering that could be tendered by the noblest in the land.

I speak to you, ladies, as women; and I do think and feel that the present political crisis has to do not only with human interests at large, but especially with those interests which are most appropriate, and ought to be most dear, to you. The harder, and sterner, and drier lessons of politics are little to your taste. You do not concern yourselves with abstract propositions. It is that side of politics, which is associated with the heart of man, that I must call your side of politics. When I look at the inscription which faces me on yonder *Peace, Re-* gallery, I see the words ' Peace, Retrenchment, and Reform.' *trenchment,* All of these words, ladies, are connected with the promotion *Reform.* of human happiness; and what some would call the desert of this world, and of the political world in particular, would be an arid desert indeed if we could not hope that our labours are addressed to the increase of human happiness; that we try to diminish the sin and the sorrow in the world, to do something to reduce its grievous and overwhelming mass, to alleviate a little the burden of life for some, to take out of the way of struggling excellence those impediments at least which the folly or the graver offence of man has offered as obstacles in his progress. These are the hopes that cheer, that ought to cheer, the human heart amidst the labours and struggles of public life.

Of all these words—peace, retrenchment, and reform—the one word upon which I will say a few more special words on this occasion is the word peace. Is this, ladies, a time of peace? Cast your eyes abroad over the world. Think what has taken place in the last three or four years. Think of the events which have deluged many a hill and many a valley with blood; and think, with regret and pain, of the share, not which you individually, but which your country collectively has had in that grievous operation.

South Africa. If we cast our eyes to South Africa, what do we behold? That a nation whom we term savages have in defence of their own land offered their naked bodies to the terribly improved artillery and arms of modern European science, and have been mowed down by hundreds and by thousands, having committed no offence, but having, with rude and ignorant courage, done what were for them, and done faithfully and bravely what were for them, the duties of patriotism. You may talk of glory, you may offer rewards—and you are right to give rewards to the gallantry of your soldiers, who, I think, are entitled not only to our admiration for courage, but to our compassion for the nature of the duties they have been called to perform. But the grief and the pain none the less remain.

Go from South Africa to the mountains of Central Asia. Go into the lofty hills of Afghanistan, as they were last *Afghanistan.* winter, and what do we there see ? I fear a yet sadder sight than was to be seen in the land of the Zulus. It is true that with respect to the operations of the war in Afghanistan you have seen none but official accounts, or hardly any but official accounts; and many of the facts belonging to that war have not been brought under the general notice of the British public. I think that a great misfortune. I know that it may be necessary and wise under certain circumstances to restrain what might be the injudicious and exaggerated, and therefore the dangerous communications that might proceed from irresponsible persons. At the same time, I deeply regret that we were not more fully *Our want of* informed of the proceedings of the war in Afghanistan, especi- *information.* ally as we must bear in mind that our army is composed in great part of a soldiery not British, and not under Christian obligations and restraints. What we know is this, that our gallant troops have been called upon to ascend to an elevation of many thousand feet, and to operate in the winter months—I am going back to a period of nine or twelve months—amidst the snows of winter. We know that that was done for the most part not strictly in the territory of Afghanistan proper, but in its border lands, inhabited by hill tribes who enjoy more or less of political independence, and do not own a regular allegiance to the Afghan ruler.   You have seen during last winter from time to time that from such and such a village attacks had *The horrors of* been made upon the British forces, and that in consequence *war.* the village had been burned.   Have you ever reflected on the meaning of these words ?   Do not suppose that I am pronouncing a censure, for I am not, either upon the military commanders or upon those who acted subject to their orders. But I am trying to point out the responsibility of the terrible consequences that follow upon such operations.   Those hill tribes had committed no real offence against us.   We, in the pursuit of our political objects, chose to establish military positions in their country.   If they resisted, would not you have done the same ?   And when, going forth from their villages they had resisted, what you find is this, that those who went forth were slain, and that the village was burned.   Again I say, have you considered the meaning of these words ?   The meaning of the burning of the village is, that the women and the children were driven forth to perish in the snows of winter.   Is not that a terrible supposition ?   Is not that a fact— for such, I fear, it must be reckoned to be—which does appeal to your hearts as women, which does lay a special hold and make a special claim upon your interest, which does rouse in you a sentiment of horror and grief, to think that the name of England, under no political necessity, but for a war as frivolous as ever was waged in the history of man, should be associated with consequences such as these ?

I have carried you from South Africa to Central Asia.   I *Eastern* carry you from Central Asia to Eastern Europe, and in the *Europe.* history of Eastern Europe in the last few years do you not again feel that this is no matter of dry political argument ; that there was a wider theatre upon which for many genera- *The oppressive* tions a cruel and a grinding oppression, not resting upon *government of* *the Turk.* superior civilisation, not upon superior knowledge, but a domination of mere force, had crushed down to the earth races who, four or five hundred years ago, greatly excelled our own forefathers in civilisation—had crushed these races to the earth, had abated in them the manhood and the nobler qualities that belong to freedom—had ground these qualities, it appeared, in some cases almost out of their composition—had succeeded in impressing upon them some of the features of slaves ; and in addition to this, when from time to time the impulses of humanity would not be repressed, and an effort was made by any of these people to secure to themselves their long-lost liberties, these efforts had been put down with a cruelty incredible and unequalled, almost and perhaps entirely unequalled in the annals of mankind ; and not only with that cruelty, but with a development of other horrors in the treatment of men, women, and children, which even decency does not permit me to describe ? I will not dwell further on these matters than to say that I think in all these scenes, if peace be our motto, we must feel that a strong appeal is made to you as women—to you specially, and to whatever there is in men that associates itself with what is best and most peculiar in you.

Ladies, I am not here before you as one of those who have ever professed to believe that the state which society has reached permits us to make a vow of universal peace, and of renouncing, in all cases, the alternative of war. But I am here to say that a long experience of life leads me, not towards any abstract doctrine upon the subject, but to a deeper and deeper conviction of the enormous mischiefs of war, even under the best and most favourable circumstances, and of the mischiefs indescribable and the guilt unredeemed of causeless and unnecessary wars. Look back over the pages of history ; consider the feelings, with which we now regard wars that our forefathers in their time supported with the same pernicious fanaticism, of which we have had some developments in this country within the last three years. Consider, for example, that the American War, now condemned by 999 out of every 1000 persons in this country, was a war which for years was enthusiastically supported by the mass of the population. And then see how powerful and deadly are the

A long experience deepens the conviction of the evil of war.

fascinations of passion and of pride ; and, if it be true that the errors of former times are recorded for our instruction, in order that we may avoid their repetition, then I beg and entreat you, be on your guard against these deadly fascinations ; do not suffer appeals to national pride to blind you to the dictates of justice.

Remember the rights of the savage, as we call him. Remember that the happiness of his humble home, remember that the sanctity of life in the hill villages of Afghanistan among the winter snows, is as inviolable in the eye of Almighty God as can be your own.   Remember that He who has united you together as human beings in the same flesh and blood, has bound you by the law of mutual love ; that that mutual love is not limited by the shores of this island, is not limited by *The mutual* the boundaries of Christian civilisation ; that it passes over the *love of* whole surface of the earth, and embraces the meanest along *humanity should not be* with the greatest in its unmeasured scope.   And, therefore, I think *bounded by the* that in appealing to you ungrudgingly to open your own *limits of Christian* feelings, and bear your own part in a political crisis like this, *civilisation.* we are making no inappropriate demand, but are beseeching you to fulfil a duty which belongs to you, which, so far from involving any departure from your character as women, is associated with the fulfilment of that character, and the performance of its duties ; the neglect of which would in future times be to you a source of pain and just mortification, and the fulfilment of which will serve to gild your own future years with sweet remembrances, and to warrant you in hoping that, each in your own place and sphere, you have raised your voice for justice, and have striven to mitigate the sorrows and misfortunes of mankind.

A vote of thanks was, on the motion of Mr. Tod, by acclamation accorded to Mr. Gladstone, who then left the town, passing down rows of torch-bearers drawn up to illuminate the streets in his honour.

THURSDAY, NOVEMBER 27, 1879.

THIRD MIDLOTHIAN SPEECH.

Delivered at West Calder to the Electors of the Parishes of Kirknewton, Ratho, Kirkliston, Midcalder, and West Calder.

These Parishes embrace a district partly agricultural and partly mining.

WEST CALDER MEETING.

ON Thursday, November 27, Mr. Gladstone drove from Dalmeny Park to address the electors at West Calder. The route lay through the villages of Ratho, East Calder, West Calder, and Bell's Quarry, in all of which triumphal arches had been erected, and the popular excitement and enthusiasm were intense. A building had been specially prepared for the meeting at West Calder, and it was crowded by a very large assemblage of electors and non-electors. West Calder was illuminated at night.

Amongst those present were the following gentlemen :— Messrs. P. M'Lagan, M.P.; John Ramsay, M.P.; E. Jenkins, M.P.; Colonel Gillon of Wallhouse; Messrs. Young of Kelly; James Houldsworth of Coltness; James Melvin, Bonnington; Alexander Smith of Muirhouse, Vice-President of the Local Association; J. Calderwood, West Calder; R. G. Smith, Midcalder; the Executive Committee of the West Calder Liberal Association, etc. etc.

Mr. M'Lagan of Pumpherston, M.P., having been called to the chair, briefly introduced Mr. Gladstone, who said :—

Mr. M'Lagan and Gentlemen,—In addressing you to-day, as in addressing like audiences assembled for a like purpose in other places of the county, I am warmed by the enthusiastic welcome which you have been pleased in every quarter and in every form to accord to me.   I am, on the other hand, daunted when I recollect, first of all, what large demands I have to make on your patience ; and, secondly, how inadequate are my powers, and how inadequate almost any amount of time you can grant me, to set forth worthily the whole of the case which ought to be laid before you in connection with the coming election.

To-day, gentlemen, as I know that many among you are interested in the land, and as I feel that what is termed *Agricultural* 'agricultural distress' is at the present moment a topic too *distress.* serious to be omitted from our consideration, I shall say some words upon the subject of that agricultural distress, and particularly, because in connection with it there have arisen in some quarters of the country proposals, which have received a countenance far beyond their deserts, to reverse or to compromise the work which it took us one whole generation to achieve, and to revert to the mischievous, obstructive, and impoverishing system of Protection.   Gentlemen, I speak of agricultural distress as a matter now undoubtedly serious.   Let none of us withhold our sympathy from the farmer, the culti-*The farmer* vator of the soil, in the struggle he has to undergo.   His *has to compete* struggle is a struggle of competition with the United States. *with the* *United States.* But I do not fully explain the case when I say the United States.   It is not with the entire United States, it is with the western portion of these States, the portion remote from the seaboard ; and I wish, in the first place, gentlemen, to state to you all a fact of very great interest and importance, as it seems to me, relating to and defining the point at which the competition of the Western States of America is most severely felt. I have in my hand a letter received recently from one well known, and honourably known, in Scotland, Mr. Lyon Playfair, who has recently been a traveller in the United States, and who, as you well know, is as well qualified as any man upon earth for accurate and careful investigation. The point, gentlemen, at which the competition of the Western States of America is most severely felt is in the Eastern States of America. Whatever be agricultural distress in Scotland, whatever it be, where undoubtedly it is more felt, in England, it is greater by much in the Eastern States of America. In the States of New England the soil has been to some extent exhausted by careless methods of agriculture, and these, gentlemen, are the greatest of all the enemies with which the farmer has to contend. But the foundation of the statement I make, that the Eastern States of America are those that most feel the competition of the West, is to be found in facts,— in this fact above all, that not only they are not in America, as we are here, talking about the shortness of the annual returns, and in some places having much said on the subject of rents and of temporary remission or of permanent reduction ; that is not the state of things ; they have actually got to this point, that the capital values of land, as tested by sales in the market, have undergone an enormous diminution. Now I will tell you something that actually happened, on the authority of my friend Mr. Playfair,—I will tell you something that has happened in one of the New England States,—not, recollect, in a desert or a remote country,—in an old cultivated country, and near one of the towns of these States, a town that has the honourable name of Wellesley. Mr. Playfair tells me this : Three weeks ago—that is to say, about the first of this month, *The prices of land in the* so you will see that my information is tolerably recent,—three *Eastern States.* weeks ago a friend of Mr. Playfair bought a farm near Wellesley for thirty-three dollars an acre, for £6, 12s. an acre —agricultural land, remember, in an old settled country. That is the present condition of agricultural property in the

old States of New England.   I think by the simple recital of
that fact I have tolerably well established my case, for you
have not come in England, and you have not come in Scotland, to the point at which agricultural land is to be had—not
wild land, but improved and old cultivated land, is to be had
for the price of £6, 12s. an acre.   He mentions that this is
by no means a strange case, an isolated case, that it fairly
represented the average transactions that have been going on;
and he says that in that region the ordinary price of agricultural land at the present time is from twenty to fifty dollars
an acre, or from £4 to £10.   In New York the soil is better,
and the population is greater; but even in the State of New
York, land ranges for agricultural purposes from fifty to a
hundred dollars, that is to say, from £10 to £20 an acre.

I think those of you, gentlemen, who are farmers will perhaps derive some comfort from perceiving that if the pressure
here is heavy, the pressure elsewhere and the pressure nearer
to the seat of this very abundant production is greater and far

The pressure is greater still.   It is most interesting to consider, however, what
felt most
severely in this pressure is.   There has been developed, in the astonishing
America itself. progressive power of the United States—there has been
developed a faculty of producing corn for the subsistence of
man with a rapidity, and to an extent, unknown in the experience of mankind.   There is nothing like it in history.   Do not
let us conceal, gentlemen, from ourselves the fact, I shall not
stand the worse with any of you who are farmers if I at once
avow, that this greater and comparatively immense abundance
of the prime article of subsistence for mankind is a great
blessing vouchsafed by Providence to mankind.   In part I
believe that the cheapness has been increased by special
causes.   The lands from which the great abundance of
American wheat comes are very thinly peopled as yet.   They
will become more thickly peopled, and as they become more
thickly peopled a larger proportion of their produce will be
wanted for home consumption, and less of it will come to you,

and at a higher price. Again, if we are rightly informed, the price of American wheat has been unnaturally reduced by the extraordinary depression, in recent times, of trade in America, and especially of the mineral trades, upon which many railroads are dependent in America, and with which these railroads are connected in America in a degree and manner that in this country we know but little of. With a revival of trade in America, it is to be expected that the freights of corn will increase, and all other freights, because the employment of the railroads will be a great deal more abundant, and they will not be content to carry corn at nominal rates. In some respects, therefore, you may expect a mitigation of the pressure, but in other respects it is likely to continue. Nay, the Prime Minister is reported as having not long ago said,—and he ought to have the best information on this subject, nor am I going to impeach in the main what he stated,—he gave it to be understood that there was about to be a development of corn production in Canada, which would entirely throw into the shade this corn production in the United States. Well, that certainly was very cold comfort, as far as the British agriculturist is concerned, because he did not say—he could not say—that the corn production of the United States was to fall off, but there was to be added an enormous corn production from Manitoba, the great province which forms now a part of the Canada Dominion. There is no doubt, I believe, that it is a correct expectation that vast or very large quantities of corn will proceed from that province, and therefore we have to look forward to a state of things in which, for a considerable time to come, large quantities of wheat will be forthcoming from America, probably larger quantities, and perhaps and frequently at lower prices than those at which the corn-producing and corn-exporting districts of Europe have commonly been able to supply us. Now that I believe to be, gentlemen, upon the whole not an unfair representation of the state of things.

How are you to meet that state of things ? What are your fair claims ? I will tell you. In my opinion your fair claims are in the main two. One is to be allowed to purchase every article that you require in the cheapest market, and have no needless burden laid upon anything that comes to you and can assist you in the cultivation of your land. But that claim has been conceded and fulfilled. I do not know whether there is an object, an instrument, a tool of any kind, an auxiliary of any kind, that you want for the business of the farmer, which you do not buy at this moment in the cheapest market. But beyond that, you want to be relieved from every unjust and unnecessary legislative restraint. I say every unnecessary legislative restraint, because taxation, gentlemen, is unfortunately a restraint upon us all, but we cannot say that it is always unnecessary, and we cannot say that it is always unjust. Yesterday I ventured to state—and I will therefore not now return to the subject—a number of matters connected with the state of legislation in which it appears to me to be of vital importance, both to the agricultural interest and to the entire community, that the occupiers and cultivators of the land of this country should be relieved from restraints under the operation of which they now suffer considerably. Beyond those two great heads, gentlemen, what you have to look to, I believe, is your own energy, your own energy of thought and action, and your care not to undertake to pay rents greater than, in reasonable calculation, you think you can afford. I am by no means sure, though I speak subject to the correction of higher authority—I am by no means sure that in Scotland within the last fifteen or twenty years something of a speculative character has not entered into rents, and particularly, perhaps, into the rents of hill farms. I remember hearing of the augmentations which were taking place, I believe, all over Scotland,—I verified the fact in a number of counties,— about twelve or fourteen years ago, in the rents of hill farms, which I confess impressed me with the idea that the high

The farmer has two fair claims—(1) to purchase in cheapest market.

(2) Relief from unnecessary legislative restraint.

prices that were then ruling, and ruling increasingly from year to year, for meat and wool, were perhaps for once leading the wary and shrewd Scottish agriculturist a little beyond the mark in the rents he undertook to pay. But it is not this only which may press. It is, more broadly, in a serious and manful struggle that you are engaged, in which you will have to exert yourselves to the uttermost, in which you have a right to claim everything that the Legislature can do for you; and I hope it may perhaps possibly be my privilege and honour to assist in procuring for you some of those provisions of necessary liberation from restraint; but beyond that, it is your own energies, of thought and action, to which you will have to trust.

Now, gentlemen, having said thus much, my next duty is to *A warning against quack remedies.* warn you against quack remedies, against delusive remedies, against the quack remedies that there are plenty of people found to propose, not so much in Scotland as in England; for, gentlemen, from Midlothian at present we are speaking to England as well as to Scotland. Let us give a friendly warning from this northern quarter to the agriculturist of England not to be deluded by those who call themselves his friends in a degree of special and superior excellence, and who have been too much given to delude him in other times; not to be deluded into hoping relief from sources from which it can never come. Now, gentlemen, there are three of these remedies. The first of them, gentlemen, I will not call a quack remedy at all, but I will speak of it notwithstanding in the tone of rational and dispassionate discussion. I am not now so much upon the controversial portion of the land question—a field which, Heaven knows, is wide enough—as I am upon matters of deep and universal interest to us in our economic and social condition. There are some gentlemen, and there are persons for whom I for one have very great respect, who think that the difficulties of our agriculture may be got over by a fundamental change in the land-holding system of this country. I do not mean, now pray observe, a change as to the law of entail and settlement, and all those restraints which, I hope, were tolerably well disposed of yesterday at Dalkeith; but I mean those who think that if you can cut up the land, or a large part of it, into a multitude of small properties, that of itself will solve the difficulty, and start everybody on a career of prosperity.

Small pro-
prietors.

Now, gentlemen, to a proposal of that kind I, for one, am not going to object upon the ground that it would be inconsistent with the privileges of landed proprietors. In my opinion, if it is known to be for the welfare of the community at large, the Legislature is perfectly entitled to buy out the landed proprietors. It is not intended probably to confiscate the property of a landed proprietor more than the property of any other man; but the State is perfectly entitled, if it please, to buy out the landed proprietors as it may think fit, for the purpose of dividing the property into small lots. I don't wish to recommend it, because I will show you the doubts that, to my mind, hang about that proposal; but I admit that in principle no objection can be taken. Those persons who possess large portions of the spaces of the earth are not altogether in the same position as the possessors of mere personalty; that personalty does not impose the same limitations upon the action and industry of man, and upon the well-being of the community, as does the possession of land; and, therefore, I freely own that compulsory expropriation is a thing which for an adequate public object is in itself admissible and so far sound in principle. Now, gentlemen, this idea about small proprietors, however, is one which very large bodies and parties in this country treat with the utmost contempt; and

A comparison
with France.

they are accustomed to point to France, and say, 'Look at France.' In France you have got 5,000,000—I am not quite sure whether it is 5,000,000 or even more; I do not wish to be beyond the mark in anything — you have 5,000,000 of small proprietors, and you do not produce in France as many bushels of wheat per acre as you do in England. Well, now, I am going to point out to you a very

remarkable fact with regard to the condition of France. I
will not say that France produces—for I believe it does not
produce—as many bushels of wheat per acre as England does,
but I should like to know whether the wheat of France is
produced mainly upon the small properties of France. I
believe that the wheat of France is produced mainly upon the
large properties of France, and I have not any doubt that the
large properties of England are, upon the whole, better cultivated, and more capital is put into the land, than in the large
properties of France. But it is fair that justice should be
done to what is called a peasant proprietary. Peasant proprietary is an excellent thing, if it can be had, in many points of
view. It interests an enormous number of the people in the
soil of the country, and in the stability of its institutions and
its laws. But now look at the effect that it has upon the
progressive value of the land—and I am going to give you a
very few figures, which I will endeavour to relieve from all
complication, lest I should unnecessarily weary you. But
what will you think when I tell you that the agricultural
values of France—the taxable income derived from the land,
and therefore the income of the proprietors of that land—has
advanced during our lifetime far more rapidly than that of
England ? When I say England, I believe the same thing is
applicable to Scotland, certainly to Ireland ; but I shall take
England for my test, because the difference between England
and Scotland, though great, does not touch the principle ; and
because it so happens that we have some means of illustration
from former times for England, which are not equally applicable
for all the three Kingdoms.

Here is the state of the case. I will not go back any farther *Progressive*
than 1851. I might go back much farther, it would only *value of land in England*
strengthen my case. But for 1851 I have a statement, made *and France.*
by French official authority, of the agricultural income of
France, as well as the income of other real property, viz.
houses. In 1851 the agricultural income of France was

£76,000,000. It was greater in 1851 than the whole
income from land and houses together had been in 1821.
This is a tolerable evidence of progress; but I will not enter
into the detail of it, because I have no means of dividing the
two—the house income and the land income—for the earlier
year, namely 1821. In 1851 it was £76,000,000—the agricultural income; and in 1864 it had risen from £76,000,000
to £106,000,000. That is to say, in the space of thirteen
years the increase of agricultural values in France—annual
values—was no less than 40 per cent., or 3 per cent. per
annum. Now I go to England. Wishing to be quite accurate,
I shall limit myself to that with respect to which we have
positive figures. In England the agricultural income in
1813–14 was £37,000,000; in 1842 it was £42,000,000,
and that year is the one I will take as my starting-point.
I have given you the years 1851 to 1864 in France. I could
only give you those thirteen years with a certainty that I was
not misleading you, and I believe I have kept within the mark.
I believe I might have put my case more strongly for France.

In 1842, then, the agricultural income of England was
£42,000,000; in 1876 it was £52,000,000—that is to say,
while the agricultural income of France increased 40 per
cent. in thirteen years, the agricultural income of England
increased 20 per cent. in thirty-four years. The increase in
France was 3 per cent. per annum; the increase in England
was about one-half or three-fifths per cent. per annum. Now,
gentlemen, I wish this justice to be done to a system where
peasant proprietary prevails. It is of great importance. And
will you allow me, you who are Scotch agriculturists, to assure
you that I speak to you not only with the respect which
is due from a candidate to a constituency, but with the
deference which is due from a man knowing very little of
agricultural matters to those who know a great deal? And
there is one point at which the considerations that I have
been opening up, and this rapid increase of the value of the

soil in France, bear upon our discussions. Let me try to explain it. I believe myself that the operation of economic laws is what in the main dictates the distribution of landed property in this country. I doubt if those economic laws will allow it to remain cut up into a multitude of small properties like the small properties of France. As to small holdings, I am one of those who attach the utmost value to them. I say that in the Lothians; I say that in the portion of the country where almost beyond any other large holdings prevail; in some parts of which large holdings exclusively are to be found; I attach the utmost value to them. But it is not on that point I am going to dwell, for we have no time for what is unnecessary. What I do wish very respectfully to submit to you, gentlemen, is this. When you see this vast increase of the agricultural value of France, you know at once it is perfectly certain that has not been upon the large properties of France, which, if anything, are inferior in cultivation to the large properties of England. It has been upon those very peasant-properties, which some people are so ready to decry. What do the peasant-properties mean? They mean what, in France, is called the small cultivation; that is to say, cultivation of superior articles, pursued upon a small scale—cultivation of flowers, cultivation of trees and shrubs, cultivation of fruits of every kind, and all that, in fact, which rises above the ordinary character of farming produce, and rather approaches the produce of the gardener.

Gentlemen, I cannot help having this belief, that, among other means of meeting the difficulties in which we may be placed, our destiny is that a great deal more attention will have to be given than heretofore by the agriculturists of England, and perhaps even by the agriculturists of Scotland, to the production of fruits, of vegetables, of flowers; of all *The cultiva-* that variety of objects which are sure to find a market in a *tion of new* rich and wealthy country like this, but which have hitherto *products.* been consigned almost exclusively to garden production. You know that in Scotland, in Aberdeenshire,—and I am told also in Perthshire,—a great example of this kind has been set in the cultivation of strawberries—the cultivation of strawberries is carried on over hundreds of acres at once. I am ashamed, gentlemen, to go further into this matter, as if I was attempting to instruct you. I am sure you will take my hint as a respectful hint,—I am sure you will take it as a friendly hint. I do not believe that the large properties of this country, generally or universally, can or will be broken up into small ones. I do not believe that the land of this country will be owned, as a general rule, by those who cultivate it. I believe we shall continue to have, as we have had, a class of landlords and a class of cultivators, but I most earnestly desire to see—not only to see the relations of those classes to one another harmonious and sound, their interests never brought into conflict; but I desire to see both flourishing and prospering, and the soil of my country producing, as far as may be, under the influence of capital and skill, every variety of product which may give an abundant livelihood to those who live upon it. I

A change in distribution of landed property is not a remedy for agricultural distress.
say, therefore, gentlemen, and I say it with all respect, I hope for a good deal from the small culture, the culture in use among the small proprietors of France; but I do not look to a fundamental change in the distribution of landed property in this country as a remedy for agricultural distress.

But I go on to another remedy which is proposed, and I do it with a great deal less of respect; nay, I now come to the region of what I have presumed to call quack remedies. There is a quack remedy which is called Reciprocity, and this

Reciprocity is a quack remedy.
quack remedy is under the special protection of quack doctors, and among the quack doctors I am sorry to say there appear to be some in very high station indeed; and if I am rightly informed, no less a person than Her Majesty's Secretary of State for Foreign Affairs has been moving about the country, and indicating a very considerable expectation that possibly by Reciprocity agricultural distress will be relieved. Let me test, gentlemen, the efficacy of this quack remedy for your,

in some places, agricultural pressure and generally distress, the pressure that has been upon you, the struggle in which you are engaged. Pray watch its operation; pray note what is said by the advocates of Reciprocity. They always say, We are the soundest and best Free-traders. We recommend Reciprocity because it is the truly effectual method of bringing about Free-trade. At present America imposes enormous duties upon our cotton goods and upon our iron goods. Put Reciprocity into play, and America will become a Free-trading country. Very well, gentlemen, how would that operate upon you agriculturists in particular? Why, it will operate thus: If your condition is to be regretted in certain particulars, and capable of amendment, I beg you to cast an eye of sympathy upon the condition of the American agriculturist. It has been very well said, and very truly said, though it is a smart antithesis—the American agriculturist has got to buy everything that he wants at prices which are fixed in Washington by the legislation of America, but he has got to sell everything that he produces at prices which are fixed in Liverpool—fixed by the free competition of the world. How would you like that, gentlemen,—to have protective prices to pay for everything that you use—for your manures, for your animals, for your implements, for all your farming stock, and at the same time to have to sell what you produce in the free and open market of the world? But bring Reciprocity into play, and then, if the Reciprocity doctors are right, the Americans will remove all their protective duties, and the American farmer, instead of producing, as he does now, under the disadvantage, and the heavy disadvantage, of having to pay protective prices for everything that constitutes his farming stock, will have all his tools, and implements, and manures, and everything else purchased in the free, open market of the world, at Free-trade prices. So he will be able to produce his corn to compete with you even cheaper than he does now. So much for Reciprocity considered as a cure for distress. I am not going to consider it now in any other point of view. But, gentlemen, there are another set of men who are bolder still, and who are not for Reciprocity; who are not content with that milder form of quackery, but who recommend a reversion, pure and simple, to what I may fairly call, I think, the exploded doctrine of Protection. And upon this, gentlemen, I think it necessary, if you will allow me, to say to you a few words, because it is a very serious matter, and it is all the more serious because Her Majesty's Government—I do not scruple to say—are coquetting with this subject in a way which is not right. They are tampering with it; they are playing with it. A protective speech was made in the House of Commons in a debate last year by Mr. Chaplin, on the part of what is called ' the agricultural interest.' Mr. Chaplin did not use the word protection, but what he did say was this,—he said he demanded that the malt tax should be abolished, and the revenue supplied by a tax upon foreign barley or some other foreign commodity. Well, if he has a measure of that kind in his pocket, I don't ask him to affix the word protection to it. I can do that for myself. Not a word of rebuke, gentlemen, was uttered to the doctrines of Mr. Chaplin. He was complimented upon the ability of his speech and the well-chosen terms of his motion. Some of the members of Her Majesty's Government—the minor members of Her Majesty's Government—the humbler luminaries of that great constellation—have been going about the country and telling their farming constituents that they think the time has come when a return to Protection might very wisely be tried. But, gentlemen, what delusions have been practised upon the unfortunate British farmer! When we go back for twenty years, what is now called the Tory party was never heard of as the Tory party. It was always heard of as the party of Protection. As long as the chiefs of the Protective party were not in office, as long as they were irresponsible, they recommended themselves to the goodwill of the farmer as Protectionists, and said they would set him up and put his interests on a firm foundation through Protection. We brought

Protection is an exploded doctrine.

them into office in the year 1852. I gave with pleasure a vote that assisted to bring them into office. I thought bringing them into office was the only way of putting their professions to the test. They came into office, and before they had been six months in office they had thrown Protection to the winds. And that is the way in which the British farmer's expectations are treated by those who claim for themselves in the special sense the designation of his friends.

It is exactly the same with the malt tax. Gentlemen, *The malt tax.* what is done with the malt tax? The malt tax is held by them to be a great grievance upon the British farmer. Whenever a Liberal Government is in office, from time to time they have a great muster from all parts of the country to vote for the abolition of the malt tax. But when a Tory Government comes into office, the abolition of the malt tax is totally forgotten; and we have now had six years of a Tory Government without a word said, as far as I can recollect,— and my friend in the chair could correct me if I were wrong, —without a motion made, or a vote taken, on the subject of the malt tax. The malt tax, great and important as it is, is small in reference to Protection. Gentlemen, it is a very serious matter indeed if we ought to go back to Protection, because how did we come out of Protection to Free-trade? We came out of it by a struggle which in its crisis threatened to convulse the country, which occupied Parliaments, upon which elections turned, which took up twenty years of our legislative life, which broke up parties. In a word, it effected a change so serious, that if, after the manner in which we effected that change, it be right that we should go back upon our steps, then all I can say is, that we must lose that which has ever been one of the most honourable distinctions of British legislation in the general estimation of the world,—that British legislation, if it moves slowly, always moves in one direction, —that we never go back upon our steps. But are we such children that, after spending twenty years—as I may

say from 1840 to 1860—in breaking down the huge fabric
of Protection, in 1879 we are seriously to set about building
it up again ?   If that be right, gentlemen, let it be done, but
it will involve on our part a most humiliating confession.   In
my opinion it is not right.   Protection, however, let me point
out, now is asked for in two forms, and I am next going to
quote Lord Beaconsfield for the purpose of expressing my concurrence with him.   Mostly, I am bound to say, as far as my
knowledge goes, Protection has not been asked for by the
agricultural interest, certainly not by the farmers of Scotland.
It has been asked for by certain injudicious cliques and classes
of persons connected with other industries,—connected with
some manufacturing industries.   They want to have duties laid
upon manufactures.   But here Lord Beaconsfield said—and
I cordially agree with him—that he would be no party to the
institution of a system in which Protection was to be given
to manufactures and to be refused to agriculture.   That one-
sided Protection I deem to be totally intolerable, and I reject
it even at the threshold as unworthy of a word of examination or discussion.

But let us go on to two-sided Protection, and see whether
that is any better—that is to say, Protection in the shape of
duties on manufactures, and Protection in the shape of duties
upon corn, duties upon meat, duties upon butter, and cheese,
and eggs, and everything that can be produced from the land.
Now, gentlemen, in order to see whether we can here find a
remedy for our difficulties, I prefer to speculation and mere
abstract argument the method of reverting to experience.
The argument Experience will give us very distinct lessons upon this matter.
against Pro-
tection is based We have the power, gentlemen, of going back to the time
upon experi- when Protection was in full and unchecked force, and of
ence. examining the effect which it produced upon the wealth of the
country.   How, will you say, do I mean to test that wealth ?
I mean to test that wealth by the exports of the country, and
I will tell you why, because your prosperity depends upon the

wealth of your customers—that is to say, upon their capacity
to buy what you produce. And who are your customers?
Your customers are the industrial population of the country,
who produce what we export and send all over the world.
Consequently, when exports increase, your customers are doing
a large business, are growing wealthy, are putting money in
their pockets, and are able to take that money out of their
pockets in order to fill their stomachs with what you produce.
When, on the contrary, exports do not increase, your customers
are poor, your prices go down, as you have felt within the last
few years, in the price of meat, for example, and in other
things, and your condition is proportionally depressed. Now,
gentlemen, down to the year 1842 no profane hand had been
laid upon the august fabric of Protection. For recollect that
the farmers' friends always told us that it was a very august
fabric, and that if you pulled it down it would involve the
ruin of the country. That, you remember, was the commonplace of every Tory speech delivered from a county hustings to
a farming constituency. But before 1842 another agency
had come into force, which gave new life in a very considerable degree to the industry of the country, and that was the
agency of railways, of improved communication, which short- *The effect of the introduc-*
ened distance and cheapened transit, and effected in that way *tion of rail-*
an enormous economical gain and addition to the wealth of *ways.*
the country. Therefore, in order to see what we owe to our
friend Protection, I won't allow that friend to take credit for
what was done by railways in improving the wealth of the
country. I will go to the time when I may say there were
virtually no railways—that is, the time before 1830. Now,
gentlemen, here are the official facts which I shall lay before
you in the simplest form, and, remember, using round numbers. I do that because, although round numbers cannot be
absolutely accurate, they are easy for the memory to take in,
and they involve no material error, no falsification of the case.
In the year 1800, gentlemen, the exports of British produce

were 39½ millions sterling in value. The population at that time,—no, I won't speak of the exact figure of the population, because I have not got it for the three kingdoms. In the years 1826 to 1830,—that is, after a medium period of eight-and-twenty years,—the average of our exports for those five years, which had been 39½ millions in 1800, was 37 millions. It is fair to admit that in 1800 the currency was somewhat less sound, and therefore I am quite willing to admit that the 37 millions probably meant as much in value as the 39½ millions; but substantially, gentlemen, the trade of the country was stationary, practically stationary, under Protection. The condition of the people grew, if possible, rather worse than better. The wealth of the country was nearly stationary. But now I show you what Protection produced; that it made no addition, it gave no onward movement to the profits of those who are your customers. But on these profits you depend; because under all circumstances, gentlemen, this, I think, nobody will dispute,—a considerable portion of what the Englishman or the Scotsman produces will, some way or other, find its way down his throat.

Trade was stationary under Protec- tion.

What has happened since we cast off Protection?

What has been the case, gentlemen, since we cast off the superstition of Protection, since we discarded the imposture of Protection? I will tell you what happened between 1830, when there were no railways, and 1842, when no change, no important change, had been made as to Protection, but when the railway system was in operation, hardly in Scotland, but in England to a very great extent, to a very considerable extent upon the main lines of communication. The exports, which in 1830 had been somewhere about £37,000,000, between 1840 and 1842 showed an average amount of £50,000,000. That seems due, gentlemen, to the agency of railways; and I wish you to bear in mind the increasing benefit now derived from that agency, in order that I may not claim any undue credit for freedom of trade. From 1842, gentlemen, onwards, the successive stages of Free-trade began;

in 1842, in 1845, in 1846, in 1853, and again in 1860, the large measures were carried which have completely reformed your Customs tariff, and reduced it from a taxation of twelve hundred articles, to a taxation of, I think, less than twelve.

Now under the system of Protection, the export trade of the country, the wealth and the power of the manufacturing and producing classes to purchase your agricultural products, did not increase at all. In the time when railways began to be in operation, but before Free-trade, the exports of the country increased, as I have shown you, by £13,000,000 in somewhere about thirteen years—that is to say, taking it roughly, at the rate of £1,000,000 a year.

But since 1842, and down to the present time, we have had, along with railways, always increasing their benefits, we have had the successive adoption of Free-trade measures ; and what has been the state of the export business of the country ? It has risen in this degree, that that which from 1840 to 1842 averaged £50,000,000, from 1873 to 1878 averaged £218,000,000. Instead of increasing, as it had done between 1830 and 1842, when railways only were at work, at the rate of £1,000,000 a year—instead of remaining stagnant as it did when the country was under Protection pure and simple, with no augmentation of the export trade to enlarge the means of those who buy your products, the total growth in a period of thirty-five years was no less than £168,000,000, or, taking it roughly, a growth in the export trade of the country to the extent of between £4,000,000 and £5,000,000 a year. But, gentlemen, you know the fact, you know very well, that while restriction was in force, you did not get the prices that you have been getting for the last twenty years. The price of wheat has been much the same as it had been before. The price of oats is a better price than was to be had on the average of Protective times. But the price, with the exception of wheat, of almost every agricultural commodity, the price of wool, the price of meat, the price of

The average increase of exports under Protection and Free-trade compared.

cheese, the price of everything that the soil produces, has been largely increased in a market free and open to the world; because while the artificial advantage which you got through Protection, as it was supposed to be an advantage, was removed, you were brought into that free and open market, and the energy of Free-trade so enlarged the buying capacity of your customers, that they were willing and able to give you, and did give you, a great deal more for your meat, your wool, and your products in general, than you would ever have got under the system of Protection. Gentlemen, if that be true —and it cannot, I believe, be impeached or impugned—if that be true, I don't think I need further discuss the matter, especially when so many other matters have to be discussed.

I will therefore ask you again to cross the seas with me. I see that time is flying onwards, and, gentlemen, it is very hard upon you to be so much vexed upon the subject of policy abroad. You think generally, and I think, that your domestic affairs are quite enough to call for all your attention. There was a saying of an ancient Greek orator, who, unfortunately, very much undervalued what we generally call the better portion of the community—namely, women; he made a very disrespectful observation, which I am going to quote, not for the purpose of concurring with it, but for the purpose of an illustration. Pericles, the great Athenian statesman, said with regard to women, Their greatest merit was to be never heard of. Now, what Pericles untruly said of women, I am very much disposed to say of foreign affairs—their great merit would be to be never heard of. Unfortunately, instead of being never heard of, they are always heard of, and you hear almost of nothing else; and I can't promise you, gentlemen, that you will be relieved from this everlasting din, because the consequences of an unwise meddling with foreign affairs are consequences that will for some time necessarily continue to trouble you, and that will find their way to your pockets in the shape of increased taxation.

Foreign affairs.

Gentlemen, with that apology I ask you again to go with me beyond the seas. And as I wish to do full justice, I will tell you what I think to be the right principles of foreign policy ; *The right principles of foreign policy.* and then, as far as your patience and my strength will permit, I will, at any rate for a short time, illustrate those right principles by some of the departures from them that have taken place of late years. I first give you, gentlemen, what I think the right principles of foreign policy. The first thing is to foster the strength of the Empire by just legislation and economy *(1) Just legislation and economy.* at home, thereby producing two of the great elements of national power—namely, wealth, which is a physical element, and union and contentment, which are moral elements—and to reserve the strength of the Empire, to reserve the expenditure of that strength, for great and worthy occasions abroad. Here is my first principle of foreign policy : good government *(2) To preserve peace.* at home. My second principle of foreign policy is this— that its aim ought to be to preserve to the nations of the world—and especially, were it but for shame, when we recollect the sacred name we bear as Christians, especially to the Christian nations of the world—the blessings of peace. That is my second principle.

My third principle is this. Even, gentlemen, when you do a *(3) To maintain the concert of Europe.* good thing, you may do it in so bad a way that you may entirely spoil the beneficial effect; and if we were to make ourselves the apostles of peace in the sense of conveying to the minds of other nations that we thought ourselves more entitled to an opinion on that subject than they are, or to deny their rights—well, very likely we should destroy the whole value of our doctrines. In my opinion the third sound principle is this — to strive to cultivate and maintain, ay, to the very uttermost, what is called the concert of Europe; to keep the Powers of Europe in union together. And why ? Because by keeping all in union together you neutralize and fetter and bind up the selfish aims of each. I am not here to flatter either England or any of them. They have selfish aims, as, unfortunately, we in late years have too sadly shown that we too have had selfish aims; but then common action is fatal to selfish aims. Common action means common objects; and the only objects for which you can unite together the Powers of Europe are objects connected with the common good of them all. That, gentlemen, is my third principle of foreign policy.

(4) *To avoid needless engagements.*

My fourth principle is—that you should avoid needless and entangling engagements. You may boast about them; you may brag about them. You may say you are procuring consideration for the country. You may say that an Englishman can now hold up his head among the nations. You may say that he is now not in the hands of a Liberal Ministry, who thought of nothing but pounds, shillings, and pence. But what does all this come to, gentlemen? It comes to this, that you are increasing your engagements without increasing your strength; and if you increase engagements without increasing strength, you diminish strength, you abolish strength; you really reduce the Empire and do not increase it. You render it less capable of performing its duties; you render it an inheritance less precious to hand on to future generations.

(5) *To acknowledge the equal rights of all nations.*

My fifth principle is this, gentlemen, to acknowledge the equal rights of all nations. You may sympathize with one nation more than another. Nay, you must sympathize in certain circumstances with one nation more than another. You sympathize most with those nations, as a rule, with which you have the closest connection in language, in blood, and in religion, or whose circumstances at the time seem to give the strongest claim to sympathy. But in point of right all are equal, and you have no right to set up a system under which one of them is to be placed under moral suspicion or espionage, or to be made the constant subject of invective. If you do that, but especially if you claim for yourself a superiority, a pharisaical superiority over the whole of them, then I say you may talk about your patriotism if you please, but you are a misjudging friend of your country, and in undermining the basis of the esteem and respect of other people for your country you are in reality inflicting the severest injury upon it. I have now given you, gentlemen, five principles of foreign policy. Let me give you a sixth, and then I have done.

And that sixth is, that in my opinion foreign policy, subject (6) *A love of* to all the limitations that I have described, the foreign policy *freedom.* of England should always be inspired by the love of freedom. There should be a sympathy with freedom, a desire to give it scope, founded not upon visionary ideas, but upon the long experience of many generations within the shores of this happy isle, that in freedom you lay the firmest foundations both of loyalty and order; the firmest foundations for the development of individual character, and the best provision for the happiness of the nation at large. In the foreign policy of this country the name of Canning ever will be honoured. The name of Russell ever will be honoured. The name of Palmerston ever will be honoured by those who recollect the erection of the Kingdom of Belgium, and the union of the disjoined provinces of Italy. It is that sympathy, not a sympathy with disorder, but, on the contrary, founded upon the deepest and most profound love of order,—it is that sympathy which, in my opinion, ought to be the very atmosphere in which a Foreign Secretary of England ought to live and to move.

Gentlemen, it is impossible for me to do more to-day than to attempt very slight illustrations of those principles. But in uttering those principles, I have put myself in a position in which no one is entitled to tell me—you will bear me out in what I say—that I simply object to the acts of others, and lay down no rules of action myself. I am not only prepared to show what are the rules of action which in my judgment are the right rules, but I am prepared to apply them, nor will I shrink from their application. I will take, gentlemen, the name which, most of all others, is associated with suspicion, and with alarm, and with hatred in the minds of many Englishmen—I will take the name of Russia, and at once I will tell you what I think about Russia, and how I am prepared as a member of Parliament to proceed in anything that respects Russia. You have heard me, gentlemen, denounced sometimes, I believe, as a Russian spy, sometimes as a Russian agent, sometimes as perhaps a Russian fool, which is not so bad, but still not very desirable. But, gentlemen, when you come to evidence, the worst thing that I have ever seen quoted out of any speech or writing of mine about Russia is that I did one day say, or, I believe, I wrote, these terrible words: I recommended Englishmen to imitate Russia in her good deeds. Was not that a terrible proposition? I cannot recede from it. I think we ought to imitate Russia in her good deeds, and if the good deeds be few, I am sorry for it, but I am not the less disposed on that account to imitate them when they come. I will now tell you what I think just about Russia.

I make it one of my charges against the foreign policy of Her Majesty's Government, that, while they have completely estranged from this country—let us not conceal the fact—the feelings of a nation of eighty millions, for that is the number of the subjects of the Russian Empire—while they have contrived completely to estrange the feelings of that nation, they have aggrandized the power of Russia. They have aggrandized the

power of Russia in two ways, which I will state with perfect distinctness. They have augmented her territory. Before the European Powers met at Berlin, Lord Salisbury met with Count Schouvaloff, and Lord Salisbury agreed that, unless he could convince Russia by his arguments in the open Congress of Berlin, he would support the restoration to the despotic power of Russia of that country north of the Danube which at the moment constituted a portion of the free State of Roumania. Why, gentlemen, what had been done by the Liberal Government, which, forsooth, attended to nothing but pounds, shillings, and pence? The Liberal Government had driven Russia back from the Danube. Russia, which was a Danubian Power before the Crimean War, lost this position on the Danube by the Crimean

War; and the Tory Government, which has been incensing and inflaming you against Russia, yet nevertheless, by binding itself beforehand to support, when the judgment was taken, the restoration of that country to Russia, has aggrandized the power of Russia. *The retrocession of Bessarabia.*

It further aggrandized the power of Russia in Armenia; but I would not dwell upon that matter if it were not for a very strange circumstance. You know that an Armenian province was given to Russia after the war, but about that I own to you I have very much less feeling of objection. I have objected from the first, vehemently, and in every form, to the granting of territory on the Danube to Russia, and carrying back the population of a certain country from a free State to a despotic State; but with regard to the transfer of a certain portion of the Armenian people from the government of Turkey to the government of Russia, I must own that I contemplate that transfer with much greater equanimity. I have no fear myself of the territorial extensions of Russia in Asia, no fear of them whatever. I think the fears are no better than old women's fears. And I don't wish to encourage her aggressive tendencies in Asia, or anywhere else. But I admit it may be, and probably is the case that there is some benefit attending the transfer of a portion of Armenia from Turkey to Russia. *The annexation of Armenia.*

But here is a very strange fact. You know that that portion of Armenia includes the port of Batoum. Lord Salisbury has lately stated to the country, that, by the Treaty of Berlin, the port of Batoum is to be only a commercial port. If the Treaty of Berlin stated that it was to be only a commercial port, which, of course, could not be made an arsenal, that fact would be very important. But happily, gentlemen, although treaties are concealed from us now-a-days as long as and as often as is possible, the Treaty of Berlin is an open instrument. We can consult it for ourselves; and when we consult the Treaty of Berlin, we find it states that Batoum shall be essentially a commercial port, but not that it shall be only a commercial port. Why *The provisions of the Berlin Treaty as to Batoum.*

gentlemen, Leith is essentially a commercial port, but there is
nothing to prevent the people of this country, if in their
wisdom or their folly they should think fit, from constituting
Leith as a great naval arsenal or fortification; and there is
nothing to prevent the Emperor of Russia, while leaving to
Batoum a character that shall be essentially commercial, from
joining with that another character that is not in the slightest
degree excluded by the treaty, and making it as much as he
pleases a port of military defence. Therefore I challenge the
assertion of Lord Salisbury; and as Lord Salisbury is fond of
writing letters to the *Times* to bring the Duke of Argyll to book,
he perhaps will be kind enough to write another letter to the
Times, and tell in what clause of the Treaty of Berlin he finds it
written that the port of Batoum shall be only a commercial port.
For the present, I simply leave it on record that he has mis-
represented the Treaty of Berlin.

Russian policy in Central Asia. With respect to Russia, I take two views of the position of
Russia. The position of Russia in Central Asia I believe to be
one that has in the main been forced upon her against her will.
She has been compelled,—and this is the impartial opinion of
the world,—she has been compelled to extend her frontier
southward in Central Asia by causes in some degree analogous
to, but certainly more stringent and imperative than, the causes
which have commonly led us to extend, in a far more important
manner, our frontier in India; and I think it, gentlemen, much
to the credit of the late Government, much to the honour of Lord
Clarendon and Lord Granville, that, when we were in office, we
made a covenant with Russia, in which Russia bound herself to
exercise no influence or interference whatever in Afghanistan,
we, on the other hand, making known our desire that Afghanistan should continue free and independent. Both the Powers
acted with uniform strictness and fidelity upon this engagement until the day when we were removed from office.
Russian policy in respect to Turkey. But Russia, gentlemen, has another position,—her position in
respect to Turkey; and here it is that I have complained of the

Government for aggrandizing the power of Russia; it is on this point that I most complain.

The policy of Her Majesty's Government was a policy of repelling and repudiating the Slavonic populations of Turkey in Europe, and of declining to make England the advocate for their *British policy in the East.* interests. Nay, more, she became in their view the advocate of the interests opposed to theirs. Indeed, she was rather the decided advocate of Turkey; and now Turkey is full of loud complaints—and complaints, I must say, not unjust—that we allured her on to her ruin; that we gave the Turks a right to believe that we should support them; that our ambassadors, Sir Henry Elliot and Sir Austin Layard, both of them said we had most vital interests in maintaining Turkey as it was, and consequently the Turks thought if we had vital interests, we should certainly defend them; and they were thereby lured on into that ruinous, cruel, and destructive war with Russia. But by our con- *Its effect on the Slavonic popu- lations.* duct to the Slavonic populations we alienated those populations from us. We made our name odious among them. They had every disposition to sympathize with us, every disposition to confide in us. They are, as a people, desirous of freedom, desirous of self-government, with no aggressive views, but hating the idea of being absorbed in a huge despotic empire like Russia. But when they found that we, and the other Powers of Europe under our unfortunate guidance, declined to become in any manner their champions in defence of the rights of life, of property, and of female honour,—when they found that there was no call which could find its way to the heart of England through its Government, or to the hearts of the other Powers, and that Russia alone was disposed to fight for them, why naturally they said, Russia is our friend. We have done everything, gentlemen, in our power to drive these populations into the arms of Russia. If Russia has aggressive dispositions in the direction of Turkey,—and I think it probable that she may have them,—it is we who have laid the ground upon which Russia may make her march to the south,—we who have taught the Bulgarians, the Servians, the Roumanians, the

Montenegrins, that there is one Power in Europe, and only one, which is ready to support in act and by the sword her professions of sympathy with the oppressed populations of Turkey. That power is Russia; and how can you blame these people if, in such circumstances, they are disposed to say, Russia is our friend? But why did we make them say it? Simply because of the policy of the Government, not because of the wishes of the people of this country. Gentlemen, this is the most dangerous form of aggrandizing Russia. If Russia is aggressive anywhere, if Russia is formidable anywhere, it is by movements towards the south, it is by schemes for acquiring command of the Straits or of Constantinople; and there is no way by which you can possibly so much assist her in giving reality to these designs, as by inducing and disposing the populations of these provinces, who are now in virtual possession of them, to look upon Russia as their champion and their friend, to look upon England as their disguised, perhaps, but yet real and effective enemy.

Why, now, gentlemen, I have said that I think it not unreasonable either to believe, or at any rate to admit it to *The designs of* be possible, that Russia has aggressive designs in the east of *Russia.* Europe. I do not mean immediate aggressive designs. I do not believe that the Emperor of Russia is a man of aggressive schemes or policy. It is that, looking to that question in the long run, looking at what has happened, and what may happen in ten or twenty years, in one generation, in two generations, it is highly probable that in some circumstances Russia may develop aggressive tendencies towards the south. Perhaps you will say I am here guilty of the same injustice to Russia that I have been deprecating, because I say that we ought not to adopt the method of condemning anybody without cause, and setting up exceptional principles in proscription of a particular nation. Gentlemen, I will explain to you in a moment the principle upon which I act, and the grounds upon which I form my judgment. They are simply these grounds: I look at the position of Russia, the geographical position of

Russia relatively to Turkey. I look at the comparative strength of the two Empires ; I look at the importance of the Dardanelles and the Bosporos as an exit and a channel for the military and commercial marine of Russia to the Mediterranean ; and what I say to myself is this. If the United Kingdom were in the same position relatively to Turkey which Russia holds upon the map of the globe, I feel quite sure that we should be very apt indeed both to entertain and to execute aggressive designs upon Turkey. Gentlemen, I will go farther, and will frankly own to you that I believe if we, instead of happily inhabiting this island, had been in the possession of the Russian territory, and in the circumstances of the Russian people, we should most likely have eaten up Turkey long ago. And consequently, in saying that Russia ought to be vigilantly watched in that quarter, I am only applying to her the rule which in parallel circumstances I feel convinced ought to be applied, and would be justly applied, to judgments upon our own country.

Gentlemen, there is only one other point on which I must still say a few words to you, although there are a great many upon which I have a great many words yet to say somewhere or other. Of all the principles, gentlemen, of foreign policy which I have enumerated, that to which I attach the greatest *The equality of* value is the principle of the equality of nations ; because, *nations is a* without recognising that principle, there is no such thing as *strict principle* public right, and without public international right there is no *of foreign* instrument available for settling the transactions of mankind *policy.* except material force. Consequently the principle of equality among nations lies, in my opinion, at the very basis and root of a Christian civilisation, and when that principle is compromised or abandoned, with it must depart our hopes of tranquillity and of progress for mankind.

I am sorry to say, gentlemen, that I feel it my absolute duty to make this charge against the foreign policy under which we have lived for the last two years, since the resignation of Lord Derby. It has been a foreign policy, in my opinion, wholly, or

The present
foreign policy
is regardless of
public right.
to a perilous extent, unregardful of public right, and it has been founded upon the basis of a false, I think an arrogant, and a dangerous assumption,—although I do not question its being made conscientiously and for what was believed the advantage of the country,—un untrue, arrogant, and dangerous assumption that we were entitled to assume for ourselves some dignity, which we should also be entitled to withhold from others, and to claim on our own part authority to do things which we would not permit to be done by others.   For example, when Russia was going to the Congress at Berlin, we said : ' Your Treaty of San Stefano is of no value.   It is an act between you and Turkey ; but the concerns of Turkey by the Treaty of Paris are the concerns of Europe at large.   We insist upon it that the whole of your Treaty of San Stefano shall be submitted to the Congress at Berlin, that they may judge how far to open it in each and every one of its points, because the concerns of Turkey are the common concerns of the Powers of Europe acting in concert.'

Having asserted that principle to the world, what did we do ?   These two things, gentlemen : secretly, without the knowledge of Parliament, without even the forms of official *The secret*
agreement
with Russia. procedure, Lord Salisbury met Count Schouvaloff in London, and agreed with him upon the terms on which the two Powers together should be bound in honour to one another to act upon all the most important points when they came before the Congress at Berlin.   Having alleged against Russia that she should not be allowed to settle Turkish affairs with Turkey, because they were but two Powers, and these affairs were the common affairs of Europe, and of European interest, we then got Count Schouvaloff into a private room, and on the part of England and Russia, they being but two Powers, we settled a large number of the most important of these affairs, in utter contempt and derogation of the very principle for which the Government had been contending for months before, for which they had asked Parliament to grant a sum of £6,000,000, for

which they had spent that £6,000,000 in needless and mischievous armaments. That which we would not allow Russia to do with Turkey, because we pleaded the rights of Europe, we ourselves did with Russia, in contempt of the rights of Europe. Nor was that all, gentlemen.

That act was done, I think, on one of the last days of May in the year 1878, and the document was published, made known to the world, made known to the Congress at Berlin, to its infinite astonishment, unless I am very greatly misinformed, to its infinite astonishment.

But that was not all. Nearly at the same time we performed the same operation in another quarter. We objected to a treaty between Russia and Turkey as having no authority, though that treaty was made in the light of day—namely, to the Treaty of San Stefano; and what did we do ? We went not in the light of day, but in the darkness of the night,—not in the knowledge and cognizance of other Powers, all of whom would have had the faculty and means of watching all along, and of preparing and taking their own objections and shaping their own policy,—not in the light of day, but in the darkness of the night, we sent the Ambassador of England in Constantinople *The secret* to the Minister of Turkey, and there he framed, even while the *agreement* Congress of Berlin was sitting to determine these matters of *with Turkey.* common interest, he framed that which is too famous, shall I say, or rather too notorious as the Anglo-Turkish Convention. Gentlemen, it is said, and said truly, that truth beats fiction; that what happens in fact from time to time is of a character so daring, so strange, that if the novelist were to imagine it and to put it upon his pages, the whole world would reject it from its improbability. And that is the case of the Anglo-Turkish Convention. For who would have believed it possible that we should assert before the world the principle that Europe only could deal with the affairs of the Turkish Empire, and should ask Parliament for six millions to support us in asserting that principle, should send Ministers to Berlin who declared that unless that principle was acted upon they would go to war with the material that Parliament had placed in their hands, and should at the same time be concluding a separate agreement with Turkey, under which those matters of European jurisdiction were coolly transferred to English jurisdiction; and the whole matter was sealed with the worthless bribe of the

Cyprus.   possession and administration of the island of Cyprus! I said, gentlemen, the worthless bribe of the island of Cyprus, and that is the truth. It is worthless for our purposes, worse than worthless for our purposes—not worthless in itself; an island of resources, an island of natural capabilities, provided they are allowed to develop themselves in the course of circumstances, without violent and unprincipled methods of action. But Cyprus was not thought to be worthless by those who accepted it as a bribe. On the contrary, you were told that it was to secure the road to India; you were told that it was to be the site of an arsenal very cheaply made, and more valuable than Malta; you were told that it was to revive trade. And a multitude of companies were formed, and sent agents and capital to Cyprus, and some of them, I fear, grievously burned their fingers there. I am not going to dwell upon that now. What I have in view is not the particular merits of Cyprus, but the illustration that I have given you in the case of the agreement of Lord Salisbury with Count Schouvaloff, and in the case of the Anglo-Turkish Convention, of the manner in which we have asserted for ourselves a principle that we had denied to others—namely, the principle of overriding the European authority of the Treaty of Paris, and taking the matters which that treaty gave to Europe into our own separate jurisdiction.

Now, gentlemen, I am sorry to find that that which I call the pharisaical assertion of our own superiority has found its way alike into the practice and seemingly into the theories of the

The speech of   Government. I am not going to assert anything which is not
Lord Beacons-   known, but the Prime Minister has said that there is one day
field at the
Guildhall.   in the year—namely, the 9th of November, Lord Mayor's Day

—on which the language of sense and truth is to be heard amidst the surrounding din of idle rumours generated and fledged in the brains of irresponsible scribes. I do not agree, gentlemen, in that panegyric upon the 9th of November. I am much more apt to compare the ninth of November—certainly a well-known day in the year—but as to some of the speeches that have lately been made upon it, I am very much disposed to compare it with another day in the year, well known to British tradition; and that other day in the year is the first of April. But, gentlemen, on that day the Prime Minister, speaking out,—I do not question for a moment his own sincere opinion,—made what I think one of the most unhappy and ominous allusions ever made by a Minister of this country. He quoted certain words, easily rendered as 'Empire and Liberty' *'Imperium et* —words (he said) of a Roman statesman, words descriptive of *Libertas.'* the state of Rome—and he quoted them as words which were capable of legitimate application to the position and circumstances of England. I join issue with the Prime Minister upon that subject, and I affirm that nothing can be more fundamentally unsound, more practically ruinous, than the establishment of Roman analogies for the guidance of British policy. What, gentlemen, was Rome? Rome was indeed an Imperial State, you may tell me—I know not, I cannot read the counsels of Providence—a State having a mission to subdue the world; but a State whose very basis it was to deny the equal rights, to proscribe the independent existence, of other nations. That, gentlemen, was the Roman idea. It has been partially and not ill described in three lines of a translation from Virgil by our great poet Dryden, which run as follows :—

> ' O Rome ! 'tis thine alone with awful sway
> To rule mankind, and make the world obey,
> Disposing peace and war thine own majestic way.'

We are told to fall back upon this example. No doubt the word 'Empire' was qualified with the word 'Liberty.' But what did the two words 'Liberty' and 'Empire' mean in a

The policy of denying to others what we claim ourselves.

Roman mouth ? They meant simply this—'Liberty for ourselves, Empire over the rest of mankind.'

I do not think, gentlemen, that this Ministry, or any other Ministry, is going to place us in the position of Rome. What I object to is the revival of the idea—I care not how feebly, I care not even how, from a philosophic or historic point of view, how ridiculous the attempt at this revival may be. I say it indicates an intention—I say it indicates a frame of mind, and that frame of mind, unfortunately, I find, has been consistent with the policy of which I have given you some illustrations— the policy of denying to others the rights that we claim ourselves. No doubt, gentlemen, Rome may have had its work to do, and Rome did its work. But modern times have brought a different state of things. Modern times have established a sisterhood of nations, equal, independent ; each of them built up under that legitimate defence which public law affords to every nation, living within its own borders, and seeking to perform its own affairs ; but if one thing more than another has been detestable to Europe, it has been the appearance upon the stage from time to time of men who, even in the times of the Christian civilisation, have been thought to aim at universal dominion. It was this aggressive disposition on the part of Louis XIV., King of France, that led your forefathers, gentlemen,

We have fought to resist such pretensions.

freely to spend their blood and treasure in a cause not immediately their own, and to struggle against the method of policy which, having Paris for its centre, seemed to aim at an universal monarchy. It was the very same thing, a century and a half later, which was the charge launched, and justly launched, against Napoleon, that under his dominion France was not content even with her extended limits, but Germany, and Italy, and Spain, apparently without any limit to this pestilent and pernicious process, were to be brought under the dominion or influence of France, and national equality was to be trampled under foot, and national rights denied. For that reason, England in the struggle almost exhausted herself, greatly impoverished her people, brought upon herself, and Scotland too, the consequences of a debt that nearly crushed their energies, and poured forth their best blood without limit, in order to resist and put down these intolerable pretensions.

Gentlemen, it is but in a pale and weak and almost despicable miniature that such ideas are now set up, but you will observe that the poison lies—that the poison and the mischief lie—in the principle and not the scale. It is the opposite principle which, I say, has been compromised by the action of the Ministry, and which I call upon you, and upon any who choose to hear my views, to vindicate when the day of our election comes; I mean the sound and the sacred principle that Christendom is formed of a band of nations who are united to one another in the bonds of right; that they are without distinction of great and small; there is an absolute equality between them,—the same sacredness defends the narrow limits of Belgium, as attaches to the extended frontiers of Russia, or Germany, or France. I hold that he who by act or word brings that principle into peril or disparagement, however honest his intentions may be, places himself in the position of one inflicting—I won't say intending to inflict—I ascribe nothing of the sort—but inflicting injury upon his own country, and endangering the peace and all the most fundamental interests of Christian society.

Nations are united in common bonds of right and of absolute equality.

A vote of thanks to Mr. Gladstone was moved by Mr. Young of Kelly, and carried amid loud cheers.

On Friday, November 28, an address was presented to Mr. Gladstone, at Dalmeny Park, by the Corporation of Leith; and in the afternoon, the members of the Executive Committee of the Midlothian Liberal Association were received by the Countess of Rosebery.

V.

SATURDAY, NOVEMBER 29, 1879.

SPEECHES IN THE CORN EXCHANGE AND WAVERLEY MARKET, EDINBURGH.

These great meetings were not directly connected in any way
with the Midlothian Election, though naturally the Liberal
feeling of county and city acted and reacted in a manner
beneficial alike to the political ardour of both. At the
Corn Exchange about 4700 persons assembled from all
parts of the country under the auspices of the East and
North of Scotland Liberal Association to hear Mr. Gladstone, and upwards of one hundred local associations were
represented. At the Waverley Market, a vast gathering
of more than 20,000 people met for the same purpose,
under the direction of a Committee of Working Men
representing the different trades of Edinburgh.

SPEECH IN THE CORN EXCHANGE, EDINBURGH.

THE following Peers, Members of Parliament, and Liberal
Candidates accompanied the Earl of Rosebery, President of
the East and North of Scotland Liberal Association, to the
platform :—

1. *Peers*—Marquis of Tweeddale, Earl of Elgin, Earl of
Airlie, Earl of Breadalbane, Earl of Aberdeen, Lord Napier
and Ettrick, Lord Reay, Lord Belhaven and Stenton.

2. *M.P.'s*—The Hon. Sir A. H. Gordon, Mr. J. Farley

Leith, Lord Colin Campbell, the Right Hon. W. P. Adam, Mr.
Edward Jenkins, Mr. James Cowan, Sir George Macpherson
Grant, Bart.; Messrs. John Ramsay, J. W. Barclay, Chas.
Cameron, Chas. Tennant, Geo. Anderson, J. Stewart; Sir D.
Wedderburn, Bart.; Mr. J. F. Harrison, Sir Geo. Campbell,
Sir T. Edward Colebrooke, Bart.; Messrs. And. Grant, P.
M'Lagan, S. Laing, W. Holms, Right Hon. Lyon Playfair,
Mr. C. S. Parker, Colonel Mure, Messrs. H. Campbell-
Bannerman, J. Pender, J. Fletcher; Sir Wilfred Lawson,
Bart.; Messrs. C. L. Dodds, Alexander Macdonald, W. H.
Gladstone; Lord Douglas Gordon, Sir George Balfour.

3. *Liberal Candidates*—Ayr Burghs, Mr. R. P. P. Campbell
of Craigie; North Ayrshire, Mr. J. B. Balfour; Berwick-
upon-Tweed, Hon. Henry Strutt; Berwickshire, Mr. Edward
Marjoribanks; Dumbartonshire, Mr. J. W. Burns of Kilma-
hew; Dumfriesshire, Mr. R. Jardine of Castlemilk; Fife-
shire, the Hon. R. Preston Bruce; East Kent, Mr. Edmund F.
Davis; South Lanarkshire, Mr. J. G. C. Hamilton of Dalzell;
Perthshire, Mr. D. Currie; Roxburghshire, the Hon. Arthur
Elliot; Stirlingshire, Mr. J. C. Bolton of Carbrook; Wigan,
Lieut.-Col. M'Corquodale; Wigtown Burghs, Mr. J. M'Laren;
Wigtownshire, Viscount Dalrymple.

The Committee of Arrangements was composed of the follow-
ing noblemen and gentlemen:—Marquis of Huntly, Earl of
Rosebery; Right Hon. W. P. Adam, M.P.; Charles Tennant,
M.P.; R. Cathcart of Pitcairlie; George Harrison, Treasurer
of Edinburgh; John M'Laren, Advocate; J. J. Reid, Advocate;
James Patten, Advocate.

Lord Rosebery having been moved to the chair by Mr.
Cowan, M.P., introduced Mr. Gladstone to the audience,
by whom he was received with extraordinary enthusiasm, all
present rising to their feet and cheering vehemently. Mr.
Gladstone, on silence being restored, proceeded to say:—

My Lord Rosebery, my Lords, Ladies, and Gentlemen,—I

have had the honour to receive the various addresses which
constitute the formal occasion of the present meeting; but in
the desire to avoid unnecessary ceremonial, I will pass over the
particular contents of those addresses, and will be very brief
indeed in my grateful acknowledgments for the honour which
has been done me in presenting them. For, gentlemen, you
have assembled together to-day with what you are good enough
to consider a practical purpose, and my thanks will best be
conveyed to your minds, the record of my gratitude most
deeply engraven there, if I can make myself able, through the
patience and kindness of this vast assembly, to set forth some
portion of that material which is the groundwork of the political
cause and the political campaign that we are now engaged in.
When I say, gentlemen, the political campaign, I have been
warned by our noble chairman that this is not a Midlothian
meeting. At the same time, it is a meeting the members of
which I may safely assume have some knowledge of what is
going forward in Midlothian, and it is a meeting closely allied
in heart and purpose with the people of Midlothian, having one
cause and one object with them.

And though I said, gentlemen, that I would not dwell upon
the contents of those addresses in detail, yet I observe, without
surprise, that the Liberal Associations for the west and south-
The financial west of Scotland speak of this as a time when the finance of
condition of the country is disordered. I have not yet had an opportunity
this country. of calling attention to that subject. I do not hold, gentlemen,
that good finance is the beginning and the ending of good
government, but I hold this, that it is an essential of good
government—it is a condition of good government. Without
it you cannot have good government—and with it you almost
always get good government. The things are harmonious,
though they are not identical.

The finance of the country has, however, been made the
subject of high consideration, and very unusual consideration,
before a dignified assembly in the south, within the month that

has not yet closed; for on the 10th of November was held the great annual festival of the Lord Mayor of London at Guildhall, and on that occasion the Chancellor of the Exchequer, to whom is entrusted the supreme care of our finance, used these remarkable words. He said : ' In challenging us upon our finance, our opponents are challenging us upon a point on which we are strong, and on which we can be secure of victory.' Well, gentlemen, you will feel with me that I may be too bold in venturing upon an attempt to storm the fortress at this point, at which it is so strong. If I were about to storm, gentlemen, the Castle which for so many centuries has looked down upon Edinburgh, I would endeavour to select that portion of the rock which was easiest and most accessible. I am therefore to a certain degree, perhaps, daunted by this declaration of the Chancellor of the Exchequer. At the same time, political generosity is not yet altogether dead, and I have enough of it in my nature, notwithstanding this announcement of the impregnable character, the unassailable character, of the Ministerial finance—I have enough of it in my nature to be disposed to make a trial to bring that finance under criticism, and under your clear review; and it will not be my fault, gentlemen, if I fail in the endeavour to lay it before you in such a manner that friends can sympathize with what I may conclude, and that opponents shall have the opportunity of clearly understanding what it is, and the opportunity of confuting me if they can.

Sir Stafford Northcote at the Guildhall Banquet.

There is one preliminary observation, gentlemen, with which I will trouble you, and it is this, that when you are dealing with the proceedings, either of an economical or of an extravagant Government, the present circumstances never set forth the whole case. In this country our economies are eminently prospective, because for a very long series of years, in fact ever since economies began—I may say about half a century ago— the wise practice has been to carry them into effect with the most liberal consideration for individual interests. The consequence is that the savings that they make accrue progressively

Present circumstances in finance never set forth the whole case.

This is true with economy.

and not at once, and therefore, whenever by a happy combination there is an economical Government in office, that economical Government invariably leaves to its successor a harvest of economies, and the succeeding Government derives from time to time a large portion of the benefit of what the economical Government has done, but of what that economical Government never profited by as far as public reputation is concerned.

And also with extravagance. And, gentlemen, the very same thing is the case with regard to the extravagant Government. Extravagance, also, is prospective as well as economy. Incur what charges you will, those charges do not instantly accrue as moneys to be liquidated; and therefore I warn you that everything I say to-day upon economy or upon extravagance is less than the truth, because I shall endeavour to confine myself to statements of that which actually exists, which is admitted to exist; and assuming that it is a correct description of that which now exists, it will not convey to you the whole of the mischief which has been done.

Gentlemen, I shall avoid minute details. I shall use round numbers, endeavouring to put everything in the most accessible and the most intelligible form, rather than to be in precise correspondence with the accounts, by describing to you how many shillings and how many pence in each case come at the end of the long figures of millions in which our financial transactions are expressed.

The last year of Liberal finance. The last year, gentlemen, of the Liberal Government was a year in which we were called upon to pay £800,000 for an Ashantee war, which was a melancholy necessity, not growing out of the will or the proceedings, perhaps, of any particular Government, certainly not growing out of the proceedings of the Government of the time, but growing immediately out of a necessity which was not disputed or denied. We also on that occasion in that year paid £3,200,000 on account of what were called the Alabama claims; and though I have always thought that as a mere matter between parties Great Britain was harshly treated in being called upon to pay so large a sum, I now thrust such considerations altogether aside. The object in view was twofold. It was the assertion of a great principle most valuable to mankind, and to be productive, I hope, in the future of immeasurable good. It also had in view another aim, which has been completely accomplished, viz. the aim of removing a formidable obstacle to affection and goodwill between the four-and-thirty millions of Anglo-Saxons who inhabit these islands, and the five-and-forty millions who inhabit the United States of America. Swelled in that way by £4,000,000, our expenditure for the year 1873–74 was £70,000,000 of money—not a difficult figure to remember. The present Government has had for its last year the year 1878–79. Its expenditure for that year is seventy-eight and a quarter millions of money. In order to make the comparison fair, they ought to have deductions as well as we. We were entitled to deductions bringing us down from £70,000,000 to £66,000,000. They are entitled to deductions on account of increases of charge—certainly for some of them they are responsible, but at the same time they are increases of charge that I will not assume to lie wholly at their account—to about the same amount. They have had a large increase upon the education votes, which is a legitimate expenditure, and a beneficial expenditure. They have had a large increase upon local charges, which, whether it be a beneficial measure or not, or whether or not it was in all respects wisely done, was not done by their mere motion, but was done in compliance with a desire that certainly went beyond the limits of the Conservative party. I deduct from their account on these grounds £4,000,000—I do not believe that is very far from the mark. Their war expenditure I will not deduct, because their war expenditure, so far from having been an inheritance from other Governments and from other times, has been the fruit, as we hold, of their needless and their wanton choice. In both cases alike, the charges of collection are deducted before making the comparison.

Taking, then, the deductions on the one side, and the deductions on the other, they are nearly balanced. Consequently the relation of the two figures which I first gave to you expresses fairly the relative expenditure of the two Governments as indicated by their views and their tendencies—that is to say, the Liberal expenditure at £70,000,000, and the Tory expendi-

There are eight millions of difference between 1873-74 and 1878-79 in favour of the Liberals.

ture at £78,000,000. That is a difference, gentlemen, of eight millions of money, which, in my opinion, is fairly to be set down to the account of the present Government. You may say, gentlemen, that a good article deserves a good price. But there are some prices that are too high, even for a good article, and our contention is that this is an article not good, but bad, and one for which any price would be a great deal too high. If all the millions bestowed upon giving effect to the warlike policy of the Government had, instead of being so applied, been thrown down to the bottom of the sea, you would have been better off, with such a mode of disposing of the funds, than you are now. Now, that is the amount of expenditure. But I wish you to understand that it is a vice which appears to be engrained in the Tory party of the day. As long, gentlemen, as the Tory party was in a minority when in Government, we got on very decently with them. The two first Governments of Lord Derby kept within bounds, and never made themselves remarkable by financial extravagance. But it pleased the constituencies in January 1874 to constitute that which had not been seen since 1841, and which, when it was seen in 1841, was constituted under very different auspices and worked for very different aims. However, that majority was constituted; and I may say this, the result has been a Government of which I am the first to admit that it has written its name in history. It is a Government, gentlemen, that will have plenty of memorials. And one of its first, greatest, and most undeniable is the perpetuation of the Income-tax. You were offered in 1845 the repeal of the

The Income-tax.

Income-tax by Sir Robert Peel; but he advised, and you wisely chose, not to repeal the Income-tax, but to use it for the great purpose of reforming your commercial legislation. You were

offered in 1874 the repeal of the Income-tax, and the constituencies then gave the same reply. I know the reason of their
reply in 1845, but what the reason of their reply in 1874, why
it was that they then preferred having the Income-tax to no
Income-tax, I have not yet been able to discover. But this, at
any rate, is clear—there was a clear stage upon which, on our
responsibility, we were ready to repeal the Income-tax, and it
would have been done with fairness to every class of the community. The Tories came in; the Income-tax since then has *Its increase.*
been raised from 2d. to 5d. in the pound, and when you will
get rid of it I do not know. I hope it; but it will be, perhaps,
in the days of your children or your grandchildren. This
extravagance of expenditure is due to no one cause. It bubbles
up everywhere. It is due in a great part to what has been
called a vigorous foreign policy, and a spirited foreign policy.
But when Lord Derby was in office, Lord Derby had no disposition at all to that sort of vigorous or spirited foreign policy,
and the first two or three years of the present Government
passed by without any sort of manifestation of it. If you
recollect, 1874 and 1875 showed nothing of the kind, nor did,
indeed, 1876. It has been 1878 and 1879 that have been the
grand years for the development of this new system.

But the extravagance of the Tory Government began to *Tory extrava-*
grow from the very first, as I will now show you. I will show *gance through-*
it you by taking the expenditure upon the forces, upon the *out since 1874.*
military establishments of the country. In the first year of *Military estab-*
the present Government it was £25,903,000; in the second *lishments.*
year, £26,842,000; in the third year it was £27,286,000; so
that you see, quite independently of the vigorous and spirited
foreign policy, it was walking upwards, quietly walking
upwards, at the rate of half a million, and at the rate of a
million, a year; and these first three years—two years, perhaps,
I should say—produced an augmentation in that branch of a
million and a half. I grant you that since the vigorous policy
began to be developed, they have not been satisfied with that

moderate rate of march. In the fourth year of the Government it rose from 27¼ millions to 30½; in the fifth year of the Government to 32¼. What the sixth year will do, gentlemen, we shall have the satisfaction of knowing somewhere about the month of April next; or, at any rate, we shall have the satisfaction of knowing so much as the Government may then think proper to disclose to us,—for one of my complaints is that they never do make disclosures at the time when they are wanted, and at the time when they are regular. They appear to have but one rule for the choice of their opportunity, and that is, convenience to themselves. Well now, gentlemen, this is rather remarkable. I have given you the fifth year as compared with the first, and the upshot of it is an increase on the military expenditure of £6,500,000. Therefore, gentlemen, do not allow yourselves to be put to silence by being told that the charges of the country are increased because education is so expensive. Do not be put to silence or abashed by being told that it is because they have been so very kind to the ratepayers. It is nothing of the kind. I take these hard figures, and I show you that the first year of military expenditure with the present Government, which was higher than our military expenditure, was £25,903,000, and that by the fifth year they had raised the military expenditure to £32,190,000,—that is to say, they had raised the charge by nearly six and a half millions of money. But pray observe what I am now going to tell you. So they went on while the Parliament was young, so they went on while the Parliament was middle-aged; but like other Parliaments it began to grow old, and when it began to grow old, like other offenders, it began to think a little of what might take place at its dissolution. The consequence is that this Government, which from year to year had thus gone on augmenting our charge, produced, in 1879, military estimates showing a decrease most gratifying to our feelings,—promised upon the papers a decrease of five millions in the year. Nearly the whole of this augmentation was to be got rid of. We were to have a decrease of five millions, and we were to have a surplus income of £1,900,000. That was the statement made last session. Need I tell you, gentlemen, that that statement was pure moonshine? There has been no real decrease; and this although the advantage enjoyed by the Government was enormous, because owing to the low prices of food and every description of material, there was an absolute saving in the prices of commodities necessary for the forces, amounting, as I understand, to £1,600,000 or £1,700,000. All that, gentlemen, is eaten up.

There is no decrease, there is no surplus, there is an admitted deficiency—admitted by the Chancellor of the Exchequer himself—of six millions of money, which will be presented to you in April next, and for which you will be called upon in some manner to provide. But an extraordinary method has been *A comparison between the present and the past Government.* adopted by our opponents of dealing with this matter. They call upon you to avoid altogether the consideration of expenditure, and to look to the rates of taxation, and they then take the rates of taxation per head over the United Kingdom, and they say that the taxation has not increased in proportion to the expenditure. Gentlemen, that is perfectly true. But then that is one of the things that we complain of. What we say is, that if you choose to increase your expenditure, you ought to increase your taxation; and they reply upon us, ' Ah, but you are so fond of taxation!' No, gentlemen. We are not fond of taxation, and we have shown what we thought of taxation by our proceedings when we have been in Government. But we are fond of this,—we are fond of financial honesty. We are fond of squaring the account; and no nation, in our judgment, is financially honest which does not use its best exertions to square the account. What can be more idle than to attempt to satisfy the people of this country by showing that the taxes have not been increased in proportion to the expenditure? Why, what would you think of a spendthrift in private life who incurred charges every year to the extent of £10,000, but paid his bills only to the extent of £5000, and said, ' You see

I am not very extravagant after all. I have only paid £5000'?
Now, that is the principle of computation upon which our
friends have been acting at their Tory meetings and gatherings
through the country; and I do not much blame them, for, gentlemen, I do assure you, upon my honour, I believe they have no
Their expen- choice,—they have nothing better to say and to do. But as I
diture per have spoken of this question of expenditure per head, I will
head. give you the results in the shortest and simplest form. The
gross expenditure of the country per head is this :—In our first
year it was £2, 8s. 6d. per head,—or rather in the year before
we came into office, in 1868, the expenditure we took over
was £2, 8s. 6d. per head. In the year 1872–73 we had reduced
it to £2, 4s. 5d. per head. No doubt that was raised in
1873–74, but I have shown that 1873–74 was loaded with a
very large amount of charge, the principal part of which—
namely, the Alabama payment—had nothing whatever to do
with that year. I take, then, the next year,—the first Tory
year, 1874–75,—which shows the expenditure at £2, 5s. 10d.
per head. The last of the Tory years,—but I do not say that
this will be the final close of the process,—the last of the Tory
years, 1878–79, shows the expenditure raised from £2, 5s. 10d.
to £2, 10s. 6d. per head,—that is to say, we, counting down to
the Alabama year, and before that year, show a decrease of 4s.
1d. per head in the expenditure of the country; the Tories show
a corresponding increase, or one rather greater, an increase of
4s. 8d. per head. So much, gentlemen, for the amount of the
expenditure per head.

Here is another most important and most essential item of
the financial investigation—it is the item which exhibits the
A view of sur- finance of the country under the view of surpluses and deficits.
pluses and You well know in private transactions the meaning of those
deficits. words—I need not stop to explain it. Well, in the five years
from 1869-70 down to 1873-74 we were able to present to the
country five surpluses, and these five surpluses in all amounted
in round numbers to £17,000,000 of money. The Tory Govern-

ment came into office; and I will divide the period, as I wish to *The period of* throw all the historical illumination on this subject that I can. *Tory Govern-* I will divide the period of their rule into two. I do it on this *into two.* ground, gentlemen. It is a very slow process to build up a good system of finance ; but it is difficult even to destroy a good system in a day. You must allow a certain time ; consequently *(1) The de-* you will find that the first portion of the period of this Govern- *struction of the former system* ment, although it is not satisfactory, yet it compares advan- *of finance.* tageously with the second. The surplus, which under the former Government had averaged about three and a half millions per annum, sank in the first year of the present Administration to £593,000. The next year it was £509,000, and the third year it was £439,000; so that the effect of the three first years before the spirited foreign policy, was to work down the surplus by £3,000,000 annually. Then began the great development of that new method of Government policy and finance, under *(2) The de-* which we are told our country is at length to assume its true *velopment of the new method* position in the world, a position founded upon a new creed, *of finance.* with a variety of articles, the first of which is uniform financial deficiency. In 1877–78 the deficiency is £2,640,000; in 1878–79 the deficiency is £2,291,000 ; in 1879-80, for which there was a pretended surplus of £1,900,000, we don't yet know the full extent of the blessings that are to be disclosed to us when the happy time of the financial harvest shall arrive, but we do know that it is not to be less, I mean the aggregate deficiency of these years, to be handed over, and to be provided for in some manner or other, either by the present dying Parliament or by some other Parliament—it will not be less than six millions of money. That, gentlemen, is to be compared with the £17,000,000 of the Liberal surpluses.

And strange to say, for the first time in my life, I have found that our friends of the other way of thinking have actually *The fact of a* made these surpluses an item of charge against the Liberal *surplus is made a charge* party. They say, 'You have taken seventeen millions of money *against the Liberals.* from the people more than was necessary for the carrying on of the government of the country; and we, on the other hand,

by parity of reasoning, have been so tender to the feelings of
the country, that we have actually taken from them £6,000,000
less than was absolutely necessary to carry on the government
of the country.' That, gentlemen, is their view of the matter.
They dispose of it by carrying the question out of the arid region
of the intellect, and they settle it by an appeal to the human
affections. They call upon you to denounce the hard-hearted-
ness of Liberal finance, which thus extracted from the people
those millions—those £17,000,000—in order to apply them to
the worthless and frivolous purpose of paying our debts; and
they call upon you to admire the humane, comprehensive, and
large-hearted proceedings, under which they have taken care
that whatever you spend you never should raise enough to pay
for it.

Gentlemen, that may be all very well, as far as it goes; but
then I think that this humane method and policy ought to
exhibit itself also in some other form—that is to say, ought to
be able to point out that upon the whole it has made large
remissions of taxation, and larger remissions than have been
made by the flinty-hearted people of the nature of my friend
Mr. Lowe, who was formerly Chancellor of the Exchequer. Let
A comparison us see, then, how this matter stands. It stands thus. The
of taxes re- late Government, at the time of the Franco-German War, was
mitted. called upon to meet a sudden and large expenditure. We
instantly imposed the corresponding taxation. We then
imposed £3,000,000 of taxation for the year 1871, but in
the other years of our Government we were happy enough to
repeal these £3,000,000, and a great many other millions. We
remitted £15,400,000, so that the balance of taxation remitted
was £12,400,000. We might claim credit for the remissions
of 1874, much with the revenue such as we left it. But I will
strike these out of the account. Now I take the Tory Government—and I will be equally concise. The Tory Government
has made certain remissions since 1874—I need not trouble you
with the details—I may fairly call them odds and ends; the total
sum of them would stand very well under 'sundries' in a private

account, but the whole amount of them is £487,000. But they
have imposed £6,250,000—that is to say, they have imposed a
balance of five and three-quarter millions, or in round numbers six millions of money. So that while adopting the false
and ruinous principle of shrinking from their duty in failing to
ask Parliament to lay on the taxes necessary to meet the
expenditure which they have invited it to sanction, and which
it has sanctioned—while doing that, while thus failing of their
duty to raise a sufficiency of taxation, yet they have imposed
upon you nearly £6,000,000 of taxes in order to produce their
£6,000,000 of deficiency.

I have gone very succinctly, gentlemen, over those essential
heads, with the aid of your patience, but I am sorry to say that
there is another chapter of finance which I must more suc- *Indian*
cinctly still lay before you—namely, Indian finance. Do not *finance.*
remain any longer under the delusion — if you ever have
been under the delusion—of believing that you have nothing
to do with Indian finance. Sir Robert Peel, in 1842,
with great sagacity, repudiated the idea that the British
taxpayer and the British citizen had no interest in the state of
the Indian account. He repudiated it when the debt of India
was a trifle compared with what it now is, when the deficiencies
of India were smaller than they now are, when the policy of
India had been placed by him under a wise control, and when
the prospects of India were bright and sunny as compared with
the prospects of to-day. Even then he gave that monition—
much more must you now lay the matter to heart. Now, what
is the state of India as to its public debt ? In 1874 it stood at
£107,500,000 ; in 1878 it had risen to £134,500,000. What is
the state of India with respect to surplus and deficiency of
income ? Well, I am glad to say that, down to the disappearance of the late Government, the surpluses of our administration
in India, after deducting a year of deficit, which was due to the
famine, amounted to £4,682,000. But we left behind us in India
an admirable Governor-General, and the present Administration
allowed him to continue in office for two years. For these two

years, though he had great difficulties to encounter, he had two more surpluses, and he left office with another sum of £1,988,000, or in round numbers £2,000,000, to the good, so that there was a sum of nearly £7,000,000 to the good shown upon that account. It was after the disappearance of Lord Northbrook that the new policy, of which you have had a nearer knowledge in Europe, began to develop itself in India; and with the commencement of that new policy, so fatally accurate is the machinery that is set at work, there began the reign of deficiency. In 1876–77 there was a deficiency of £2,183,000. Out of the four years there are three deficiencies, and as Lord Northbrook and the Liberal Government retired, leaving behind a balance of surplus of nearly seven millions of money, so the present Government have accumulated an aggregate deficit in the last four years of £5,831,000, or in round numbers £6,000,000 of money, in beautiful correspondence with the £6,000,000 which are promised for a deficit at home.

There, gentlemen, the same thing occurred; the same spirit of expenditure seemed to come in with the operations of the Tory Government. We left the military expenditure of India at fifteen millions and a quarter, and in four years the present Government increased that military expenditure by £1,400,000, long before they had commenced the recent course of transactions; I mean to say, apart altogether and separate from the ruinous charges of the Afghan War.

Indian military expenditure.

General expenditure of India.

If I look, gentlemen, at another subject for a moment, namely, at the general expenditure of India, I must say its increase is most alarming. I am not going to lay the whole responsibility of that increase on the Government. I cannot accurately divide the responsibility. I know not how much is due to avoidable and how much to unavoidable causes; but this I know, that the expenditure of India during our time was £50,400,000 on the average; it was £49,600,000 in our last year of office, and I know that it has now risen to £58,970,000, or not far from sixty millions of money. I do not say, gentlemen,—for pray observe I have not attempted to analyze the amount,—what share of it may be, in my opinion, due to the folly of the Government. But what are we to say to this great fact, that with those tremendous figures staring them in the face, they have not taken even those figures as a warning against the setting on foot of their most mischievous, and, in my opinion, most guilty plans for the invasion of Afghanistan? They are now heaping up deficiency upon deficiency, difficulty upon difficulty, and they have brought it to such a point that I warn you in this hall, that, if but a few years more of similar proceedings are permitted, you, the people of England, Scotland, and Ireland, will be called upon to come down and to take upon your shoulders the 134 millions of East Indian debt, and the whole responsibility for the ruinous finance of that country.

Now, gentlemen, I hope that what I have said thus far has been intelligible, and I will endeavour to be intelligible to the end. It is fair to hear what is to be said upon the other side. With that view I turn myself, gentlemen, to the highest authority, and again I name the highest authority — the Chancellor of the Exchequer. The Chancellor of the Exchequer executed a most extraordinary manœuvre on the 10th November; for the first time he made a budget speech, as I have told you, at Guildhall. In that budget speech, after having stated his deficiency at £6,000,000, he made a plea, he made two pleas, but this was the first plea,—during our period of office, he said, there has been great depression of the seasons affecting our agricultural interests. Now, I want to remove misapprehensions upon that subject. We have had this year, in the dispensation of Providence, a harvest deplorably deficient; but permit me to say that the harvest of 1879 is not the cause of the falling revenue, or of the deficit of 1878, and 1877, and the bad finance of earlier years. Now, let us look at the harvests before 1879. I have shown you the astounding contrast between the state of things as it was and the state of things as it is, and allow me before I go further to say this: I make no boast of the state of things financially as it was under the Liberal Government.

A budget speech at the Guildhall.

We did, at the outside, no more than our duty. I do not think
that our economy was an economy for which we are entitled to
claim special credit. A Government cannot carry economy
beyond the point up to which it is firmly and resolutely supported
by the people. I make no claim; this is not self-laudation;
I merely quote it as an instance of tolerable performance of duty,
and I place in contrast with it that which I call intolerable
departure from duty. But it is all to be put upon the back of

The prices of wheat from 1869-73 and from 1874-78 compared. the seasons, is it? Well, I will take the seasons, and see how
they stand. I take the price of wheat as the cardinal article
from which you may form, upon the whole, a judgment; and I
find that for the five years when we were in office the price of
wheat on the average was 53s. 5d. a quarter; for the five complete years before the present year, during which the present
Government has been in office, the price of wheat was 52s. a
quarter—it was nearly the same, but cheaper by 1s. 5d. The
food of the people was cheaper, and therefore, as far as the
price of wheat is concerned, that did not contribute to the
distress of the country, or to the deficiency of the revenue.
But, of course, it is open to say, and quite fair to say, ' Well,
well, but the price of wheat when you were in Government was
kept down by enormous foreign importations. You had good
harvests, and we had bad.' But was that so? I say that, if
there was a difference affecting the cultivation of the soil,
it was no great or extraordinary difference. Now, compare
the harvests of 1869 to 1873 with the harvests from 1874 to
1878, and again I resort to the very fairest criterion—namely,
the yield of the acre of wheat in the number of bushels it produced. I won't trouble you with the numbers for each year in
particular, I will only give you the results. The result of the
yield of the wheat harvests in our five years was, that the acre
of land produced upon the average 26 bushels of wheat and
4-5ths of the 27th bushel. I now take the five years of the
present Government, and I find that the acre of land for those
five years produced 26 bushels of wheat and 3-5ths of the 27th

bushel, so that the difference between 3-5ths of a bushel and 4-5ths of a bushel constitutes this terrible depression of the seasons. And this is what the Chancellor of the Exchequer, who ought to be by far the best informed man in the country on every detail of these questions, thinks it fit and becoming to produce before the citizens of London, whose presumed want of agricultural knowledge, I am afraid, tempted him to be less careful than usual.

Now, gentlemen, I hope you will follow me in a very short chapter of my case, as I draw near the close of it,—I am happy to say for your sakes,—in which, perhaps, it will not be so easy for those unacquainted with Parliament to appreciate fully the weight of what I have to say, though I am quite sure that my many and respected colleagues whom I see around me, who have seats even in the present House of Commons, and whose numbers in the next House of Commons it will be your duty, gentlemen, largely to reinforce,—I know very well that they will follow and comprehend the weight of what I am going to say. Mismanagement of finance is thoroughly bad; but that mismanagement may be accidental. What is even worse than mismanagement of finance is destruction or disparagement of the sound and healthy rules which the wisdom of a long series of finance Ministers, of an excellent finance department, and of many Parliaments has gradually and laboriously built up, to prevent abuse, to secure public control, to work by degrees upon the public debt of the country, and to take care that the people shall not be unduly burdened.

Now, gentlemen, I will tell you in a few words, and I do it fearlessly, because I speak as one who has had much experience, what are the rules of finance observed with almost unvarying *Rules of* uniformity until the accession of the present Government; and *finance.* not by one party alone, for this let me say, that Sir Robert Peel and Mr. Goulburn and the Conservative party of their day were, if possible, stricter, more rigid, better financiers than the Liberals of their day; that is historical. But both parties upon the whole have uniformly adhered to those rules of finance which I am going to give you in the briefest words. The first of them is, that the Chancellor of the Exchequer shall boldly uphold economy in detail; and it is the mark, gentlemen, of, I was going to say, a chicken-hearted Chancellor of the Exchequer, when he shrinks from upholding economy in detail, when, because it is a question of only £2000 or £3000, he says that is no matter. He is ridiculed, no doubt, for what is called saving candle-ends and cheese-parings. No Chancellor of the Exchequer is worth his salt who is not ready to save what are meant by candle-ends and cheese-parings in the cause of his country. No Chancellor of the Exchequer is worth his salt who makes his own popularity either his first consideration, or any consideration at all, in administering the public purse. You would not like to have a housekeeper or steward who made her or his popularity with the tradesmen the measure of the payments that were to be delivered to them. In my opinion the Chancellor of the Exchequer is the trusted and confidential steward of the public. He is under a sacred obligation with regard to all that he consents to spend. Well, there has been, I must say, one member of the present Government—and let me do him justice, it is a pleasure to do him justice—Mr. Smith, the First Lord of the Admiralty, who, when he was Secretary of the Treasury, fought like a man for the public purse; but I am bound to say hardly ever in the six years that Sir Stafford Northcote has been in office have I heard him speak a resolute word on behalf of economy. As to speaking irresolute words, gentlemen, I assure you they are all worthless. You had better spare them. They are perfectly understood. There are like the resistance of coy ladies, who are said to wish that more pressure should be used. That is the case of a Chancellor of the Exchequer who does not speak resolutely against waste. But that resistance in detail to jobbery and minute waste and extravagance is the first of wholly sound financial rules. It was violated on an early occasion by the present Government, when they executed as gross a job as,

(1) *Economy in detail.*

This has been violated by present Government.

in my opinion, has ever been made known to Parliament, on the death of Sir E. Ryan, in creating an office of £2000 a year for the present Lord Hampton, to do what had been admirably well done without that office before, and has not been, and nobody pretends that it has been, one bit better done since.

The second rule, gentlemen, is this, and this is perhaps the *(2) A financial statement to be made once only in the year.* most essential of them all: that once in the year, and only once, the Chancellor of the Exchequer shall make his financial statement, shall say such was my income, and such was my charge for the year that has expired, so that Parliament can judge me upon it; such is my estimated income and such is my estimated charge for the year that is to come, so that Parliament can form its judgment with reference to the condition of the country, whether it is reasonable, and if there be need, what measures it shall take in order to supply the means. Now there are great occasions, undoubtedly, when it is necessary for a Chancellor of the Exchequer to depart from such a rule. A war may break out which could not have been anticipated long after, months after, his budget—of course I do not speak of cases like this. But what I say is this, that as a rule, I think in nine cases out of ten, or some such proportion, for the forty years before the day of the present Government, this plan of one annual statement was observed; and the consequence of it was that Parliament was always in a condition to form a comprehensive view of the financial condition of the country. But now the whole thing is forgotten and thrown to the winds. We never have a real annual account. If you go *We never have now a real annual account.* down to the House of Commons now on the day of the statement in April by the Chancellor of the Exchequer, you will see that it is regarded with very great indifference. There is no crowd of people wishing to know, as there used to be, wishing to know what is the condition of this great Empire. They know very well that nothing will be told them as to the future which can with any kind of decency be kept back; and they know perfectly well that, as the year goes on, finance will be brought before them by driblets, so that they never will have the opportunity of truly adapting the provision that they make to the real wants of the Empire. It has now, gentlemen, come

At present we have three annual budgets.

to this. We have a budget in April; we have a second budget in July; we have a third budget in February or March, in February generally; and this year a further improvement has been effected, and a fourth budget has been interpolated on the 10th of November. Do not suppose that I am speaking lightly of this matter, though it may be well to relieve a dry subject as far as one can by a reference of that sort.

I assure you, gentlemen, upon my whole knowledge and experience, that the efficiency of the popular and Parliamentary control upon the expenditure of the ˉcountry entirely

Parliamentary control depends upon one annual budget.

depends upon the maintenance of the principle of the annual, as opposed to the triennial or tri-monthly budget. It is idle to talk of controlling the expenditure of the Government, unless you compel them to adhere to that rule.

That is bad enough, but even that is not all. The old rule of Chancellors of the Exchequer, the rule which I inherited from Sir Robert Peel, and on which I endeavoured to act, and which in my early day nobody presumed to deny, was this, that if an expenditure was uncertain, you were not entitled to come down in April and say, ' I cannot tell you precisely what

Where expenditure is to be incurred an estimate should always be made of it.

it is, but I will tell you it when I can give an exact statement.' The answer is: You are bound to estimate for it to the best of your ability, and if there is a doubt, you are bound to rule that doubt in favour of the larger side, so that your demands may be ample; and in no case, so far as human foresight can avoid it, should the public revenue be placed in a deficiency. Why, now, gentlemen, that rule has been trampled systematically under foot. A Zulu war in April. Not a figure, not a pound, not a shilling, not a penny was estimated in the budget for the Zulu war. 'I have not received the accounts from the auditors for the army and the navy, and I cannot tell you exactly what it will be.' I want to know, gentlemen, what would be your condition if you were engaged in a great European war, when the accounts often take years to make up, and when any accurate estimate cannot by possibility be formed, if the Chancellor of the Exchequer is to be permitted to keep in his pocket all those heavy charges that are none the less accruing upon you, and to leave you in virtual ignorance of what they are going to be. What is the consequence of this ? I will illustrate what I am saying. I am not using light or idle words. I have not used a word in this speech, or in any other, so far as I know, that I am not prepared to justify. What has been the consequence ? If you will look over the budgets of the last Government, you will *Our estimates were always in* see that in almost every case we spent less money than we had *excess of our wants.* asked Parliament to give us. We acted upon this old, well-established—ay, and I will venture to say, conservative principle, not in a party sense, but in a sense higher than a party sense—this conservative principle of compelling the Minister to state all the charge that he is likely to incur, in order to maintain the efficacy of popular control. But what has been the case in *What is the case with the* this Government ? Why, in the five years of this Govern- *Tories?* ment, eight millions and a quarter of money were spent—almost entirely, I think, in the last of those years—more than the Chancellor of the Exchequer had asked for in his April budget. Of course it is intended to be true, but virtually, I may say, there is no truth, inasmuch as there is no accuracy, in the account, and a system is adopted under which accuracy is impossible, and under which control is no more than a perfect phantom.

Well, here is another rule, and it is this, that when you have not money enough you must supply the deficit by taxation. But that is a rule not only not observed, but it is ridiculed. Sir Stafford Northcote told us last year—he said really to tax the country at a period like this, when there is distress, though it was not very great distress, still it would be very disagreeable to people's feelings to be called upon to undergo additional taxation; and after all, he said, an occasional deficit is no such very great matter. Now, gentlemen, what I object to is this : we are all of us—I mean, considered as taxpayers—a great deal too much given to laxity in this matter ; to spend too much, and not to insist upon a rigid rule of making a sufficient provision for what is spent. But the Constitution appoints one particular man to teach us sound doctrine, and to nail us up to that particular doctrine, and that particular man is the Chancellor of the Exchequer. And that Chancellor of the Exchequer —acting, I am bound to say, in perfect harmony with his colleagues—that Chancellor of the Exchequer is the very man who comes down to corrupt whatever there is of financial virtue in us, and to instil into our minds those seductive and poisonous ideas that it does not, after all, matter very much if there is a deficit, and that it is extremely disagreeable when commerce is not in the most flourishing state to call upon the people to pay. Was that the practice of Sir Robert Peel ?— because these gentlemen sometimes—as often as they find it convenient, which is perhaps not always—fall back upon Sir Robert Peel as a Conservative Minister. He came in upon a deficiency in 1842. He had a large deficiency. He had to deal with the people at a period of the most serious distress, grievous distress, such popular distress as has not been known within those last few years. And he came to Parliament and stood at his place in the House of Commons, pointed out the *Annual loans* figures as they stood, and said to them—I ask you, will you *form a miser-* *able expedient.* resort to the 'miserable expedient' of tolerating deficit, and of making provision by loans from year to year ? That which he denounced as 'the miserable expedient' has become the standing law, has become almost the financial gospel of the Government that is now in power.

I will not detain you, gentlemen, upon one other rule that I had noted down, because I have already had occasion to refer to it, but I may simply say it was this, to aim at annual surplus as a main instrument for the steady reduction of

the public debt. I have told you already that that rule
is now made by the Conservative Government and party the
subject of ridicule, and that if you raise money, if you aim at
having some respectable surplus for the reduction of debt, that
is denounced as a method of taking from the people more
taxation than is necessary in order to meet the public charges.

Now, gentlemen, there is yet one point more on which the
Chancellor of the Exchequer seems to place a good deal of
reliance, and after saying a few words upon it, I will release
you from the duty which you have been discharging with such
exemplary resignation—the duty of listening to me. The
Chancellor of the Exchequer said, in the speech at the
Guildhall, in winding up his argument on the finance in
which he feels himself so strong, and where he cheerily
defies all antagonists, and is ready to ' stand against the
world in arms,'—he says : ' The wealth of the country has
not diminished. A penny of the Income-tax,—and that is a *The value of*
very convenient unit and standard measure which has been by *1d. in the In-*
a sort of general consent adopted for indicating the growth of *come-tax is a*
convenient
wealth in the country,—a penny of the Income-tax is worth *measure.*
£100,000 more than it was when we came into office.' Now *A comparison*
I want to apply a very simple test to this matter, which will *of the growth*
of wealth in
exhibit to you, I think, as accurately, though very succinctly, *the country*
—will exhibit to you as accurately as anything I could say *under the pre-*
sent and
the position in which we now stand, and the happy prospects *former*
Governments
that are spread out before you. ' A penny on the Income- *tested by that*
tax,' so said the Minister, ' calculated on the same basis *measure.*
as formerly, would bring in £100,000 more than it
did at the commencement of our Administration.' I am
bound to say that I do not believe that Her Majesty's
Government have entirely stopped that growth of wealth
in this country, which the industry and enterprise of the
country has brought about. But, in order that we may
note what is the exact amount of our obligation to them
in this respect, I wish not to stop with the year when

the present Government came into office, not simply to test the value of the penny in the Income-tax in the year 1874 and in 1879, but to go back a little farther, and to inquire at what rate the value of the penny in the Income-tax increased or diminished before we had the felicity that was opened upon us by the dissolution of 1874. Now, the state of the case is this. The Income-tax was imposed in 1842 ; it was then at the rate of 7d. in the pound, and the value of the penny, after making a liberal allowance for the non-inclusion of Ireland, the value of the penny for the purposes of a fair comparison, I am confident, was less than £780,000. Well, in 1873, which we reckon the last year of our ministerial existence, at that time the value of the penny in the Income-tax had increased to £1,850,000. The thirty-one years had produced an increment in the penny of the Income-tax amounting to £1,070,000. That is to say, the annual rate of increase over the whole of those years, with their Liberal Governments and their Conservative Governments, their good harvests and their bad, their flourishing trade and their depressed trade,—the average annual increment of the penny in the Income-tax, one year taken with another, as you will perceive by dividing £1,070,000 by thirty-one, was £34,000 a year. How stands the matter now ? Since the finance of the present Government, which is their strong point, recollect, came into operation, the penny in the Income-tax has increased, as we are assured,—and I do not for a moment question it,—by £100,000 in six years. That is to say, that whereas formerly, under all Governments, it increased at the rate of £34,000 a year, since the present Government came in it has increased at the rate of £16,000 a year. It is idle for the Chancellor of the Exchequer to say he has not stopped the growth of wealth in the country. In six years he has disposed of half of it. Let them give him another six years at the dissolution, and depend upon it he will go far to dispose of the other half.

That is the state of the case, gentlemen, on the point where the Government are so strong. I will not trouble you, as a Liberal Association, upon the other points where it is admitted that they are less strong; but one thing I must still call upon you to observe—although I had promised to release you. I remember a matter, that I think of such importance that I feel myself bound to state it, in justice to you, and in justice to the Government. I have complained of the relaxation of financial rules, and the general upshot of the whole thing is that we never know where we stand; we never know whether we have heard the worst. At this time there is a belief, and a widespread belief, that the cost charged against India and made known to us on account of the Afghan war, is not the true cost; that a great deal more has been incurred, while very little has been paid; that of these large amounts have been kept back as unsettled accounts, and not made known to us in any way. Nay, further, if I am rightly informed,— and I mention it in order that it may be contradicted if it is untrue, because it is a thing upon which I cannot from its nature get positive knowledge,—I am told that the cost of that war has been kept down by drawing enormously upon the *materiel* of the Indian army,—upon the stores of ordnance, for example, and not replacing in proportion to what was withdrawn. That compels me, gentlemen, to go back to the past; and now I make a challenge to the Government upon a matter of fact which is ten years old, but which is so far applicable to the present day that, if an explanation can be given, it ought to be given. It is the case, gentlemen, of the Abyssinian war. I have told you that after all these damning figures, which I have stated to you, when I ask myself, Do I know the worst? I have no confidence whatever that I know the worst. And I am in great fear that for years there will be evolved new difficulties accruing out of transactions that have already taken place, and bringing upon you heavy charges. What happened in the case of the Abyssinian war? I am not attacking the policy of the war. That was not peculiar to a party. I am

A doubt expressed as to whether we know the real cost of the Afghan war.

The cost of the Abyssinian war was kept back in 1868.

speaking of the manner in which the charge was dealt with. Parliament was asked, in the end of 1867, to make provision for the Abyssinian war, and was told, if I remember rightly, by the Chancellor of the Exchequer of the day, that the charge would be £3,500,000, or that possibly it might reach as high as £4,000,000. In 1868,—and of this I do not seriously complain, — in 1868, the then Chancellor of the Exchequer said that he was obliged to put the figure higher, and that he thought the charge might approach £5,000,000 for the Abyssinian war. With that information, gentlemen, Parliament was left to content itself. The Abyssinian war was made, and was concluded early in 1868 ; by 'early' I mean before the summer of 1868 was much advanced. A dissolution was impending. Not a scintilla of further information was ever conveyed to the country before the dissolution. We went to the country, believing that the Government had spent upon the Abyssinian war something less than £5,000,000. The Government must have known at that time what they had spent. The dissolution passed. The new Government came in, and we found that we had to pay there and then nearly £9,000,000. Now, this matter has been made the subject of reference in the House of Commons. I have wished to make it the subject of most distinct and intelligible reference here. Let the explanation be given. Why was the country never told before the dissolution of 1868 that the Abyssinian war would cost, had cost, nearly nine millions of money? Why were we left to take the case of the Government as having spent five millions of money upon that war? Because, unless it can be explained, gentlemen, in all these financial statements that we

The inference as to present affairs. have had, and in all these financial statements that next session must bring forth, you will again have to recollect that a dissolution is impending, and when the figures are placed in your hands with which the country is to be entertained on the occasion of that dissolution, you will have to ask yourselves, ' Are these figures like the figures to which you treated us on the occasion of the Abyssinian war ? '

I have no more now to do than to say that I hope I have made good the pledge with which I began, of endeavouring to lay before you clearly and intelligibly, for friend and foe, the matter that I had to state ; and I have to discharge, as far as I can discharge by acknowledging it, my debt to you for the unexampled kindness with which you have been pleased to hear me.

A vote of thanks, on the motion of the Earl of Airlie, seconded by the Right Hon. Lyon Playfair, M.P., was accorded amid loud cheers to Mr. Gladstone.

The proceedings terminated with a vote of thanks to the chairman, proposed by Sir George Macpherson Grant, Bart., M.P.

VI.

SPEECH IN THE WAVERLEY MARKET, EDINBURGH.

This meeting immediately followed that in the Corn Exchange,
and again Lord Rosebery was called to the chair. On
rising, Mr. Gladstone met with a reception which,
alike from its enthusiasm and from the vastness of the
audience, exceeding 20,000 in number, has never been
approached, at least within the walls of any building in
Scotland. He spoke as follows :—

MY Lord Rosebery, my Lords, Ladies, and Gentlemen,—There
is nothing that I can say, or that much better and wiser men
could say, to this meeting, that is one-half as remarkable as
the meeting itself. It is no light cause that has brought
together—that has called off from their usual occupations to
stand in such compressed mass before me—this great ocean
of human life. I fear, gentlemen, you have suffered ; you
must have suffered inconvenience, notwithstanding the admirable order that prevails ; but although, gentlemen, I can tell
you nothing that, as I have said, can in the least degree
add to the intense interest of such an assemblage, yet neither
can I part from you without a brief interchange of sentiments
for a few moments on some of the questions in which our hearts
are alike engaged. I say, gentlemen, an interchange of sentiment, for you have already expressed to me what your feelings
are on behalf of the working classes at large. I am glad to see
that you do not fear to call yourselves the working men of
'Edinburgh, Leith, and the district.' In this character you have

given me your sentiments, and I wish to echo them back
with corresponding sentiments of my own. An assemblage of
this nature does not afford the place appropriate for minute
criticism. My strength would not suffice; your patience
must be exhausted. I will therefore avoid such criticisms ;
I will avoid what is in the nature of censure or blame ; I
will fall back, gentlemen, upon a positive principle upon
which I would hope there can be no difference of sentiment
among us, even if there be within the limits of this hall some
few whose opinions are not wholly those of the majority, but
still whose opinions and feelings we should endeavour, upon
so noble an occasion, scrupulously to respect.

Gentlemen, you have spoken, in one line of your Address,
of the unhappy position in which England stands, in which
Great Britain will stand—the United Kingdom will stand—
if it should be found to be in opposition to the interests of
the struggling provinces and principalities of the East. Now, *The Balkan*
gentlemen, I wish to lay before you my view upon that *Principalities.*
subject, because there are some who tell us that we are not
contending for liberty, but contending for despotism, and that
the result of our policy will be that when the power of the
Turkish Government ceases to sway the Eastern provinces of
Europe, it will be replaced by another despotic Empire—the
Empire of Russia. That, gentlemen, is not your view nor
your desire, neither is it mine, and I wish to avail myself of
this occasion for the purpose of clearly putting and clearly
answering one question of vast importance—'Who is it that
ought to possess, who is it that ought to sway, those rich and
fertile countries which are known as composing what is called
the Balkan Peninsula ? '

It seems, gentlemen, to be agreed that the time has come,
that the hour is about to strike, if it has not struck already,
when all real sway of Turkish power over those fair provinces
must cease, if it were only by reason of impotence. Who, *Who is to suc-*
then, is to have the succession to Turkey ? Gentlemen, from *ceed Turkey?*

the bottom of my heart, and with the fullest conviction of my understanding, I will give you the reply—a reply which, I am perfectly certain, will awaken a free, a generous, an unanimous echo in your bosoms. That succession is not to pass to Russia. It is not to pass to Austria. It is not to pass to England, under whatever name of Anglo-Turkish Convention or anything else. It is to pass to the people of those countries; to those who have inhabited them for many long centuries; to those who had reared them to a state of civilisation when the great calamity of Ottoman conquest spread like a wild wave over that portion of the earth, and buried that civilisation under its overwhelming force. Those people, gentlemen, are already beginning to enjoy the commencement of liberty. Four or five million Roumanians, who were formerly subject to Turkey, are now independent. Two million Servians, once political slaves, are now absolutely free. Three hundred thousand heroes such as Christendom cannot match—the men of Montenegro—who for four hundred years have held the sword in the hand, and never have submitted to the insolence of despotic power—those men at last have achieved not only their freedom, but the acknowledgment of their freedom, and take their place among the States of Europe. Bulgaria has reached a virtual independence. And, gentlemen, let me say a word on another province, that which was the scene of the terrible massacres and horrors of 1876—the province of Eastern Roumelia. It is inhabited by perhaps a population of a million. Well, gentlemen, at the Congress at Berlin we were told by Prince Bismarck and others that the Congress had restored to the Sultan a fair and rich province—namely, the province of Eastern Roumelia. Some were then afraid that the meaning of those words must be held to imply that the ancient despotism was still to prevail in Eastern Roumelia. The words that were used were ominous and dangerous words. It was said that the province was restored to the direct authority—political and military—of the Sultan. Gentlemen, I can a

The people of the Principalities.

Roumania.
Servia.

Montenegro.

Bulgaria.

Eastern Roumelia.

little console you on that subject; I hold in my hand—and if we were a less extended assembly I might be tempted to read to you—but I hold in my hand an account of the opening of the First Representative Chamber assembled in Eastern Roumelia. It has been freely elected by the people. It is, as was to be expected, a Bulgarian Chamber, but along with Bulgarians there sit in it Greeks, and, I believe, also, in one or two cases, Turks, by the title of freemen, and about to learn, as I hope, to act in that character. On the day of the meeting you will not be sorry to hear that the Governor-General entertained the representatives of this country, which four years ago was an enslaved country—he entertained them at dinner to the number of eighty-four. After dinner, toasts were drunk in our manner, and among those who proposed the toasts one was a Turk, in perfect harmony with the rest, who asked the company to drink to the health of the Sultan for having given them such an excellent Governor-General. Gentlemen, this is what I call progress. When you uproot slavery, when you put an end to suffering and shame, when you give security to life, property, and honour, which have previously only existed at the will of every representative of the Turkish power, of every one professing the Mahomedan religion, you accomplish a great and blessed work—a work in which the uttermost ends of the civilised world ought to rejoice, do rejoice, and will rejoice. The end of it all, gentlemen, is thus far, that not less than eight or ten millions of people have in one form or another been brought out of different degrees of political servitude, and have been made virtually freemen.

Gentlemen, I appeal to you to join me in the expression of the hope that under the yoke of no Power whatever will those free provinces again be brought. It is not Russia alone whose movements ought to be watched with vigilance. There are schemes abroad of which others are the authors. There is too much reason to suspect that some portion of the statesmen of

Austria will endeavour to extend her rule, and to fulfil the evil prophecies that have been uttered, and cause the great change in the Balkan Peninsula to be only the substitution of one kind of supremacy for another.   Gentlemen, let us place the sympathies of this country on the side of the free.   Rely upon it, those people who inhabit those provinces have no desire to trouble their neighbours, no desire to vex you or me. Their desire is peacefully to pass their human existence in the discharge of their duties to God and man ; in the care of their families, in the enjoyment of tranquillity and freedom, in making happiness prevail upon the earth which has so long been deformed in that portion of it by misery and by shame. But we say, gentlemen, that this is a fair picture which is now presented to our eyes, and one which should not be spoiled by the hand of man.   I demand of the authorities of this country, I demand it of our Government, and I believe that you will echo the demand, that to no Russian scheme, that to no Austrian scheme, to no English scheme, for here we bring the matter home, shall they lend a moment's countenance ; but that they shall with a kindly care cherish and foster the blessed institutions of free government that are beginning to prevail—nay, that are already at work in those now emancipated provinces.   So that if we have been late in coming to a right understanding, if we have lost many opportunities in the past, at least we shall see and lay hold on those that remain, so that when in future times those countries again shall arrive at the prosperity and civilisation which they once enjoyed, they shall have cause to remember the name of Great Britain among the names of those who have contributed to the happy and the blessed change.

I think, gentlemen, that I have had sufficient evidence in the demeanour of this meeting that this is your opinion.   I hope I am right in saying that such a meeting is not a mere compliment to an individual, or a mere contribution to the success of a party.   Your gathering here to-day in almost countless thousands I regard as a festival of freedom, of that rational freedom which is alone secure, of that freedom best known to us, which is essentially allied with order and with loyalty. And I hope, gentlemen, that you will carry with you a determination, on the one hand, to do all you can in your civil and your social capacities for maintaining that precious possession of yours, and for handing it down to your posterity ; and, on the other hand, for endeavouring by every lawful and honourable means, through the exercise of the vast moral influence of this country, and through all instruments which may from time to time be conformable to the principle of justice, for the extension of that inestimable blessing to such races and nations of the world as hitherto have remained beyond the range of its happy and ennobling influence.

Gentlemen, I thank you for the extraordinary kindness which has enabled me to convey the remains of a somewhat exhausted voice I hope even almost to the farther limits of this enormous building. That kindness is only a portion of the affectionate reception, for I can call it no less, which has been granted to me at every turn since my arrival in this country ; and through you I desire, I will not say to discharge, for a discharge there can never be, but at least warmly, truly, cordially to acknowledge the debt that I owe to the people of Scotland.

Votes of thanks to the various deputations presenting addresses, between sixty and seventy in number, and a formal vote of thanks to the chairman, terminated the proceedings of what must be regarded as one of the most remarkable political gatherings ever witnessed in this country.

VII.

MONDAY, DECEMBER 1, 1879.

SPEECHES AT DUNFERMLINE, PERTH, AND ABERFELDY RAILWAY STATIONS.

Mr. Gladstone left Dalmeny Park on the morning of Monday, December 1, and, crossing the Forth at Queensferry, proceeded by special train to Inverkeithing. There an address was presented to him by the Magistrates and Town Council of the burgh. On arriving at Dunfermline, the next stoppage, a large crowd, numbering about 9000 persons, was found awaiting the train at the railway station. Provost Walls, in the name of the Corporation, presented an address.

SPEECH AT THE RAILWAY STATION, DUNFERMLINE.

Mr. Gladstone, who, on accepting the address, was enthusiastically cheered, said :—Mr. Provost and Members of the Town Council, and Ladies and Gentlemen,—I have to thank you very heartily for the address that has been placed in my hands, and I feel that even that address affords not so striking a testimony of your feelings, as the numbers in which you have gathered together before me. Believe me, that though I am grieved to pass by this historic spot with such rapidity, yet I shall carry away with me a long and lively recollection of the remarkable demonstration you have been pleased to give me of your sympathy and kindness. I do not receive it, ladies and gentlemen, as a personal matter. I receive it as a tribute to a common cause, in which we are all alike engaged. The Provost has well said that we are endeavouring to strike a blow on behalf of Liberalism in the stronghold of Toryism. I trust that blow will be effective. At any rate, the delivery of it will be as earnest, as steady, and as strong as I, for one, can help to make it. For you, the men of Fife, I have only to say that you may be satisfied with the position, the happy position, in which you have hitherto been, of returning to Parliament a member acting in conformity with your views, and promoting the progress of sound Liberal opinions. For, ladies and gentlemen, if all had done as Fife has done, if England and Ireland had done as Scotland has done, even the Scotland of 1874, which I trust will be greatly improved upon by the Scotland of 1879 and 1880—if they had done even as the Scotland of 1874 did, we should not now have had to face a deficiency of six millions in England, confusion of finance in India, war in South Africa, war in Afghanistan, and in Europe a state of turbulent expectation, which, if it do not bear the name of war, yet, unfortunately, too much resembles it in effect and substance.

Ladies and gentlemen, I bid you farewell, cordially hoping that your industries may continue to flourish, and that under the shade of that ancient church whose melodious bells we now hear in the distance, you may prosecute those industries with satisfaction and with advantage; further, that you may prosecute another industry which at this moment I do not undervalue—the industry of maintaining those sound political principles which, depend upon it, lie at the root of our national greatness and our national prosperity.

Mr. Campbell-Bannerman, M.P., then presented sets of damask table linen, in the name of the manufactories of the town, to Mrs. Gladstone, the gifts being acknowledged by Mr. Gladstone, amid continuous cheering which lasted until the train left the platform. Crowds had assembled at various wayside stations, but only at Cowdenbeath was a stoppage made, to take up the Right Hon. W. P. Adam, M.P.

SPEECH AT THE RAILWAY STATION, PERTH.

When the special train reached Perth the station was found to be crowded, and Mr. Gladstone was received with the most vehement expressions of joy. Accompanied by the Lord Provost and Magistrates, the right honourable gentleman and his friends proceeded to the City Hall, and there received the freedom of the Fair City. Mr. Gladstone, in returning thanks, made a graceful allusion to the death of Mr. Roebuck, M.P. After the ceremony a start was made for the railway station, around which by this time an enormous crowd from the city and the surrounding districts had assembled. Immediately adjoining the station a small platform had been erected, and cheer followed cheer when, after receiving addresses from the City and County Liberal Associations, Mr. Gladstone, introduced by Mr. Parker, M.P., began to reply as follows :—

My Lord Provost, Sir James Ramsay, Ladies and Gentlemen,—Sir James Ramsay has not read, has not caused to be read, the county address out of consideration for the limited time which is at our disposal. That was most considerate on his part, and I think that we do not lose hereby all that might be supposed on this account, that we can form some idea of what is in it. Let me say, ladies and gentlemen, I have had a varied experience during my short stay in Perth. In the City Hall just now I fell in with a Lord Provost Richardson who in that City Hall was no politician. Neither was I. But I come here, and here I find a Lord Provost Richardson who is perfectly intelligible in his statements of public opinion, and I really believe he is the same man. My friend Mr. Parker spoke of the influence that this visit might have on the city and county elections. But, gentlemen, I am not here to interfere in your elections. You don't want any advice from me. Your city is a virgin city. It has never been stormed by the adversary, and I believe it never will be. And as to the county, no doubt I am a spectator, a spectator only, but I am

much mistaken if it does not, on the earliest occasion, follow
the example of the city. I was very glad to hear the address
of the city Liberals read, but the address of the city Liberals
said that while it was pleasant to welcome me, their pleasure
would be still greater if Scotland should make me one of her
representatives. Now, gentlemen, I want to get rid of that
' if.' You may depend upon it, except for the uncertainty of
my life, or of human life, there is no ' if ' at all in the matter.
The county of Midlothian, if it had not spoken sufficiently
already, has spoken in this last week in a manner perfectly
intelligible to us, and, depend upon it, perfectly well understood by those who are to oppose us.

Gentlemen, I came down here upon a very grave errand,
and upon that errand I will say a few words, because the
business is a common business, for us, for the men of Midlothian, and for you all. I came to advance a most serious *The serious*
indictment. The declarations that I have made have covered *indictment*
against the
a very wide field; they have exposed a large open front. I *Government.*
have not been able, I admit, to read with perfect care all that
has been written in the newspaper press of the country upon
this interesting occasion. But so far as I have read, or so far
as friends have informed me, there is only one statement of
fact,—and I have made a great many,—there is only one
which has been seriously challenged. I stated, gentlemen, in
Edinburgh that it was an established usage for a great length
of time that the Parliaments of this country should only *The normal*
duration of
address themselves to the regular transaction of the business *Parliaments.*
of six and not of seven sessions. I wish here to repeat that
statement, and to say that so far as the time of my own
experience goes, and I believe so far as an earlier experience
is concerned,—but I will not now speak of that, because I
have not had time to re-examine the whole of the facts,—but
so far as the last half-century is concerned, I say I will hereafter shatter to pieces the allegations of those who have impugned my statement. And the matter is of much importance;

because my point, gentlemen, is this. I have never said that the Parliament might not, for grave cause, go through the regular business of a seventh session. I can conceive circumstances which would render it right and expedient, but the rule being that seven regular sessions should not be taken, I am entitled to ask why it is that rule is to be departed from on the present occasion. That is a most instructive question for us, because there is but one answer. The Government do not like to dissolve, because they dare not dissolve. They do not like to dissolve, because they naturally and not dishonourably, not culpably, wish to prolong their Ministerial existence. They think, gentlemen, that they are conferring immense blessings on the country, and they very naturally desire that the flow of these blessings—which we may almost call a deluge—should not be arrested one day sooner than is necessary. But the practical point of the whole discussion is this; I omit the investigation of the facts for the present, I will deal with it before I go out of Scotland, if life and breath are given me. But the practical point is this. They do not dissolve because they dare not dissolve; and the fact that they do not dissolve is and must be to you an additional incitement, an additional ground of confidence, because it amounts to a moral demonstration that we are those who now represent the mature convictions of the majority of the constituencies.

Gentlemen, I came down here with a set of very ugly charges to sustain, for notwithstanding that, as I have said, Her Majesty's Government believe themselves to be the authors and parents of innumerable blessings and benefits to the country, we have the misfortune to believe exactly the reverse. In fact, gentlemen, their speeches could be made into speeches suitable for us by a very simple process. I will tell you what it is. If you would strike out the word 'not' wherever they insert it, and if you would put it in wherever they do not use it, their speeches, depend upon it, would in a great degree save us the trouble of making speeches for ourselves. I will

Special circumstances may be conceived rendering seven full sessions necessary.

read to you, gentlemen, because it is very short, the charges
that I came to Scotland to sustain. I advanced them in a
letter in which I accepted the offer of the Liberals of Midlothian, and I wish to be pinned to what I then said; it is a
very good thing for public men to be so pinned. I charged *Mr. Glad-*
them, first, with the mismanagement of finance; secondly, with *against the*
an extravagant scale of expenditure; thirdly, with having *Government.*
allowed legislation, which is always in arrear in this country,
from the necessary pressure of the concerns of so vast an
Empire, with having allowed that legislation to come into such
a state that its arrears are intolerable and almost hopeless. I
charged them with a foreign policy which has gravely compromised the faith and honour of the country. I charged them
with having, both through their ruinous finance, and through
their disturbing measures, broken up confidence in the commercial community, and thereby aggravated the public distress.
I charged them with having contributed needlessly and wrong-
fully to the aggrandisement of Russia. I charged them with
having made an unjust and dangerous war in Afghanistan, and
I further charged them in these terms: ' By their use of the
treaty-making and the war-making powers of the Crown, they
have abridged the just rights of Parliament, and have presented
prerogative to the nation under an unconstitutional aspect,
which tends to make it insecure.' Now, gentlemen, I was
very anxious to go about the concerns of this Midlothian contest, which is, in fact, in some degree a Scotch contest,—I am
very anxious to go about it like a man of business; yet I
grieve to say that, so many are the counts of the indictment,
and so heavy—so copious is the matter which it is necessary
to bring out fully before the country in connection with the
coming dissolution, that I have not yet discharged myself,
though I have been pretty liberally heard on various occasions,
I have not yet discharged myself of all that requires to be
said. And, therefore, with your permission, I will avail myself
of the quarter of an hour that is at my disposal, before the

time appointed for the departure of the train for the North, in order to explain to you one of the phrases that I have used in this letter to the electors of Midlothian.

The abuse of the war-making power. I charged the Government with having abused the war-making power and the treaty-making power. Of the war-making power I will not now speak further than to say that I allude especially to the war in Afghanistan, on which I yet hope to find some opportunity of explaining myself more at length. To you I will speak, within the narrow limits I have described, *The abuse of the treaty-making power.* of the treaty-making power; and, gentlemen, though you are a vast assembly, meeting here in circumstances of some inconvenience, and though the subject is one not free from difficulty, I have so much reliance on your intelligence, as well as upon your patience, that I am confident you will clearly understand what I want to convey to you.

Consider, gentlemen, I entreat you, what is meant by the treaty-making power. It is a power under which the Crown of the United Kingdom is entitled to pledge the faith and honour of the country to any other State whatever, and for any purpose whatever, unless I except the payment of money, but the exception is more apparent than it is real. Now that is a power so large, that it must be most dangerous unless very discreetly used. It is so large, gentlemen, that at various times it has attracted the jealousy of patriotic men; and attempts have been made in Parliament to limit the action of that power, by requiring that treaties should be submitted to Parliament before they are finally concluded. (Cheers.) I do not wonder for a moment that you are disposed to receive with some favour a suggestion of that kind. The objections to that suggestion are not objections of principle. In principle I cannot say it would be unsound. They are objections entirely, in my opinion, of practice, and they come to this, that the nature of negotiation with foreign States is frequently *The treaty-making power was formerly safe and useful.* so complicated and so delicate that it hardly can be carried on except by a single agency concentrated, like the agency of Ministers, and that agency invested with the exercise of a large discretion. Now, my opinion is that the treaty-making power of the Crown, as it has been used by former Governments, was a safe and a useful power. About a year or two ago —I forget exactly how long—Mr. Rylands, a well-known member of Parliament, made a motion in the House of Commons to the effect that some control ought to be placed on this power. I, gentlemen, opposed that motion, upon grounds which I wish to state to you. I said the Crown, and the Crown acting through its responsible Ministers, is by far the most effective agent for the conclusion of the difficult subjects that are necessarily involved in the making of treaties. But then I said—No doubt you will object that it is a vast power which is thus placed in the hands of Ministers, and that it would be most dangerous if it were exercised without reference to the known convictions and desires of the nation; but, gentlemen, I also said my reply to the objection is, that after all the long *Treaties* years of my public life, I cannot now recollect a case in which *should be* any treaty has been made except in conformity with the well- *with the con-* understood general tendencies and convictions of the people. *the people.* The subjects have usually been long before the public. It may not be known what the precise materials of the treaty are, but it is known within certain bounds what they must be, and any right-minded Government has no difficulty whatever—as I can say from practical experience—in so conducting itself in these delicate matters as to have a moral certainty that though they have had no formal communication with the Parliament or the people, yet they are truly expressing the convictions of the Parliament and the people.

I will not now trouble you with references to instances, but if, gentlemen, you were to go back to the time of the Crimean War, and the treaties at the close of that war,—if you were to take the treaty made in 1870 with respect to Belgium, or, in fact, a whole multitude of instances upon which we might proceed,—I do not hesitate to say that these treaties were instruments which in each case were agreeable to the national feeling

Upon that ground alone the treaty-making power is defensible.

at the time. Now, that was the express ground on which I defended the treaty-making power. I said in Parliament that it was impossible to defend that power upon any other grounds. I want to tell you what then happened. Sir Stafford Northcote, as the leader of the Government in the House of Commons, and as the man who, upon the highest subjects, is entitled to speak the sense of the Government—Sir Stafford Northcote rose after me, and he said—I do not quote his words, but I state their effect—he said, such was his concurrence with the opinions I had given as reasons for not entertaining the motion of Mr. Rylands, that it would save him the trouble of entering at length upon the subject. Therefore, gentlemen, I hold that the Government were bound, in making treaties, to do nothing of importance except upon the principles to which Sir Stafford Northcote then assented. They were bound to make no treaties upon questions of a novel character and of vast importance with regard to which the country had had no opportunity of making up its mind. Now I want to know what it was that happened a very short time after that debate. To the perfect astonishment alike of Tories and Liberals, it was announced, without almost the notice of a day, that Her Majesty's Government

What the Anglo-Turkish Convention involved.

had contracted what is called the Anglo-Turkish Convention. No human being had heard of the subject-matter of that Convention. Neither Tories nor Liberals had had the slightest opportunity of considering it. We were told, one fine day, that we had become responsible for the good government of the whole of Turkey in Asia. Look at your maps, gentlemen, and see what that vast country is, seething, I am afraid, with all the consequences of bad government. And here we, whose own affairs properly belonging to us are beyond our power to deal with, so that they are constantly running into arrear, by the act of the Government, taken and done in the dark, were involved suddenly and without notice in the provisions of this Convention.

(1) The protectorate of Asia Minor.

Now, what are these? I have given you one. We were to be responsible for the good government of the whole of Turkey

in Asia. You are sometimes told it is Asia Minor. It is not
Asia Minor peculiarly; it is all Syria, all Palestine, Assyria,
Turkish Arabia. The whole of those vast countries are placed
under our responsibility; and if, gentlemen, any functionary
of the Turkish Empire misconducts himself in any of those
countries, that is now your affair. But that is not all, gentlemen.
You have also undertaken by this treaty—made on a sudden
and in the dark, while the Powers of Europe were assembled at
Berlin, but without the knowledge of any of those Powers—you
have also undertaken to defend the frontier of Armenia against *(2) The defence*
the Russian arms. You, at a distance of three thousand miles, *of the Armenian fron-*
have undertaken to send your fleets and armies to that country *tier.*
to meet Russia on her own borders, and to repel her from the
Turkish territory. And, moreover, you have made that covenant
irrespectively of the goodness or badness of her cause; for it does
not say that you will defend Turkey against Russia on the
Armenian frontier after convincing yourselves that she is in the
right, but you are placed under an unconditional engagement.
But then, along with all this, what other great provision is there?
There is this provision, that you have become practically the
masters of the island of Cyprus. (Laughter and jeers.) Well, *(3) The ac-*
gentlemen, I find this—I cannot name the island of Cyprus in *quisition of*
Cyprus.
any assembly of my fellow-countrymen without immediately
drawing forth a flood of derisive laughter. But, gentlemen,
this is no laughing matter. You have undertaken responsibility
for that island. You have undertaken the good government
of that island. And what have you done? I have no doubt
that in many matters of administration we may have improved
the government. It would be very difficult indeed to take over
any Turkish island and not to improve the government. But
I am sorry to say, gentlemen, that we have imported some new
scandals into that island. I will tell you of two ordinances that
have been passed by British authority. First of all, I ask you,
was it a right or a proper thing, without the knowledge of the
people of this country, to take over an island of that kind? I
think it a very shabby trick to play the Turk. But, indepen-

dently of that, was it right for you people, who were a free
people, to take over that island and govern it despotically?
You are governing that island despotically by the hands of
military officers.   Is that a proper position for a free people to
be placed in without its knowledge as well as without its consent?   But you have done these things already.   Under the
Turk, any man could buy land in the island of Cyprus and go
and cultivate it.   We in our wisdom—because it is the nation
after all, this is a self-governed country,—I do not mean the
people of Perth,—not at all, the people of Perth would not
have done it,—but I mean the people of the country—have
passed an ordinance, under which no man is allowed to buy
land in Cyprus unless he is either an English or a Turkish
Cyprus under   subject.   Before Cyprus became ours, any Greek of the king-
British rule.   dom of Greece might have bought land in Cyprus; and
remember Cyprus is inhabited by Greeks.   Nothing could
have been more natural and proper than the purchase of land
by a Greek.   That we have forbidden.   But I will tell you
what else we have done that is a great deal worse, and you will
hardly believe it.   Under the Government of this free nation,
an ordinance has been passed, the effect of which is that the
authorities of the island, who are chiefly military authorities
appointed by us, have power to banish from the island any
man they please without putting him on trial for any offence.
(Cries of shame.)   Yes; you are justified in crying shame.   It
is a shame—it is a disgrace to this country; it is a scandal
before the world.   Gentlemen, I have given you three leading
points.   I will not speak now upon the worthlessness of Cyprus
for the purpose for which we were told it was to be so valuable,
because time would forbid it.

But now observe, I come to my practical conclusion—that
the treaty-making power has been abused.   It has been used for
purposes in themselves objectionable, and it has been so used
in contempt, as I should say, of the moral title of Parliament
and of the nation to be aware of the principles on which a
Government is acting, and of the ends it has in view.   That

treaty-making power, in my opinion, is good while it is rightly and wisely used; it is evil and indefensible when used as it has been used by the present Administration. On that account, gentlemen, I say that this in its effect, whatever its intention may be, is, on the part of the Government, a disloyal conduct; because the effect of it is to prejudice the prerogatives of the Crown, and to impair their foundation by making them odious in the sight of the nation at large. That is all, gentlemen, that I will now say, because it is true that our time is about exhausted. But I wish you to see even from this brief exposition that I did not speak lightly when I said that prerogative had been presented to the country in a light which tended to make it insecure, and thereby to import organic disturbance among us,—among a people who love their institutions, among a people who desire only to turn them to the best account, and not to be brought into the condition of countries that, less fortunate than ourselves, are obliged to be considering from day to day in what manner they shall remake the Government of the land. I beg your pardon, I want to remake the Government of the land,—but by 'remake the Government,' I meant the institutions of the land.

The effect of the abuse of the treaty-making power is to prejudice the prerogatives of the Crown by rendering them odious.

These are, gentlemen, a small part of the whole case that is before you. It is a most grave case. Some portions of it, I think, I have been able in some degree to develop and explain in the county of Midlothian. I very much doubt whether it will be again very confidently asserted by any Minister that finance is the strong point of the Government. That was so stated. That very word was used at the meeting in the Guildhall on the 10th of November; and when I read it, I recollected that there is a passage found in a book of highest authority, and commonly cited in these words, 'Oh that mine enemy would write a book!' With a very slight change, I am disposed to alter that line, and to say, 'Oh that mine enemy would speak a speech!' He could not have done better. Gentlemen, I want you to understand that the claim of the Government is that finance is their strong point. Pray understand it when they produce their deficits; pray understand it when they propose their taxes; or pray understand it when they present to you the figures which will measure the accumulation of debt upon the country. Gentlemen, let us all do our best to make clear the issue that is to be placed before the nation.

The issue is whether in this way we wish to be governed. That issue is—Is this the way, or is this not the way, in which the people of the United Kingdom desire to be governed? Gentlemen, I bid you a grateful farewell.

Mr. Donald Currie said, Within a minute or two we have to proceed by the train to Breadalbane, and I now ask you kindly to give three cheers for Mr. Gladstone, thanking him for having come to Perth.

This call was most heartily responded to, and with cheers for Mr. Currie, Mr. Parker, M.P., and the Earl of Breadalbane, the proceedings in the open air concluded.

Mr. Gladstone, amidst the greatest enthusiasm, at once entered the train and proceeded to the North.

SPEECH AT THE RAILWAY STATION, ABERFELDY.

At Dunkeld, during a stoppage of a few minutes, Mr. Barry, merchant, in the name of the assembled inhabitants, gave Mr. Gladstone a hearty welcome to the Highlands, and received a few words of thanks in reply.

On the arrival of the special train at Aberfeldy at about 4.30, Lord Breadalbane, with Lord Colin Campbell, M.P., Mr. C. S. Parker, M.P., and Mr. Donald Currie, Liberal Candidate for Perthshire, were ready to receive the distinguished guest. An address from the inhabitants of Aberfeldy and district having been presented by Mr. Rankin, banker, Mr. Gladstone, who on coming forward to acknowledge the presentation was loudly cheered, said :—

Mr. Rankin, Lord Breadalbane, Ladies and Gentlemen, Inhabitants of Aberfeldy and the district,—I accept with very great pleasure an address which has been as spontaneous in its character
as it is warm and earnest in its language. I assure you, ladies
and gentlemen, that it is to me an unexpected pleasure. I had
no idea, when I accepted the courteous and kindly hospitality of
Lord and Lady Breadalbane, that I should give you an occasion
to meet together in public for the purpose of expressing your
sentiments on what is now going on, and has been going on, in
Midlothian. But I am the more gratified in proportion as I
feel that this movement was unexpected,—in proportion as I
feel it has come entirely from yourselves. Gentlemen, I have
not now received for the first time an expression of similar
sentiments from the people of Scotland. I am bound,—I will
not say in modesty,—but I am bound in truth to state that I
regard many of the kind words that you are pleased to use with
respect to myself, and with respect to my past public life, as
proceeding from your indulgence rather than from my own
deserts, and, at any rate, as being used towards myself, not
merely with reference to the past, not merely on personal
grounds, but because you are aware that, as a member of the
Liberal party, I have undertaken an arduous contest in the
metropolitan county of Scotland ; and you not unnaturally
regard this contest as an occasion on which you may well and
suitably express sentiments that you conscientiously entertain.

Ladies and gentlemen, I cannot find words to express to *The serious*
you my feelings of the serious nature of the occasion. I do *nature of the*
not use the language of exaggeration ; I do not act under the *occasion.*
impulses of party. Those impulses would not lead me,
advanced in years, to undertake a labour of this kind, were
it not that I feel that the issues are so grave. They so deeply
involve the character as well as the happiness of the country,
that, in my opinion, it is the duty of every man to use his
utmost exertions, to contribute all that he can, towards causing
it to be rightly understood and rightly decided; and I, who have

preached this doctrine indefatigably to others, am bound not
to shrink from acting upon it myself.   Ladies and gentlemen,
I must frankly tell you as regards the issue of that contest in
Midlothian, that unless I am deceived in the grossest manner,
there can be no doubt.   There is even reason to believe that
some of the shrewdest among our opponents are perfectly well
aware that they cannot win; and let me tell you, gentlemen,
that our opponents in electioneering matters are frequently
very shrewd indeed.   We have much to learn from them in
that respect; and, ladies and gentlemen, I trust we shall
learn from them many useful and valuable lessons, not as
to the ends exactly that they have in view, but as to the
judicious and careful use they make of the means of obtaining
these ends.   The mind of this country, ladies and gentlemen,
has been led abroad and over the whole earth.   It really
seems as if under the present sway our business was not to
regulate the concerns of our own land and of our own firesides,
but the concerns of the people of Europe, Asia, Africa, and
the rest of the world.   That is not my view of the matter at
all.   My view of the matter is, that the promotion of good
government among and for a people is a great, and noble,
and arduous work, that taxes all their energies.   I wish to
get rid of a great deal of the nonsense—the mischievous
nonsense—that has been introduced into our politics.   None
of us can forget the enormous responsibilities, the extended
duties, that attach to such an Empire as this country has
erected, stretching forth into every quarter of the world,
and having relations with the whole of its inhabitants
far and near.   But while we duly estimate these relations,
while we will never shrink from those duties, let us avoid
'The thea- that system of meddling those theatrical displays and tricks,
trical policy.' which are aimed, apparently, at drawing off the minds of the
people of this country from their own interests, and from
their own necessities, and at blinding them to the fact that,
while they are inflamed and flattered by high-sounding dis-

courses about the great position of England, and the necessity
that England should become the teacher and the instructor of
every nation in the world, we are in danger of falling into a
condition in which we shall be conspicuous for the neglect of
our own affairs, and in which all the reasonable wants and
wishes we entertain for the improvement of our laws and
institutions will remain entirely unfulfilled.

Gentlemen, I will not further detain you at this time. I
assure you I rejoice to think that so lively a sympathy exists
among you for the cause in which we are engaged; and,
gentlemen, I hope when the county election in Perthshire
comes, you will show that you are aware that Scotland, as well
as England, ' expects every man to do his duty;' you will
contribute your part towards the constitution of a Parliament
sounder and wiser than that which now exists; and rely upon
it, we shall see, in the course, I hope, of a very limited time,
some progress made towards undoing the many mischiefs that
have been brought upon us in recent years, and towards giving
some satisfaction to the reasonable wants and wishes of the
people.

———————

Hearty cheers for Mr. Gladstone and for Lord and Lady
Breadalbane concluded the proceedings, after which the party
drove through the illuminated village of Aberfeldy, past bonfires
blazing on the adjoining hills, and on between rows of torch-
bearers towards Taymouth Castle, where fireworks and rejoic-
ings closed the eventful day.

VIII

TUESDAY, DECEMBER 2, 1879.

TAYMOUTH SPEECH.

ON Tuesday morning, December 2, Mr. Gladstone received, in the Banner Hall, Taymouth Castle, a deputation from the Killin Breadalbane Liberal Association, by whom an address was presented. The deputation was introduced by the Earl of Breadalbane, President of the Association.

Mr. Gladstone, in acknowledging the presentation, said :— Gentlemen, I accept the address in the name of the Killin and Breadalbane Liberal Association, but I think that you give yourselves a modest name in this respect, that so far as I am able to judge, at least in this portion of the country, the Liberal Association really means the people of the district. I am glad to think it should be so—not that it is not well that we should be braced in our political training by some differences of opinion; not that it is not well, as no party is perfect, that each party should, as it were, supply what is wanting in the other party, but that undoubtedly at this moment in particular it is a matter of very great interest, and very great satisfaction, to come among those communities where the principles which we conceive to be sound bear commanding sway. I rejoice to think, gentlemen, that among you, and I hope in Perthshire, there can be little doubt of the result which will be achieved by your united efforts. No doubt the efforts will be serious. We cannot question that they will require to be serious efforts.

We cannot afford, gentlemen, as a party at this crisis of

the national history, to indulge ourselves in those innocent *The necessity* and sometimes benevolent diversities of opinion which have *for united* *action.* on many occasions led to diversity of action on the part of the Liberal party, with very injurious consequences to the welfare of the country. I have a good while ago remarked in print, and I really think that at this time it is not inopportune to repeat the remark, that at the last election, in 1874,— that which we considered to have been a somewhat disastrous election,—there was a majority returned—setting aside the party calling themselves the Home Rule party, or reckoning them, for argument's sake, for the moment as a portion of the Liberal party, which up to that time they had been—there was a majority returned over those who were called Liberals in favour of the Government of somewhere about fifty,—I think a little over fifty,—and out of that number of a little over fifty, nearly one-half was simply due to the fact that the Liberals had chosen to run candidates against one another. That is to say, that suppose in a particular constituency the Liberals were three to two, they would run two candidates, they would divide their three into two parties of one and a half each, and naturally the man who had the united two came to the head of the poll, although he represented but a minority of the constituency. Now it is in the nature of the Liberal party to be subject to those diversities, and we ought not to wish to get back to the absolute uniformity of the Tory party. It would impair that freedom of thought, that healthy, active atmosphere, what Shakespeare calls the 'nimble air,' that prevails in the Liberal sphere, if we should endeavour to get rid of them; but there ought to be a limit beyond which they ought not to be pushed. I am not, gentlemen, blaming you as if locally you required that lesson; I have never heard of any such disposition in the county of Perth; at least I am quite sure if it exists, it will not be allowed to go beyond its proper bounds. But undoubtedly there is great danger, in a party constituted as our party is, lest in a variety of sectional objects, however important, we should divide ourselves, and by doing so we should, without really advancing our sectional objects, inflict the greatest detriment on those objects which we have in common, and which appertain to the general welfare of the whole party.

Gentlemen, there are a few words at the close of this address which you will forgive me for a moment referring to. You hope that Midlothian will do its duty, and upon that subject I don't think you need entertain any doubt or misgiving. I feel convinced that Scotland will do its duty, and will set a brilliant example. I believe, also, that the country at large will do its duty. It is most desirable that it should. I really think that almost all we have to wish of the people on this great occasion is that they should seriously think, and should seriously realize to themselves, that what they ought to set before their eyes and their minds is the public and national good. We know that a great many individuals—and I am bound to say, without wishing to do them injustice, especially the Tory party—will give votes from personal attachments, local attachments, and a great variety of accidental circumstances; but if ever, gentlemen, there was an occasion on which all those personal and local attachments ought to recede into the shade, on which the mind ought to address itself to the general interests of the Empire, this is the occasion. We cannot help seeing—I defy any one to lay his finger upon a point in our history, choose it where he will, in the course of the last half-century, at any period, in fact, since the peace of 1815—I defy him to find any situation in the least degree parallel to the present situation. This little island, inhabited undoubtedly by a race of enormous energy, but charged also with responsibilities which have always been sufficient to absorb that energy, finds itself gradually entangled from year to year in a multitude of new responsibilities, and is encouraged and flattered by the adulations of a portion of the press, and by the interested language of party, to

The country will do its duty.

This is an occasion on which all personal and local feelings should recede into the shade.

believe that all this is safe, and prudent, and wise. Can it, gentlemen, be so? Is it in the nature of things—is it in the design of Providence, that besides the concerns of the vast Empire over which this little island rules, we should be meddling in the business of almost every portion of the globe? Now let us take a lesson from across the water. *The example set us by the United States.* Our friends, our natural relations in America, are gifted with energies quite as great as ourselves. But they find enough to do in developing the interests of the enormous territory committed to them. They do not allow themselves to be bewildered by the dangerous nonsense that is constantly talked to us about the necessity of our interfering here and interfering there, with cause or without cause, setting up fictitious interests, claiming to do this, that, and the other thing, and vaunting that we are so strong that we will get through it all, for ' we've got the ships, we've got the men, we've got the money too.' This is the sort of trash, that is the sort of poison upon which, unfortunately, a large portion of the people—a small portion in Scotland, a more considerable portion in England, and a larger portion still, I am sorry to say, in London, where they ought to be better instructed—have allowed themselves to be led astray. I hope this period of delusion is coming to an end. You call it Tory misrule; that is a very homely phase, but we know very well what it means, and most people are beginning not only to know it in the abstract, but to have what I may call an experimental sense of it. It is coming home to them through the intelligence and through the brain, it is coming home to them through the heart, and it is likely very shortly indeed to come home to them through another department not so dignified as either of these two, still a department which is material to the comfort and happiness of your lives; I mean the pocket.

Gentlemen, I am very grateful to you for having taken the pains to make this long journey on this cold morning. The coldness of the morning suggests to me to say that I see in your proceedings all the briskness of a bracing atmosphere, such as belongs to winter; but, on the other hand, in the fervour of your feelings and the display of them given here, I see a temperature not only mild but warm, such as summer itself cannot exceed. It seems to run through all Scotland. I can draw no distinction. Let it be a great metropolitan city or let it be a rural village—let it be a mining district or let it be a district perfectly and absolutely agricultural—I find no division; I find the sense of Scotland proclaiming itself by signs that cannot be mistaken; by signs that, as I said at the outset in speaking to you, the Liberal Association, as representing a community—by signs that are truly national signs. This, gentlemen, is what the country needs, what it needs in a degree such as has never in ordinary times, in what we call times of peace, been equalled. The time is near when the matter must come to issue. Rely upon it, what we have most to desire is to make our countrymen think. If we can get them to think, can bring them to weigh in the scales of prudence all the principles, all the interests at stake, and so consider the courses which are before them, then I am certain that we need not entertain the smallest apprehension, and that we shall have a brilliant victory for our cause.

During the remainder of his stay at Taymouth Mr. Gladstone did not deliver any political speeches.

Mr. Gladstone left Taymouth Castle on Thursday, December 4, and proceeded direct to Glasgow. At the station there an immense crowd patiently awaited the arrival of the train, and received the right honourable gentleman on his appearance with a perfect ovation, again and again renewed.

FRIDAY, DECEMBER 5, 1879.

SPEECH IN ST. ANDREW'S HALL, GLASGOW.

ON Friday morning Mr. Gladstone delivered to the students at the University his address as Lord Rector, and subsequently took luncheon at the University with the Senatus Academicus. Mr. Gladstone then returned to the residence of Sir James Watson, where he remained till the hour fixed for the public meeting in St. Andrew's Hall.

This great meeting was composed of nearly 6000 persons, the great majority standing in the area of the hall, from which, in order to accommodate a larger number, all the seats had been removed. At half-past five Mr. Gladstone left the house of Sir James Watson, his host, and, amid loud cheers from crowds collected along the route, drove to the Hall.

There a reception certainly in no degree less enthusiastic than any the right honourable gentleman had received in Scotland awaited him.

Among those who occupied places on the platform were :— The Earls of Breadalbane, Airlie, and Rosebery ; Lord Napier and Ettrick ; Right Hon. W. P. Adam, M.P. ; Sir T. E. Colebrooke, Bart., M.P. ; Dr. Charles Cameron, M.P. ; Mr. George Anderson, M.P. ; Mr. Charles Tennant, M.P. ; Mr. W. H. Gladstone, M.P. ; Colonel Mure, M.P. ; Mr. R. W. Duff, M.P. ; Mr. William Holms, M.P. ; Mr. James Stewart, M.P. ; J. W. Burns of Kilmahew, Donald Currie, H. E. Crum-Ewing, J. B. Balfour, advocate ; John M'Laren, advocate, etc. etc.

Lord Breadalbane introduced Mr. Gladstone, whom the audience greeted with loud and prolonged cheering. He said:—

My Lord Breadalbane, my Lords, Ladies, and Gentlemen,— I meet you, I hope, this evening under good auspices. I mean, in the first place, the auspices of the noble Lord who has taken the chair, and who, representing an illustrious family in Scotland, promises to walk in the steps of those distinguished noblemen who have given to aristocracy its true and most permanent strength throughout the land, by associating it at every point with the liberties and privileges of the people. Under good auspices, because the feeling of the people of Scotland, which has been exhibited during the last fortnight in a manner not to be mistaken, has, I think, nowhere arrived at a more forcible expression than in the city of Glasgow, and in the great Hall where we are now assembled.

I wish, gentlemen, that I felt myself worthy and capable of doing justice to an occasion, which I describe as a good and a great occasion. But I find that the work in hand, instead of dwindling as I proceed, always seems to grow, from day to day. The subject is so large, the points to be argued so unusual, I may say, though it is not a very significant portion of the case, that I should have liked, with regard to one or two even insignificant points, even small points, such, for example, *The creation of* as that which related to the creation of a new Civil Service *a new Civil* Commissionership and to Lord Hampton, had time permitted, *Service Com-* *missionership.* to show to you that I spoke within the bounds of truth in the matter which I stated, and that the character which I attached to that transaction was warranted by its nature. But I cannot detain you on that subject. There is, however, another matter, on which comment has been made, that I cannot pass without notice. It is, gentlemen, the question *The ordinary* of dissolutions of Parliament, and of the ordinary life of *duration of a* *Parliament.* a Parliament. The reason why I cannot pass this by is because it bears in an important manner on our present position. My argument is that there must be some reason why, in the face of an established usage, the Government do not advise the Sovereign to dissolve the Parliament;

and I can find no reason except one, and that is, that they fear the verdict of the people. I am met, gentlemen, by the assertion that there is no such usage. It might, perhaps, be sufficient for me to fall back upon the declaration—the published declaration—of the two highest authorities on constitutional matters—one of them Mr. Hallam ; the other, happily still spared to us, Sir Thomas Erskine May. Both of these have declared that six years, and not seven, are the established modern rule for the duration of Parliaments. But, gentlemen, there has been a cavil, and I must say a quibble, in this matter. The word session has been taken advantage of. The word session has a technical meaning. Everything that follows a prorogation, and that ends with a prorogation, is a session, although it should only last seven days. I had not time—I had other matter to deal with—I could not enter into the technical account of a session. But what I tell you is this, gentlemen, that there is not a case upon record since the Reform Act—that is to say, that there is no case within fifty years, and I am of opinion that there is no real case for fifty years before that—in which one and the same Parliament has approached the work of seven integral or real sessions. Now, that is the question, and that is the point of usage. Remember, we in the present Parliament have now done the work of six integral sessions. We are told by agents of the Government that we are to sit for another twelve months. The meaning is, we are to go through a seventh integral session. Two cases are quoted against me— one is that of 1841, the other that of 1859. In neither of *The duration* them did the Parliament perform the work of seven integral *of Parliaments in* 1841 *and* sessions. What they did was this : In 1841, and again in 1859. 1859, the old Parliament was dissolved in the middle of a session,—near the close of it,—but before the necessary work of the annual session had been accomplished. I won't dwell upon 1859, because the two cases are virtually identical, and we have no time to spare.

In the session of 1841 the Government of the day had been declared by a vote of the House of Commons to have lost its confidence. The consequence was that it was impossible for that Government to ask for the supplies for twelve months. Accordingly, they took the supplies for three months, and they dissolved the Parliament, I think, in the month of June. Why, after that, you will see yourselves it was matter of absolute necessity that the Parliament should meet after the dissolution, should determine who should be the Ministers, and, having come to that determination, should vote the annual supplies for the Government that had its confidence. That is exactly what was done ; and that having been done, the Parliament separated. Technically that was a session, but really and in substance it was no session at all. It was simply winding up what remained undone of the essential, necessary, formal business of the year. Why, gentlemen, if I found my way into a shop in Glasgow, and took part along with the young men when they were putting away the goods in the evening for the night, you would not call that serving for the day in the shop ; and yet that is just as much serving for the day in the shop as those pretended sessions—that is to say, those technical and formal sessions—are real sessions in the sense that we have now before us.

I return, then, to my point. I do not detain you on the case of 1859, which is substantially just the same ; but I return to my point, and I say—no Parliament, at any rate for the last fifty years—I will not detain you with complicated explanations on the earlier case of the Parliament of 1820, long before the Reform Act—no Parliament under the modern system of Government, which dates from the Reform Bill, has ever done more than the regular work of six sessions. There must therefore be a reason why the Government, deviating from rule and usage, are going, as they say, to give us a seventh. There can be but one reason, and that is, that they dread condemnation by the people, and dismissal from their offices.

Now, gentlemen, I frankly own to you one of the motives that has led me, in coming to Glasgow, to undertake addressing you on political subjects, after it might well be supposed that the patience of all Scotland was thoroughly exhausted in listening to me, has been that in this constituency, placed as it is by Act of Parliament in a peculiar position, I might venture humbly to point out to you the enormous importance of your holding together. The three-cornered representation *The three-* is eminently adverse to the expression—the clear and effective *cornered repre-* expression—of the interests of a majority. Where there is, as *Glasgow.* there is in Glasgow, a very large majority, it may well happen that that large majority shall fail to command the three seats; and if they do not the effect is this, that though you may be three to one compared with your Conservative opponents, yet in your representation by your three members one neutralizes the other, and Glasgow, this vast community, has virtually but one representative. Gentlemen, I will not go over the commonplaces, though they are very important commonplaces, respecting the tendency of the Liberal party to defeat its own objects by allowing the attachment of an undue importance to aims which are partial and which are sectional; but this I will say, that if we cannot be brought to act heartily together, and *The necessity* to make great sacrifices of our own personal and sectional *for united* views, in a crisis like this, if the picture that the Empire and that the world now present to us does not at this moment drive home upon the breast the consciousness of that great necessity of union, I for my part should despair; I should say the evil was incurable. And in that case what is the result? The result is this, that the Liberal party, although, as I think, a decided and a considerable majority of the whole people of the country, would be handed over for another six years, or perhaps, gentlemen, for another seven years, to that under which I believe we have been for the last six years, namely, the domination of what is really a minority of the constituencies of the country.

Well now, gentlemen, I must endeavour to-night, with your

permission, to present to you one or two more touches of that picture. You have been told that there is no picture at all which need excite the uneasiness of anybody. It is all owing to Liberal prejudice ; and when the great voice was raised three years ago from earth to heaven against the horrors that were enacted in the Turkish Empire, you were asked, and you are now asked, to believe that that was no better than a party manœuvre. We have said that we never compound the sense of party with the duties of humanity ; but foolish indeed it would have been if, because we were a party, we were to have renounced our obedience to those duties. But who are they that appear to make a combination of the kind ? Gentlemen, *An illustration* we have lately had the most extraordinary illustration that *of the connec-* ever met my eyes—and, in truth, unless it had met my eyes I *tion between the* *objects of party* should have said it had been quite impossible—with respect to *and the duties* *of humanity.* the connection between the objects of party and the duties of humanity. Such illustrations are not to be drawn from within the Liberal precincts. This comes, gentlemen, from the opposite camp. I will not quote, I would not venture to quote a statement such as I am going to read from the *Daily News,* or the *Echo,* or the *Scotsman,* but I am going to quote it where I am safe in my source. I am going to quote it from the *Standard* and the *Times.* Gentlemen, you know well that we have heard much of the efforts that have lately been made to induce the Turkish Government to amend the condition of the Christians in Asia Minor ; and you are aware that the menace of sending Admiral Hornby to the East with a British fleet has been averted ; and averted how. By authorizing Baker Pasha to make a tour of inspection through that country, and to write a paper embody- ing an account of what he may have seen ! But how came, *The recent dis-* gentlemen, this extraordinary zeal ? I quote from the *Standard* *satisfaction of* *the Govern-* of November 29, and I think it was in the *Times* of Novem- *ment with the* *Turkish delay* ber 19. It appears that there was dissatisfaction on the *to carry out* *promised re-* part of the English Government with the Turkish Govern- *forms.* ment ; and two despatches, says the correspondent of the

Standard,—two despatches were written to Musurus Pasha in order to disarm the displeasure of Great Britain. The first despatch did not contain any matter which appears to require our particular attention, but the second despatch was one which, it appears, has been published in a foreign newspaper called the *Political Correspondence,* and I am going to read to you the passage as I find it in the *Standard.* This is the apology of the Turkish Government, and the promise of the Turkish Government by which it averted the displeasure, apparently, of the English Government, and made it ready to accept the declarations so transmitted :—' The Porte must certainly acknowledge that the position of the English Cabinet would be extremely difficult if the promised reforms are not immediately introduced. On the other hand, the Sultan's Ministers lay great stress on the maintenance of the Beaconsfield Cabinet.' As I go by, gentlemen, I interpolate a few words ; and I recommend every Tory candidate in Glasgow and elsewhere to print at the head of his address, in capital letters at least, perhaps it ought to be done in letters of gold, these words which I have just read, ' The Sultan's Ministers lay great stress on the *The Turks re-* maintenance of the Beaconsfield Cabinet,'—I resume the perusal *gard the inten-* —' which has given so many proofs of its benevolent intentions *tions of the* for the Turkish Empire. It also is not unknown to the Porte *for their* that a Liberal English Cabinet would make common cause with *Empire.* Russia and the other enemies of Turkey. The Cabinet presided over by Said Pasha therefore recognises that its fate, and that of Turkey itself, is connected with the maintenance of the Conservative Cabinet in England ; and, therefore, has decided on lightening the task of Her Majesty's Ministers by introducing without delay the reforms which are needed.' Therefore it appears that the motive of the reforms which Turkey has promised is to improve the position of the Beaconsfield Cabinet at the general election ; and the nature of those reforms is summed up to you in this, that Baker Pasha is to travel through Asia Minor, and to write a paper describing what he sees. In the *Times* the connection with party interests was still more largely assumed by the Turkish Government. And I must say I think that exhibition of facts proceeding from their friends in Turkey, and casting so strange a light on the origin of the recent movement professedly on behalf of the Christian population, ought to meet with some explanation from the Tory party generally, and from the Ministers of the Crown.

But now, gentlemen, it may be said, and it has been said, they have been exerting themselves to procure reform ; why do not you give them credit for so exerting themselves ? I will give you the answer. I will assume that they have been so exerting themselves ; I will assume, if you like, that their exertions have not had reference, as the Turkish Government in the *Times* was made to say they had, to the coming dissolution. What, then, have they been about ? They have *A single- handed advo- cacy of the interests of the Christians in Turkey.* been about a single-handed advocacy of the interests of the Christians in a portion of the Turkish Empire, and have threatened to support that single-handed advocacy by force. That would be the statement of the case, as they themselves would make it. Now, gentlemen, I want you to remember this. Why did you make the Crimean War ? You made the Crimean War purposely to prevent that single-handed advocacy on the part of Russia. Russia said in 1853, by the mouth of Prince Menschikoff, ' We demand from the Porte a Convention which shall enable us to enforce the redress of Christian grievances, and, if they are not redressed, to resort to force.' For that declaration you made war against Russia. For the same declaration you are now asked to give credit to the Government. And why, gentlemen, was this done in 1853, and done with the general and enthusiastic consent of the country ? Because it was felt that all this *Its dangers.* single-handed advocacy was full of danger, that it excited the jealousy of Europe, that it gave scope for selfish intrigue, that there was no security of its efficacy for its purpose, that it laid down exceptional rules on behalf of particular Powers, and thereby tended to subvert the public law of Europe. These grounds were the very grounds you thought fit to make war in 1853, and they are exactly the grounds upon which, and modes of action to which, you are now asked to accord confidence and praise.

After, with a perverse obstinacy, difficult to understand, the concert of Europe had once and again been broken up by the action of the Government, this attempt at single-handed advocacy is that for which they are now claiming praise. But, gentlemen, with regard to this single-handed advocacy, there is more in the case than I have stated.

I told the people of Midlothian, in my letter of acceptance, that one of the charges against Her Majesty's Government, which had repeatedly been made, but which had not been, and which could not be answered, was the breach of the public law of Europe. I am here to make good that charge, and to make it good by a brief, and, I hope, intelligible exposition. This interference in Asia Minor,—of which all I can say is this, that, right or wrong, I should be very glad if any good results are produced, whatever I may think of the means, — this interference in Asia Minor purports to be justified by what is called the Anglo-Turkish Convention. I will not inquire whether it is so supported, but I will assume it in favour of the Government, for the sake of the argument. My contention is that the Anglo-Turkish *The Anglo-* Convention was in itself a gross and open breach, or rather *Turkish Convention was a* a gross and manifest breach, of the public law of Europe. *gross breach of* I corrected myself at the word 'open,' for open it was not. *the public law* It was secret and clandestine. But why was it a breach of the public law of Europe? Because, by the Treaty of Paris, the result of the Crimean War, it was solemnly enacted that everything that pertained to the integrity and independence of Turkey, and to the relations between the Sultan and his subjects, was matter, not for the cognizance of one particular

Power, but for the joint cognizance of the great Powers of Europe. And what did we do in 1878? When the Russian war with Turkey came to a close, we held Russia rigidly to that principle, and we were right in so holding her. We insisted that the treaty she had made should be subject to the review of Europe, and that Europe should be entitled to give a final judgment on those matters which fell within the scope of the Treaty of Paris. We did that, and we even wasted six millions in warlike preparations for giving effect to that declaration. We then brought together at Berlin, or assisted to bring together at Berlin, the Powers of Europe for the purpose of exercising this supreme jurisdiction; and while they were there, while they were at work, and without the knowledge of any one among them except Turkey, we extorted from the Sultan of Turkey,—I am afraid by threatening him with abandoning the advocacy of his cause before the Congress,— we extorted from the Sultan of Turkey the Anglo-Turkish Convention. But the Anglo-Turkish Convention was a Convention which aimed at giving us power, in the teeth of the Treaty of Paris, to interfere between the Sultan and his sub-

It interfered with the integrity of the Sultan's dominions. It violated the Treaty of Paris.

jects; and it was a Convention which virtually severed from his Empire the possession of the island of Cyprus. It interfered with the integrity. It interfered with the independence. It broke the Treaty of Paris, and the Treaty of Paris was the public law of Europe.

The Government and Cyprus.

Now, gentlemen, I will proceed with as much rapidity as I can; but I have yet a word to say upon the subject of Cyprus. I want you briefly to contrast in your minds the promises that were made to you about Cyprus, and the position in which those promises now stand. What was Cyprus to be, gentlemen? You recollect the exultation that went abroad throughout the land at the time when the virtual acquisition was announced. What was Cyprus to be? Why, in the first place, it was to be a naval harbour, better than the harbour and arsenal of Malta. That was a declaration which,

unless I am much mistaken, proceeded on a solemn occasion
from the mouth of the Prime Minister. And not only so,
but you were to have this wonderful harbour with
great rapidity, for, on the 28th or 23d July 1878, the
Prime Minister made a promise to the House of Lords in
these words: — 'By this time next year' — that is, July
1879—' your Lordships will find that there are ports suf- *The harbour*
ficient to accommodate British ships;' that means, of course, *of Cyprus.*
British ships of war. There is no such port. There is not the
slightest prospect of such a port. They are not making such
a port. They have no money to make such a port. I have no
doubt that if you will give them some millions of your money,
—that money, the total store of which they have not much
contributed to increase,—if you will give them some millions
of your money, in time they will make a port there, or anywhere else. And most probably, gentlemen, it will turn out,
when made, to be like the port of Alderney. There we were
assured, that if we would spend a few hundred thousand pounds
—we were told by the unanimous opinion of all the military,
naval, scientific, engineering authorities—we should have an
admirable harbour that would seal up the port of Cherbourg.
Gentlemen, we spent, not a few hundred thousands, but a few
millions ; we made a ruinous place, useless, I believe, for any
purpose of commerce or of war ; and the port of Cherbourg is as
open as it ever was. So much for the harbour in Cyprus. But
it was also to be a place of arms. There was there to be a great
military force that was to overawe Russia, and was in case of
need to march across the mountains of Asia Minor, I suppose
by the aid of the instrument which used to be called seven-
league boots; and to intimidate Russia on the Armenian
frontier. Is it, gentlemen, a place of arms ? Well, it is a *A place of*
place of arms, but it is a place, I believe, only of the arms of *arms.*
about 200 men. They began, indeed, with sacrificing the health
of some thousands of British troops in Cyprus ; but they knew
very well that could not be continued. That would not serve

on the hustings, nor would it serve for any other good purpose.
So, instead of being a place of arms, it is a place in which we
have not a force sufficient to defend it against the meanest
armament that ever undertook the most trivial operation.

Cyprus a safe-
guard of the *
road to India.

But besides this, gentlemen, there was another object to be
gained by the possession of Cyprus, and that was—it was to
be a safeguard of the road to India.   Now I want to say a word,
if you will allow me, upon this safe-guarding of the road to India.
I want to know what is the meaning of that claim.   In the
principles of foreign policy, gentlemen, as I have professed
them from my youth, it is a fundamental article that we are
to set up no claim for ourselves which we do not allow to
others, and that he who departs from that principle is com-
mitting treason against public law and the peace and order of
the world.   What is the meaning of safe-guarding the road to
India ?   It seems to mean this ; that a little island at one end
of the world, having possessed itself of an enormous territory
at the other end of the world, is entitled to say with respect
to every land and every sea lying between its own shores and
any part of that enormous possession, that it has a preferential
right to the possession or control of that intermediate territory, in order, as it is called, to safe-guard the road to India.
That, gentlemen, is a monstrous claim.

We have no title with regard to any land or any sea,
other than that within the allegiance of Her Majesty, except titles equal to those of all other Powers.   Do not
suppose that I am saying that the route to India is a

This doctrine
began with the
Suez Canal.

matter of no importance.   This doctrine of safe-guarding the
road to India began with the purchase of the shares in the
Suez Canal, and I must say that manœuvre was most successful.
I do not deny, I confess with sorrow, that though I with
some others resisted it from the first, it was admirably de-
vised for hoodwinking the people of the country, for catching
them on their weak side ; and it did carry with it undoubtedly
approval at the time.   But, gentlemen, it was a mere delusion.

No doubt the Suez Canal is of importance ; but if war breaks out, and if the channel of the Suez Canal becomes vital or material to your communications with India, you will not secure it one bit the better because you have been foolish enough to acquire a certain number of shares in the Canal. You must secure it by the strong hand. You must secure it by the superiority of your naval power. That superiority would secure it whether you are a proprietor in the Canal or not, and won't secure it a bit the better because you have chosen to complicate your already too complicated transactions with a new financial operation of that ridiculous description.

The Suez Canal can only be secured by naval supremacy.

But, gentlemen, suppose that I am entirely wrong; suppose the purchase of the shares in the Suez Canal was the desire of consummate human wisdom ; suppose that you are entitled to lay hands on all the countries that lie between you and India, under the pretext of what is called safe-guarding the road to India. Does the island of Cyprus safe-guard the road to India ? Nothing of the sort, gentlemen. It is 300 miles off the road to India. How in the world, if the question of maintaining the road to India depends upon possessing the Suez Canal, how in the world are you the better by choosing to encumber yourselves with the trust and the defence of a foreign island, with people of another race not sympathizing in your purposes, not connected with your nationality, and lying more than 300 miles from the point—not simply from the point, but off the route to the point—where your naval force is to be applied ? Well, gentlemen, the truth is this, that Cyprus is to us—whatever it may be in itself, it is to us a valueless encumbrance. The getting of it offended Europe. The getting of it, I don't hesitate to say, was even a wrong to Turkey. The governing of it by despotic means has been dis-honourable to the British Power ; and the fact that it is value-less does not in the least exempt us from the responsibility of the transaction. No doubt it was a possession gotten by a clandestine treaty, in violation of public law; and whether it be

Cyprus is a ' valueless en-cumbrance.'

precious, or whether it be worthless, if it was so gotten by clandestine means and in breach of public law, the getting of it is a deed as much tainted with secrecy and corruption as was that, which sent forth Gehazi from the presence of Elisha a leper white as snow.

I might, gentlemen, quote to you an important authority upon that subject, the authority of Sir Samuel Baker, a traveller of great courage and enterprise, well and honourably known to us by his researches and his discoveries in Africa; but I will not detain you. It is certainly remarkable that he should give his authority, as he has done in a recent and interesting work, against, entirely against, the possession of Cyprus on the footing on which we now hold it; because he is a gentleman who evidently in the main agrees with the principles of what have been called the Jingo party in this country. Therefore his evidence is the more remarkable; but I will not detain you further on this head.

I have another matter on which I wish to speak. It is one on which I have, as yet, hardly opened my mouth in Scotland. *India and* It is the question, gentlemen, of India, and of Afghanistan. *Afghanistan.* Now there is, I think, a great propriety in speaking of India before a Glasgow audience. I find a most legitimate ground for the assertion of that propriety in the great interests connected with India that subsist in Glasgow. You will recollect, gentlemen, that on a former occasion a Conservative Government gave a most emphatic acknowledgment of the title of Glasgow to be heard on Indian matters. It was in the year 1858 that a Government bearing that title brought in a bill for the government of India, which was considered at the time to be of a highly comic description. If you remember, there were to be in the Indian Council four members who were to be chosen for that Council by the £10 householders of Liverpool, of Manchester, if I recollect aright, of Belfast, and of Glasgow. In virtue of many titles, gentlemen, I ask you to consider with me what has been and what is going on in India. Very faintly and imperfectly, indeed, can I on this occasion open up the question; but yet I hope to say something which may serve to draw your attention to it, and to beget in the minds of some the conviction that unless an effectual attention be given to that portion of Her Majesty's dominions by others than those who are now in the direction of affairs, the greatest danger overhangs our connection with India, and with that danger the greatest dishonour that this country can undergo, in the failure to fulfil the most arduous and perhaps the noblest trust, that ever was undertaken by a nation.

Gentlemen, about three or four years ago Parliament was asked, and Parliament consented, to supersede the title under which up to that time Her Majesty, whom God preserve, had governed the whole of her dominions, so far as India was concerned, by empowering her to assume the title of Empress of India. Well, gentlemen, I am not about to re-argue the matters, which were largely discussed with respect to the policy of the assumption of that title. We thought it partook in a measure of those theatrical elements, which have since been much more fully and much more ruinously developed. But I will now assume that it was right; and if it was right, gentlemen, I call upon you to agree with me in this, that in order to complete the transaction, that assumption of a higher title ought to have been accompanied, in the face of the vast Indian people, by increase of franchise or of privilege, by augmentation of benefit, by redress of grievances and correction of abuse. Is that the course of government, which has since been pursued in India?

I must call your attention, gentlemen, to three, or rather to four topics, on none of which will I dwell with the particularity that their importance deserves. The first of them is what was called 'The Arms Act.' This was one of the early accompaniments of the assumption of the title of Empress. Before that time the importation of arms, and the use of gunpowder and other explosives, had been either wholly or to a great extent free in India. It was most desirable that that freedom should not be restricted or withdrawn. First, because special laws for the restraint of the possession of arms always indicate a mis-

The title of Empress of India.

'The Arms Act.'

trust of the people ; and the assumption of the Queen's title of Empress had been accompanied with the most high-sounding declarations as to her confidence in the universal loyalty of the people and the chiefs of India.   Next to that it is important, because in India the possession of arms is necessary for a cause of which we know nothing in this country—for the defence of the people against dangers to life, which you will understand when I tell you that I believe, according to a moderate estimate, no less than 20,000 persons lose their lives every year in India by wild beasts and serpents.   It was, thirdly, desirable that this use should be free, because commercial enterprise, such as public works, railroads, and almost every engineering work depends in a large degree upon the large use of explosive material ; and I have had the most striking statements of the impediments, which have been placed in the way of enterprise in India, from gentlemen whose case I cannot know, but who state it in a manner that commands attention, and invites assent.   I have had these statements, showing how this mischievous Act, as it appears to me, restricts the application of capital, and the development of industry and of useful works in India.

The freedom of the native press in India.   Gentlemen, the next head is, in my judgment, yet more serious. Half a century, or very nearly half a century, has elapsed since Lord William Bentinck, whom Glasgow did herself the honour of sending to Parliament, when he was appointed—I believe it may be more than half a century since—Governor-General of India, conferred upon the popular press of that country practical freedom.   That freedom never was misused.   That freedom was not a freedom to be eyed with jealousy.   It was of immense advantage to us.   The difficulty of every superior race which has to exercise political domination, and which wishes to exercise it well, is this—that timidity checks the full expression of opinion, and that those who rule cannot get at the true mind and meaning and desires of those who are ruled.   This native press was invaluable for the purpose of giving insight into the native mind ; but, a very short time after the assump-

tion of the title of Empress, when benefit and franchise ought
to have been enlarged in India in every way that wisdom could
devise, this ill-omened Act was introduced—an Act which
placed every newspaper of the vernacular tongues in India at
the absolute mercy of the Viceroy of the country. Now,
gentlemen, just think what this is. No doubt it was a serious
measure to grant that liberty. It ought not to have been done
without consideration. Neither was it done without consideration. It subsisted for half a century. It was made the subject *Its abolition.*
of investigation by different sets of distinguished men holding
office in India. Lord Macaulay, Sir Fitzjames Stephen, and all
the eminent men who held in succession the office of Viceroy,
were thoroughly favourable to that liberty. Nay, more, gentlemen, the Tory Duke of Buckingham, and a stauncher Tory
there is not in the country, having in him the sense, and spirit,
and feeling of an Englishman—the Tory Duke of Buckingham
when consulted by the Viceroy, remonstrated energetically
against the abolition of the freedom of the native press. Notwithstanding that, it was done. And how was it done? It
was done in a day. It was done without the slightest opportunity of opposition or discussion. It was done in a manner
which could not but suggest, and which goes far to prove that
even at that time the fatal policy since pursued was in full
view—that it was known or feared the policy would bear hard
on the people of India—that it was apprehended, if it so bore
upon them, it might lead to remonstrance; and therefore, beforehand, they were gagged by imposing upon the press a law that
is a contradiction to the spirit of the age in which we live,
and a disgrace to British authority.

These, gentlemen, so far, have been two of the accompaniments of the assumption of the Imperial title in India.
Another is of a very intelligible description. The third of *The increased*
taxation in
its accompaniments has been increased taxation upon that *India.*
impoverished population. Nor do these words convey the
whole truth, and the brief explanation of them that I will
give, and which I can only give in summary form, will show

you that even increase of taxation does not convey to the mind
the whole mischief of the case. The taxation was increased,
but it was increased with the most solemn, the most specific
and reiterated declarations, that it was increased not to supply
the ordinary purposes of the Government, but simply for the
purpose of a provision against famine. It was pointed out,
and pointed out with truth, that those famines, the scourge of
which seems to be becoming more terrible in India, — that

Indian famines. those famines when they arise import a derangement into the
finances, such as can hardly occur consistently with their due
and orderly management. And, therefore, this inceased taxation at the time when famine expenditure was not expected
was to be laid by, to be held apart as a sacred sum, marked for
the one exclusive purpose of meeting destitution, and meeting
starvation, when the next famine should arrive. Not a word
was dropped as to the intention to invade it in case of political
difficulty or war. These were the terms, — I will not quote,
because I cannot afford to take up your time to that extent,—
but these were the terms, as broad and unconditional as they
could be, according to all that I have read or seen upon the
subject, in which that pledge was given. Has that pledge been
kept ? The taxation was levied. The pledge was given. The

The money intended to meet famine has been spent upon the Afghan War. pledge has utterly been broken. The money has been used.
It is gone. It has been spent upon the ruinous, unjust
destructive war in Afghanistan. Nay, it has not even brought
expenditure and income together; because, after spending the
resources sacredly and solemnly pledged to the exclusive
purpose of meeting famine, you still will have, according to
the figures that are before us, at the close of the existing year,
a deficiency which I stated, and I believe it is not disputed, as
approaching six millions of money. Gentlemen, I want to
know whether you think this is the way in which to govern
India ? Is this the way in which we are to attach to us the
minds of the millions over whom we have assumed an Empire,
—an Empire, the origin of which will in many cases ill bear
examination, but which we who inherit it ought to

endeavour to redeem from discredit; ought to endeavour to elevate into honour; ought to endeavour, I will say, to consecrate to the Almighty by the strict application of the principles of justice and goodwill, of benevolence and mercy, towards a people of whom, I think, we must in fairness say that from first to last they have been distinguished by an extraordinary docility, and a disposition, wonderful in an Asiatic population, to submit to the restraints of order and of law.

Well, gentlemen, it would indeed have been a most painful and a grievous circumstance, if we had been obliged to consume and absorb the provision made for a purpose so urgent as that of preventing or limiting starvation,—if we had been compelled to absorb that fund by a war of justice and necessity. We have absorbed it to support a war of wilfulness, of injustice, and of folly. And, gentlemen, I think that the pulpit rather than the platform is the place from which to impress upon the minds of a Christian nation the enormous guilt, the immeasurable responsibility, which is undertaken by those countries that indulge themselves with levity, nay, even with something like exultation, in those wilful, unjust, and destructive wars. What has been the foundation of the causes for the Afghan war? It has lain, first of all, in the reversal of an Indian policy which had received the sanction of a number of successive Viceroys,—men variously trained: some of them in the transactions of India, some of them in the heavy trials of the Mutiny, some of them in the high traditions of English noblemen, many of them in the healthful discipline of the British House of Commons. All these men, with one accord, laid it down as a fundamental principle that we were to leave to the Afghan people—ay, and to the hill tribes between us and the Afghan people—the undisputed possession of those rude mountainous regions in which their lot was cast. The wisdom of those statesmen looked forward — and they were right in looking forward—to the possibility of a calamity, which I trust never may be realized, but which has come nearer to us, not by steps only, but by strides, under the disastrous policy of the last two years,—I

What has been the foundation of the causes for the Afghan War?

The possibility of a conflict with Russia in Asia. mean a conflict with Russia in Asia. Their doctrine was that the strength of a nation engaged in war is measured by nearness to its base of supply, and by easy communication with that base. Remain where you are, they said, in the plains of India. The farther the Russian has to come to attack you, the weaker he will be, and the more easily you will be able to prevail over *The safe way to prepare for this.* him, should he be mad enough to make the attempt. That was the doctrine established in policy, not by one authority alone; for immediately before Lord Northbrook had the honour of supporting it, it was supported with equal zeal, with equal ability, by his predecessor Lord Mayo, whose life fell a sacrifice to his duty, but whose political trustworthiness was assured in our eyes by his admirable conduct of the Government of India; in the eyes of our opponents by the fact that he had been a steady and a loyal member of the party of Lord Derby. Well, gentlemen, when I think of the grounds upon which that wise policy has been departed from, and of the results that have already been produced, the recital of the grounds might make one laugh; the recital of the results might better make one weep. It seems to me, gentlemen, that for the last two years we have been under what calls itself a policy; but it is no policy. It is what is better known by an outlandish term, yet one not inapplicable —it is a phantasmagoria. We have gone up into the mountains; we have broken Afghanistan to pieces; we have driven mothers and children forth from their homes to perish in the snow; we have spent treasure, of which a real account has never yet been rendered; we have undergone an expenditure of which as yet I believe we are aware of but a fraction; we have renewed and redoubled the wrong which our fathers did to Afghanistan forty years ago, in the time of Dost Mahomed, and which it had been the constant object of the wise Viceroys of India to obliterate from recollection by good deeds and kindly treatment, and the resolute endeavour to restore their confidence in a people whose historical relations with the Afghan country had been marked with so dark a stain. Much had been done in that sense. Distrust had greatly disappeared. The Afghan rulers were disposed to cling to us. No doubt the last of them, Shere Ali whom we have sent in sorrow to his grave, endeavoured at times, as civilised Powers too will do, to make the most of his connection with us. But he never committed an offence against us; he never gave us the slighest cause even for distrust of his ultimate intentions. It was our wilful action, and our wilful action alone, that raised the cause of quarrel. And, gentlemen, what is true of Cyprus on a small scale, is true of Afghanistan on a greater scale. The fact that the result of our enterprise is nothing to ourselves but mischief and embarrassment, does not in the slightest degree redeem us from the charge of a guilty cupidity under which that enterprise was undertaken.

It was our wilful action alone that raised the cause of quarrel.

Now, gentlemen, what happened? There were two gentlemen, men of distinguished names, who supported the Indian policy of advance into Afghanistan. Who were they? Sir Henry Rawlinson and Sir Bartle Frere. These were the two great authorities. Sir Henry Rawlinson was, I believe, a distinguished officer; he is a scientific man—a man of high character and great ability. Sir Bartle Frere, except that I believe he is entirely a civilian, deserves the ascription to him of all those qualities in the highest degree. But neither the one nor the other has ever been in a position of real responsibility; neither the one nor the other has ever imbibed, from actual acquaintance with British institutions, the spirit by which British government ought to be regulated and controlled. That they are men of benevolence I do not doubt; but I am afraid they are gentlemen who are apt, in giving scope to their benevolent motives, to take into their own hands the choice of means in a manner which those who are conversant with free government and with responsible government never would dream of. Sir Bartle Frere's mode of action at the Cape of Good Hope does not tend to accredit his advice in Afghanistan. Against these two gentlemen there are the judgments of all the Viceroys from Lord Ellenborough to Lord Mayo, of most distinguished generals, of a whole host of Indian authorities, and of responsible British statesmen.

Our conduct to Shere Ali.

Well, now, gentlemen, what has been our conduct to the late Ameer of Afghanistan? We were bound by treaty to that Ameer—the Treaty of 1857, made by Sir John Lawrence. We were bound, and admitted, I think, by every Viceroy down to Lord Northbrook to be bound, not to force upon Shere Ali the reception of British envoys of European birth. Remember this, gentlemen; there never was the least difficulty about having envoys at the Court of Shere Ali. Shere Ali was perfectly willing to receive native envoys, because he could receive native envoys—men of his own religion—without their exciting jealousy; and consequently the lives of those envoys were perfectly safe. He did not receive our native envoy; it was Lord Lytton's wilful act that withdrew him. But after what had happened before, Shere Ali, wiser far than we, remonstrated against the attempt to send British envoys into Afghanistan, for he said it was impossible to answer for their safety. But we

The sending of an envoy to Cabul.

insisted on sending our British envoys. Nay, even that did not satisfy us; for when in 1857 the subject was discussed between Sir Lewis Pelly on our part, and the Minister of Shere Ali, it was known to the Viceroy, or apprehended by him after the death of his Minister, that the Ameer, in his terror and despair, was sending a new envoy to concede all our demands rather than quarrel with us; and with that fact in his view the conferences were closed, and Shere Ali was not permitted even the opportunity of making this mischievous and forced concession.

And why, gentlemen, did we make war upon Shere Ali? I will now read to you in the fewest words two declarations —who sentences, one from the speech of one of the confidential advisers of the Crown, and another from the speech of another of those advisers. Lord Cairns, a man of great ability, said in the House of Lords in the Afghan debate—I believe I quote the report correctly—' We are not going to war with Afghanistan for receiving a Russian envoy. We are going to war with him for not receiving our envoy.' While Lord Cairns gave that account in the House of Lords, another Minister is said to have given the following account in the House of

Commons :—' We did not quarrel with the Ameer because he *The contradic-* did not receive the British Mission at Cabul ; we quarrelled *tory reasons given for the* with him for having received the Russian Mission at Cabul *quarrel.* with great pomp.' This contradiction, gentlemen, may well amuse you. I am not at all surprised at it. It appears to me, that gentlemen who undertake to justify policy like the Afghan policy, must of necessity, unless their stars be highly favourable to them, fall into many contradictions. But I want to ask you which of those two reasons do you prefer; which do you think is the best ? Lord Cairns has said to us, we are going to war with him for not receiving our envoy. But, in the first place, it is an understood principle of public law that nobody has a right to fasten an envoy upon an independent ruler, and the declarations of the Government— the declaration especially of Sir Stafford Northcote as lately as twelve months ago—was that the object of their policy was to make Afghanistan free, strong, friendly, and indepen- dent. You see how that policy has been fulfilled. But you had no title to force an envoy upon Shere Ali. Does, then, Lord John Manners relieve us from our embarrassment by giving us a better reason than the lame reason of Lord Cairns ? He says we made war because the Ameer received a Russian Mission at Cabul with great pomp. Why did he receive the Russian Mission ? Because the Russian Government, as a mea- sure of hostility to us, most unjustifiably as regards the Ameer, when they apprehended a quarrel with England, sent word to the Ameer that he must receive their Embassy. It was im- possible for the Ameer to resist. He received that Embassy under compulsion. He did no wrong, therefore, in receiving it if under compulsion. But supposing he had done wrong, which was the greater offender—the feeble Ameer who re- ceived the Embassy of Russia because he could not help it, or the great white Czar—the Emperor of all the Russias, who forced him to receive that Embassy. And what was our con- duct ? You have heard much, gentlemen, about a vigorous foreign policy, and a spirited foreign policy. A meaner act, a shabbier act, a more dastardly act is not to be found upon record than that by which this Government, forbearing to punish Russia, forbearing even to remonstrate with Russia—that is to say, accepting from Russia the most feeble and transparent excuses with an ostensible satisfaction, reserved all its force and all its vengeance for the unfortunate Ameer of Afghanistan. And, gentlemen, is not the result worthy of the origin. Some credit has been given by some writers to us, who took part in strong protestation, from the first, against those most iniquitous proceedings, for having prophesied their disastrous result. There was no merit in those prophesies. The deeds done were deeds that could have none other but a disastrous result.

If you failed in Afghanistan, I mean in a military sense, which was most improbable,—your permanent military failure, almost impossible,—if you failed in Afghanistan, even for a time, you disgraced yourselves in the eyes of the world, and lost that military repute and credit which undoubtedly is of the highest importance to an Asiatic Power. But if you succeeded in Afghanistan, you broke Afghanistan to pieces.

The Govern-
ment has
destroyed the
barrier between
Russia and us.
The barrier—the firm barrier, well defended by its mountain ranges—which we and which former Governments had striven to place between Russian and English possessions, now exists no more. Afghanistan is no longer a kingdom. Province after province has broken away. You are in possession of its most important strongholds to the south and to the east. Other persons are in possession of its severed fractions in other quarters; and your possession—useless, fruitless, hopeless—brings upon you a large military charge which you do not dare to ask the people of England, and of Scotland, and of Ireland to pay, and which you are imposing, with an injustice never surpassed in the history of the world, on the impoverished population of India.

Well, gentlemen, what then is the general upshot of this review, in which I have been engaged since I came to Scotland; which I have had, I feel it more than any can, no power adequately to conduct, but yet which I hope I have not gone through without bringing out into the light, and bringing home to the mind and the heart, some truths at least which it is material for this nation to know? What is the general upshot? Let us look at it together. I will use the fewest words. We have finance in confusion; we have legisla- *A summary of our position now under a Tory Government.* tion in intolerable arrear; we have honour compromised by the breach of public law; we have public distress aggravated by the destruction of confidence; we have Russia aggrandised and yet estranged; we have Turkey befriended as we say, but mutilated, and sinking every day; we have Europe restless and disturbed—Europe, which, after the Treaty of Paris, at all events so far as the Eastern Question was concerned, had something like rest for a period approaching twenty years, has, almost ere the ink of the Treaty of Berlin is dry, been agitated *The Treaty of Berlin.* from end to end with rumours and alarms, so that on the last 10th of November we were told that the Prime Minister thought that peace might be preserved, but on the previous 9th of November—namely, four months after the Treaty—it had been much more doubtful. In Africa you have before you the memory of bloodshed, of military disaster, the record of 10,000 Zulus—such is the computation of *The Zulu War.* Bishop Colenso—slain for no other offence than their attempt to defend against your artillery with their naked bodies their hearths and homes, their wives and families. You have the invasion of a free people in the Transvaal; and you *The annexation of the Transvaal.* have, I fear, in one quarter or another,—I will not enter into details, which might be injurious to the public interest,— prospects of further disturbance and shedding of blood. You have Afghanistan ruined; you have India not advanced, *The Afghan War.* but thrown back in government, subjected to heavy and unjust charges, subjected to what may well be termed, in comparison with the mild government of former years, a system of oppression; and with all this you have had at home, in matters which I will not now detail, the law broken, and the rights of Parliament invaded. Gentlemen, amidst the whole of this pestilent activity,—for so I must call it,—this distress and bloodshed which we have either produced or largely shared in producing, not in one instance down to the Treaty of Berlin, and down to the war in Afghanistan,—not in one instance did we either do a deed, or speak an effectual word, on behalf of liberty. Such is the upshot, gentlemen, of the sad enumeration. To call this policy Conservative is, in my opinion, a pure mockery, and an abuse of terms. Whatever it may be in its motive, it is in its result disloyal, it is in its essence thoroughly subversive. There is no democrat, there is no agitator, there is no propounder of anti-rent doctrines, whatever mischief he may do, who can compare in mischief with possessors of authority who thus invert, and who thus degrade, the principles of free government in the British Empire. Gentlemen, I wish to end as I began. Is this the way, or is this not the way, in which a free nation, inhabiting these islands, wishes to be governed? Will the people, be it now or be it months hence, ratify the deeds that have been done, and assume upon themselves that tremendous responsibility? The whole humble aim, gentlemen, of my proceedings has been to bring home, as far as was in my power, this great question to the mind and to the conscience of the community at large. If I cannot decide the issue,—and of course I have no power to decide it,—I wish at least to endeavour to make it understood by those who can. And I cherish the hope that

> ‘ When the hurly-burly’s done,
> When the battle’s lost and won,’

I may be able to bear home with me, at least, this consolation, that I have spared no effort to mark the point at which the roads divide,—the one path which plunges into suffering, discredit, and dishonour, the other which slowly, perhaps, but surely, leads a free and a high-minded people towards the blessed ends of prosperity and justice, of liberty and peace.

SPEECH AT MOTHERWELL STATION,

SATURDAY, DECEMBER 6, 1879.

MR. GLADSTONE, on Saturday morning, December 6, proceeded by rail from Glasgow to Motherwell, where he was received with every demonstration of joy by about 600 persons within the station itself, and by a crowd estimated at fully 2000 immediately outside the gates. The various deputations from the Liberal Committees of the Middle and Upper Wards of Lanarkshire were introduced by Mr. Hamilton of Dalzell, the Liberal candidate for South Lanarkshire, in the absence, from ill-health, of Sir T. E. Colebrooke, Bart., M.P., and an address was presented by Mr. Houldsworth of Coltness. Then followed addresses from the Magistrates of Motherwell and of Wishaw, presented by the Provosts of those burghs.

Mr. Gladstone, who was received with loud cheers, in acknowledging these presentations, said:—Gentlemen, the business on which I came to Scotland is substantially for the present at an end. That business was not the mere seeking of a seat in Parliament, and still less a desire to evoke personal honours for myself. It was to be enabled, in the face of a patriotic people, to make something like a detailed exposition of a difficult and complicated case, extending over the transactions of many years, reaching to the various quarters of the globe, and yet necessary, as it seemed to me, to be placed with unusual fulness before the people of the country for their consideration and decision. Gentlemen, after the efforts of yesterday, which were considerable, I should not be in a

condition to resume that work even were we not assembled
at a spot where we are of necessity, to a certain extent, in
competition, so far as sound is concerned, with some of the
ordinary operations of a railway station. I will only, then,
ask you to believe with me that the errand which has brought
me here is a most serious errand. I find confirmation of that
view in the language of the address from the Liberal Associations
which has been read in your hearing. These Associations feel
that the time has arrived when the country should be freed
from the disastrous policy of the present Government. At
that phrase, gentlemen, I will stop to say that undoubtedly
the liberation of the country from the present Government is
a main and capital object of my pilgrimage. After the
demonstration which the conduct of the present Parliament
has afforded, and in particular, far beyond the rest, after the
demonstration which the last two disastrous years have afforded,
I tell you frankly that unless you effect that you will effect
nothing. That removal of itself is but a part of the work.
What will come afterwards, for those who may be selected to
guide the affairs of this country, will be a matter of the utmost
Party triumph complexity and difficulty. Don't suppose that party triumph
is not the end,
but the essen- is the end of all things in my view. No, gentlemen; but it is
tial beginning. the necessary, the essential, indispensable beginning. And
here let me say, with respect to the kind expression that was
used in one of the speeches just addressed to me, that a return
to place and power is no part of the purpose for which I have
come here for myself.

But for the public interest, gentlemen, what you have here
stated is that you want statesmen who will uphold the constitutional privileges of the people, and the meaning of that is,
that during these latest years the constitutional privileges of
the people represented in their Parliament have not been
upheld. It is perfectly true that they have been compromised
with the willing, nay, the eager consent of Parliament, and
that is the very reason why you should long for the moment

when you will have the opportunity of choosing a Parliament of a different complexion. You say you want statesmen who will maintain the national honour. Gentlemen, if national honour could be maintained by boasting and by brag, then indeed it has been splendidly maintained. But if national honour depends upon a firm decision to accord to others the rights you claim for yourselves—if national honour is the everlasting principle of equal right to all—if national honour requires that wherever strong words are used they shall be followed by strong acts, then, indeed, we are of opinion that national honour has not been maintained. Finally, you want statesmen who will be guided by the great principles of justice, economy, and reform. It is needless for me to do more than say that in my firm and sad belief those principles of justice, those principles of economy, those principles of reform, have been either neglected or gravely compromised, and even trodden under foot. So, gentlemen, this work is a serious work. It is the work of to-day, and of not to-day alone. The firm and manly purpose which has been indicated, so far as my observation has gone, at every point during the last fortnight, is a purpose which it will be your duty and your necessity to maintain in its full vigour till the day of trial comes.

The national honour has been maintained by boasting and by brag.

This, gentlemen, is not the first time in our history when the first effort for liberty—the first illuminating ray that has spread over the land—has come from Scotland. I reflect with joy that many places in England have distinctly shown that they are already alive ; but something, gentlemen, is left to you. You will have a forward place in the work to be done, in the triumph to be achieved ; and it is because I believed that none were better qualified to take that forward place than the people of Scotland, that on this occasion I came among you with the firm determination not to fall short in any effort that my humble energies could afford to be a sharer in your labours, and to assist you towards gaining their triumphant end.

Colonel Buchanan of Drumpellier called for three cheers for Mr. Gladstone, which were most heartily given. The right honourable gentleman drove off to Dalzell House amid hearty demonstrations of good feeling, which were not allowed to die away till he had passed out of the town.

In the afternoon the freedom of the Burgh of Motherwell was presented to Mr. Gladstone by a deputation of Magistrates specially appointed for the purpose.

During the fortnight he spent north of the Tweed, Mr. Gladstone addressed on various occasions personally upwards of 75,000 people; and were the vast crowds who assembled in various places to do him honour computed, it may fairly be said that something like a quarter of a million of persons took some part in the demonstrations everywhere evoked by the mere announcement of an intended visit. The only event in the least degree comparable to the progress of the right honourable gentleman is the historical visit of Earl Grey to Edinburgh in 1834, not long after the first Reform Bill became law; and it may be doubted whether even that memorable journey witnessed such a thrill of the enthusiasm of a nation as Scotland but the other day felt, ay, and still feels.

APPENDIX.

SPEECHES IN REPLY TO CORPORATION
ADDRESSES.

SPEECH AT EDINBURGH IN REPLY TO AN ADDRESS
PRESENTED BY THE CORPORATION, ON TUES-
DAY, NOVEMBER 25, 1879.

MR. GLADSTONE, who was received with loud cheers, said:—
My Lord Provost, and gentlemen of the Town Council, I accept with great pleasure this flattering address. I have been
speaking of myself to-day as in some sense a stranger to the
county of Midlothian. That confession I felt bound to make
as regarded the county as a political entity or combination.
But I really will not altogether speak of myself as a stranger
in the city of Edinburgh. This is not the place to commit
the act of autobiography. But I have exceedingly early and *Early recollec-*
rather extended recollections in connection with this ancient *tions of Edinburgh.*
city—this most interesting and beautiful city. On the occa-
sion of my first visit to it I heard the glass of the windows of
the Royal Hotel rattle to the guns of the Castle, as they
announced one of the great victories won over Napoleon the
Great, in the year 1815. Therefore I am afraid, sir, that I
have the advantage of many of you in respect at any rate of
the date when my recollections of Edinburgh begin. But I
do not stop there, for it has been my lot, I will say my very
happy lot, to spend on no less certainly than four or five occasions of my life several months at a time within the precincts
of Edinburgh. That also is at a date so remote as to go back
beyond the recollections of most men. I knew Edinburgh, I
may say I knew it well. I knew almost every street and
every corner in the days when the curious old wynd led down

from the Castle to the Grassmarket, of which, I am ashamed to say, now I forget the name.   (Turning to the Lord Provost) —What do you call it ?

The Lord Provost—The West Bow.

Mr. Gladstone—Yes, the West Bow ; that most curious winding street.   I may say I knew Edinburgh when Edinburgh was, in fact, in what I may call the virgin purity of its ancient beauty, with which, I am afraid, you have been compelled, in worshipping the great goddess Convenience, as is the necessity of modern times, in various places seriously to interfere.   I knew Edinburgh in the days of Lord Moncreiff, of Dr. Gordon, of Dr. Thomson, of Bishop Sandford, and many other remarkable men.   And I may say that I have had the honour, for I think it a great honour, of having had many walks in Edinburgh and its neighbourhood with a man whose name will always remain amongst you as that of the most distinguished son and the greatest ornament of the Presbyterian system — I mean Dr. Chalmers.

I am very glad, my Lord Provost, to have this opportunity of recalling the feelings of disappointment with which I found myself, in the year 1853, through political circumstances, prevented from having the great honour of seeing the Lord Provost of that date, and of addressing the citizens of Edinburgh on the occasion of being enrolled upon their list of burgesses.   It was a very great disappointment, but I know it was not imputed at the time to any indifference to that honour.   It was subsequently a great pleasure to me, not only to serve the office *The Lord* of Lord Rector of the University, but to serve it at a time of *Rectorship of* *the University.* peculiar interest, when its new constitution was first taken into action, and to hold that office for six years with the accompaniment of not infrequently attending the meetings of the University Court, and bearing a practical part in the proceedings.   And although you are not here strictly an academical audience, yet I know the kindly and official connection which prevails in the city of Edinburgh between the Municipality and the University ; and I therefore heartily congratulate you, my Lord Provost, on the flourishing state of that University, *The flourishing state of the University.* and the important recent accession to its numbers. In the position of the University I read a good omen for the future of Scotland, and I feel the greatest confidence that she is not likely to lose the high place that she occupies on the great roll of nations. For myself, my Lord Provost, naturally, within the limits of strict truth, I wish to make the most on the present occasion of whatever I can claim to associate me with Scotland, and in one point I can vie with any of you, because there is not a man in this room, or out of this room, whose blood is more exclusively Scotch in its character than *His Scottish descent.* my own. I have not, and, as far as I know, none of my forefathers ever had, any relations but were of pure Scottish extraction. So that you have in me, so far as that is concerned, what may be called the genuine article. My Lord Provost, I have often admired, in conjunction with the world at large, the spirit and energy with which the proceedings of *The spirit and energy of the Municipality.* the great municipal bodies of Edinburgh have been carried on. Always a most interesting city, presenting to the artist, archæologist, and the antiquarian such a combination of points of interest as hardly are to be found elsewhere combined within the same limited surface, Edinburgh has within the present century planted herself out in every direction, and under the fostering influence of its powerful local institutions, it has become a great and splendid city, vieing undoubtedly with any city that can be named within the British dominions, as regards its beauty, its great natural advantages, and all those features in respect of which cities may justly claim our admiration. In the sister municipality of Glasgow you have had a formidable rival, one with which it is an honour to compete, because that municipality too has been distinguished by zeal, making it an example—almost, indeed, a model ; and I believe that the recent transformation of a large portion of Glasgow under municipal auspices has been an operation such as is an honour to Scotland, and has conferred a very useful model for Parliament in one of the most useful Acts which in recent years it has passed. I, therefore, my Lord Provost, both wish and confidently anticipate that the ancient body over which your Lordship worthily presides, will continue to enjoy the full confidence of the city, and to answer all those important purposes which are associated with our local institutions,—purposes which belong to the life of citizenship, purposes which have to do with the manner in which public duty is associated in this country with individual responsibility, and with that of individual fitness.

We see in other countries the lack, and the damage that they suffer for want of efficient local institutions of self-government. We see on the other side of the Atlantic the large portion of the wonderful energy of our American brethren and friends, as I am glad to think we may call them, the *The value of* large portion of their wonderful expansion there, due to the *habits of self-* habits of self-government in local institutions which they *government* carried with them from this country. It is not for me to *in local* *institutions.* offer you any exhortations on that subject, but I assure you that I feel most cordially the dignity and importance of the functions that you are called upon to discharge, and I trust and believe that they will always be so esteemed by the populations of our country. I would wish, my Lord Provost, to make one other observation, without trespassing over the limits to which an address such as this is naturally confined. Your Lordship and your brethren of the Town Council have given me the credit of patriotic motives, and of having been a friend, in my public conduct, of what is termed in your excellently drawn address, oppressed nationalities. Well, my Lord and gentlemen, I venture to give you this assurance, that I am sustained and encouraged, and I may almost say driven on in political life, at the present time particularly, by the sentiment, believed and entertained by me most sincerely, whether erroneously or not, that the principles at issue are much broader than those of ordinary contention, and involve more serious issues; I do believe, and I humbly ask for confidence when I state my own belief, that the objects which we have in view at the present time are objects connected with the welfare of mankind upon the widest scale. We live in times when there is an inter-communion, a close inter-communion, between country and country, such as was comparatively little known to our forefathers. Whatever we may say, amidst the clash of arms and amidst the din of preparations for warfare in time of peace, which really when they come to be considered seem almost universal war itself, such is the continuous suggestion and peril of war which they contain,—amidst all this, yet there is going on a profound, mysterious movement, that, whether we will or not, is bringing *The mysterious* the nations of the civilised world, as well as the uncivilised, *movement which is* morally as well as physically nearer to one another, and *drawing* making them more and more responsible before God for one *nations nearer* another's welfare. Considerations of that kind, not limited to *together.* these shores, but going far beyond them, enter profoundly into the daily action of States, and of all who are concerned with the direction of that action in Parliament, or in office, or whenever they come to exercise that political power.

I make no assumption at this moment as to the justice of the manner in which I have understood these greatest and world-wide considerations. I may be entirely in error in the view I have taken, or in the view I may take, and this is not the place to raise that question. But I do most heartily thank you for having given me the credit of being actuated at least by the desire to consider in public transactions the wider interests of mankind, and I venture to assure you that, so far as my will and intention are concerned, objects of that nature, and nothing meaner or narrower, will ever be taken as the pole-star of my life.

REPLY TO ADDRESS FROM THE CORPORATION
OF GLASGOW.

MR. GLADSTONE, who was loudly cheered, said:—My Lord Provost, Bailies, and Town Councillors of Glasgow, my Lords, Ladies, and Gentlemen,—I am sure that all who are here present will feel that it has been my lot to-day considerably to tax that portion of strength which is lodged within any one human frame; and that, on that account, you will not, my Lord, measure the sincerity or the depth of my gratitude for this renewed mark of your confidence and kindness by the comparative brevity of the reply which I may address to you. My Lord Provost, the address of the city manifestly expresses the sentiments of the Magistrates and Town Councillors; and as they are the elected of the people, I may believe them presumptively to convey the sentiments which are those of this great community at large. I am bound to say that, in the most emphatic passages of that address, and likewise of the speech with which you were good enough to preface it, I find the ringing cheers of the vast audience assembled in your City Hall, echoing many of the sentiments, many of the most glowing sentiments, to which the address, and to which your own speech, gave utterance. Now, my Lord Provost, if there is anything that should abate pride and vanity in a man, if there is anything that should make him feel how poor are his best exertions when measured with the importance of the interests on which he is called to exercise an influence, how much he must leave undone, how far short in every endeavour he must fall of the mark he has wished to attain—if there is anything that would have the effect of realizing and bringing home these sentiments, it is the glowing eulogy which, in your address and in

your speech, has been conveyed to me, because I feel that it is
in reality your warm sentiment and your favourable disposition
which have led you to draw a picture far more highly coloured
than the reality to which it refers.   But this, my Lord Provost,
I will say, that when you were good enough to sum up, if I
may so put it, your words of eulogy in the expression of the
belief that you have presented this address to an honest man,
at least I feel that there is, or there ought to be, in that
generous manifestation of confidence a very powerful incentive
to try, in some measure, to deserve the commendation you
have been good enough by anticipation to give.   If ever I am
conscious of deliberately swerving from the path of duty, this
eulogy, this kind and warm expression, will be the very first
witness to rise up in judgment against me, and call me back
to duty.

My Lord Provost, I have great satisfaction in meeting
again this Corporation.   It was on this very spot that fourteen
years ago I had the honour to receive the freedom of the city,
and to address an audience, not perhaps quite so numerous,
for I think it was a seated audience,—but an audience
which crowded your City Hall.   I then felt, I then knew
that I was addressing one of the most efficient and one of the
most distinguished among the municipal bodies of this country.
But, my Lord, I rejoice to think, and I am glad to bear my
impartial testimony, that within the fourteen years that have
since elapsed, your municipality has established new claims,
not only to the confidence of the great local community, but
likewise to the acknowledgments and the approval, and, I
will venture to say, to the admiration of the country at large.
If, my Lord, there has been heretofore one subject of reproach
more patent and telling than another in the government
of our great towns, it has been the comparative indifference
with which the welfare of the mass of the community was
regarded in respect to the important article of their habita-
tions, at those particular periods when there was a call for
what are described as public improvements.   My Lord, in too

many cases, I do not hesitate to say, I know not whether in Glasgow, but certainly in the metropolis of the land with which I have been conversant as an old resident, those public improvements were, I grieve to confess, the infliction of public cruelties—a displacement and a dislodgement of humble populations dependent on local access to their labour, or dependent entirely upon the custom of those whose local access to their labour enabled them to support the small tradesmen of the place. So that often, with changes which, when they met the eye, appeared to bear testimony to a spirit of progress and of reform, there lay within that which vitiated the whole process, because underneath fair appearances there was an insufficient feeling of what was required by the real welfare of the people, and a disposition, for the sake of a greater and better show, to sacrifice both the comforts and necessaries of those dependent on their daily labour. My Lord, we have lived into a better time, and I hope that nowhere will it hereafter be found practicable to pass these improvement schemes, and to give them effect, without an obligation to have regard to the effect of the scheme on those whom they displace, as well as upon the general convenience and beauty of our cities. My Lord, if the change has been, as I trust it has been, brought about, I am bound to say I believe it is due to no one single cause, to no single body, in so large, and I may say dominant, a degree, as to the action of the Corporation of Glasgow. The scheme, which was then in its embryo, for effecting a large removal of your population, embodied, I believe, for the first time, the absolute condition that you should find for those who were dislodged equivalent and fully as convenient accommodation within reasonable distance. This was a truly reforming principle, under which we may safely prosecute our town improvements, and it is, my Lord, a conspicuous honour to this municipality if it has had a foremost place in setting such an example to the country. I may go one step further, and say, as I believe it to be the truth, that you have actually supplied the Government and the Parliament with the basis of a useful measure: you have thus been the means of obtaining the sanction of the Legislature to principles which were formerly quite out of mind, and to which you were first to give a conspicuous and authoritative place in the views and practice of the community. My Lord Provost, I need not say that I am glad that my renewed visit, after the interval of those fourteen years, has enabled me to bear this marked and definite testimony, which renders it needless for me to dwell upon the general subject of the importance of the office that you hold, and the satisfactory spectacle that is afforded by the regular election, through the free choice of the community, of those who are to exercise authority in this great town. But, my Lord, I may be permitted to say, in reference to the experience of the last twenty-four hours, that I have had the honour and the pleasure of seeing poured forth into your streets your population by thousands, by scores of thousands. I have had the opportunity of observing with lively satisfaction the feelings of kindliness, of good humour, that have prevailed, the respect for order, the self-command and self-government of the people, even when under the influence of an enthusiasm I certainly should be the last to disparage or deny.

My Lord, I will now only further say that I cherish among the archives of my family, and that I shall pass on with satisfaction to my descendants, the box in which you were good enough to enclose the instrument conferring upon me the freedom of this city; that I receive with equal satisfaction the proof that after fourteen years you have seen no reason to repent of the mark of kindness and regard that you then were good enough to bestow, and that among the warmest and most pleasing recollections of my life will be the reception, and especially the present reception, that I have met with in the city of Glasgow. Among my holiest desires will also be the desire for its continued prosperity, and its eminence in all that can give alone true greatness or true happiness to a Scottish community.

The audience repeatedly and loudly called upon the Earl of Rosebery to address them, but, under the circumstances, that was of course out of the question.   Mr. Gladstone and his party then left the hall amid loud cheering.   During the drive back to the residence of Sir James Watson, Mr., Mrs., and Miss Gladstone were loudly cheered by the people who remained in the street to witness the return journey.

It is stated that the Liberal students have resolved to ask Mr. Gladstone to allow himself to be again nominated for the Lord Rectorship, and that, through the generosity of a number of Liberal gentlemen, a 'Gladstone annual prize' is to be endowed in the University.

LORD RECTOR'S ADDRESS.

LORD RECTOR'S ADDRESS.

THE immediate occasion of Mr. Gladstone's visiting Glasgow was to make personal acquaintance with the students, who two years ago elected him Lord Rector of the University, and the reception accorded him at the hands of his academical constituents was such as did honour alike to him and to themselves. No sooner had the opening words of the Lord Rector's address reached the ears of the vast assemblage in the Kibble Palace, than they resigned themselves to the spell of its smooth-flowing periods, and followed with closest attention the lessons of mature wisdom so pleasantly conveyed.

Mr. Gladstone spoke as follows :—

Gentlemen,—For six years I had the honour to hold the office of Rector in the University of Edinburgh, and to take part in the government of that University as the presiding member of its Court, and otherwise. Upon agreeing that my name should be submitted to you for the corresponding office in 1877, I stated my inability to engage myself for the performance of any active duty whatever, including in this renunciation the time-honoured function which has been exalted by the unwilling efforts of so many distinguished men—the function of delivering a Rectorial address to the students of the University. In so stipulating, I was not governed by any disposition to undervalue the honour solicited on my behalf, or the dignity of this ancient and noble institution ; but I had in view partly my increased and increasing years, partly the fact that I had already travelled over the

The Lord Rector's Address.

field of such topics as had occurred to me in connection with such an occasion and such a duty. It was, in truth, a high and not a low estimate of the office, then in prospect and since conferred, which led me to guard myself by this reservation ; for I was unwilling to run the risk of being obliged to offer you the mere leavings of an exhausted store, or the commonplaces of that routine which cannot always be shut out even from academical precincts, or thoughts, or language. In truth, I find it more easy to offer you my reasons for having eschewed the performance of this particular duty than to vindicate my now undertaking to discharge it. In this respect, after what I have said, I must be content rather to excuse than to justify myself. I excuse myself mainly by saying that I have perceived among you signs of a strong attachment to the established custom of an address from your Lord Rector, such as I am unwilling to disappoint. And as the stars seem to multiply after prolonged and earnest gaze, so I must admit that upon reflection the field of topics appropriate to your condition and prospects continually gathers new elements of fertility from the movement and tendencies of the time, as the well-ploughed soil progressively acquires them from the passing breeze. I will only, then, invoke your indulgence, in case the matter of my address should suggest or prove that I had better have adhered to my first intention.

English and Scotch students. In some respects, gentlemen, your position and that of the sister establishments in Scotland is more normal than that of two larger and yet more ancient and powerful Universities of England. Of the governing and teaching bodies as known to you on this side of the Border we can say with truth, what we cannot as yet say with universal truth of Oxford and of Cambridge, that their members are all of them working bees. Of your modest endowments you may boast, what is still to a limited extent open to question in the South, that they are without exception applied, rationally and directly, to the promotion of true academic purposes. You have also a great advantage in this, that among your students there is hardly a sprinkling, or at all events there is a much thinner sprinkling, of youths who, unhappily for themselves and for others, arrive at the University without any adequate sense of its mission or of their own. Such youths contemplate it as a pleasant lounge, subject to the drawback of lessons of routine, which it is their chief care to keep down to a minimum; or accept it as a condition of their social standing, or as a promotion from their school life; or turn it physically to account as a school of corporal exercises, without any higher care. The rapid growth of wealth in the country tends to enlarge the numbers of these pseudo-students, but it is the aim of reform, and the constant care of the authorities in England, if they cannot be exterminated, to keep them down. Among you, gentlemen, I trust that these anomalous varieties of the academic sub-kingdom of the human species are scarcely known. May they long be strangers to your precincts, for they foreshadow in youth, and they feed in after life, that heavy mass of idlers among our wealthy men, who, though not reckoned statistically among our dangerous classes, yet are in truth a class both mischievous and dangerous to the intellectual and moral vigour of . society, and even to the institutions of the country. Oxford and Cambridge have a noble office, and in its own way an unrivalled position; but the Scottish Universities have also their own proper and admirable work. To them it is given, far more than elsewhere, to draw forth freely from that grand and inexhaustible repository, the mass of the people, the human material capable of being moulded into excellence, and to earn in the most honourable of all modes the title of national by serving most and best the needs of the nation at large.

And I rejoice to know, gentlemen, that if this title has been *University facts and figures.* legitimately won in other days, you are not likely to lose it now. While the population of your country is fast growing, the population, so to speak, of your Universities is growing faster still. I find that the students of Glasgow, who in 1861 were 1140, had grown, in the last annual session, to be 2096. Nor will you observe with envy, for there can be no envy in the fair sisterhood of Universities, that Edinburgh exhibits an increase no way less remarkable, and has risen, within the same sixteen years, from 1462 to 2591. In all, it would appear that Scotland, with her population of three millions and a half, has for her four Universities more than 5500 students. A noble testimony this, gentlemen, to the wisdom of the Act of 1858; to the careful government and efficient instruction of your able and, I must add, indefatigable Principals and Professors; and, not least, to the unexhausted appetite of the Scottish people for the benefits which Universities confer. Through the kindness, however, of your Principal and your Professor of Humanity, seconded by the intelligent willingness of his students, I have been allowed the privilege of a nearer insight into the structure of your academic society. It is with the deepest interest and pleasure that I place upon record the main heads of knowledge thus attained. Of 647 students in the Humanity Class, information has actually been obtained as follows from no less than 590 as to their position and destiny in life :—Of these, 229 are studying with a view to the ministry; 116 to the profession of teachers; 110 for the law; for medicine no more than 38 are in the Humanity Class; 23 for various branches of business; and 74 are as yet undetermined, of whom, I am informed, it is probable that a large proportion will enter on some one of the walks of commercial life. Still more interesting than this exhibition of the connection between the greatest among the professions and the pursuit of general culture, is the view, I will say the deeply touching view, of the amount of resolute, unsparing, personal effort, through which alone it is that the youth of Scotland come so extensively to the benefits of academic training. These are not the children of wealth and ease, grudging whatever is given to study as stolen from luxury and amusement. They are the hardy offspring of a hardy land, who win by toiling the privilege of further toil, and in thus cumulating effort give a doubled strength to the fibre of their faculties and their will. Of the 590 students, who may be taken, I understand, fairly to represent the average of the University, about one-third, or, more exactly, 199, are so far independent in their means that they are not diverted from their academic work by any other occupation. But there are no less than 391, or about two-thirds of the whole, who keep their place in the University almost in all cases by one form or another of paid employment, added on through the whole or a portion of the year to the burden of their studies. 240 were thus engaged in extraneous work both during the session and throughout the summer; 135, without doubling their task during the session, are variously employed through the summer; the remaining 16 join a business to their academic pursuits in the winter. The intending lawyers are clerks in writers' offices; the teachers to be and others are employed in teaching, and some as pupils in the training colleges. Some youths are exercised in mission work. 'The remainder,' says Professor Ramsay, 'are distributed over every conceivable kind of employment. In the Humanity Class this year are included joiners, miners, brassfounders, bootmakers, tailors, grocers, engineers, shipbuilders, drapers, stewards of steamers, a toll-keeper (who may, I suppose, well be said to levy toll first of all upon himself), a pocketbook-maker, a blacksmith, and others. Of this statement, gentlemen, I will only say that I do not know, and hardly can conceive, one in itself more striking, more touching, or one more full of promise for the future of your country.

These facts and figures, gentlemen, present to us more than an interesting fragment of statistics, more than a case of legislative success and wise and prosperous administration. They supply a sign, and one among the most interesting signs, bearing upon the relation between the special wants of the

Modern progress and its causes.

age and the present extent and efficacy of the provision for meeting them; for the wants of this age are indeed very special and very urgent. It is a time of rapid progress; and rapid progress is in itself a good. But when the velocity is great, then, as in the physical so in the moral world, the conditions of equilibrium are more severe, and the consequences of losing it are more disastrous. The changes that have taken place among us within the compass of a generation, as to the external and material conditions of life, have been far greater changes than at any previous period of recorded history have been crowded into a similar space of time. Capital and industry, if they could be regarded as persons, and as persons who had gone to sleep fifty years back and were now suddenly awakened, would be at a loss to identify the world they remembered with the world they found. At the commencement of that period, the laws which were miscalled Protective, and which were really laws for the promotion of scarcity and the prevention of abundance, had so completely attained their purpose, that notwithstanding the growth of population and of mechanical invention, notwithstanding a few initial efforts of enlightened statesmen, never to be sufficiently commended, the exchange of British produce with the produce of other countries remained at the point where it had stood at the commencement of the century. At the close of that period the commerce of the country was multiplied fivefold. Our shipping, which at the close of the war in 1815 had amounted to two and a half million tons, and by dint of protective' fostering stood at the same figure in 1830, had in 1878 passed six and a half millions of tons, navigated at a much smaller expense per ton, and also, through the agency of steam, performing relatively to tonnage from twice to three times the amount of work. Goods, which had been used to travel from place to place at two miles an hour, now principally go at twenty. Persons who travelled at four, six, or

ten, now, at one-third or one-fourth the cost, accomplish four
times the speed. Private correspondence had been a luxury
forbidden to the less wealthy classes, for a letter from Edinburgh to London paid, I think, fifteenpence-halfpenny for each
separate piece of paper it contained; while it now passes in a
fourth part of the time for a penny or a halfpenny. Messages,
while I speak, are passing with the speed of lightning along a
thousand wires; and, further, we are cheered or threatened, as,
according to our several temperaments, the case may be regarded, with inventions of which the joint effect seems likely
to be that everybody will speak to everybody at all times
and to all places and upon all subjects. Materials and instruments of production, which nature had supplied to us
grudgingly and from a distance, are now produced at will by
art in quantities only limited by demand. But it would be
vain to attempt a complete enumeration of the changes which
—often, it must be sorrowfully confessed, in deforming the
fair face of creation—have during this wonderful period
passed upon our industry and trade. I will only sum up the
results by stating, from an able paper by Mr. Giffen of the
Statistical Department ('Recent Accumulations; Statistical
Society, January 15, 1878'), that the annual income, taxable
to Income-tax, which was 130 millions in 1813, was 571
millions in 1874–5; that the annual increment of personal
property, without allowing for capital laid out upon the soil,
is 150 millions; that the amount added in a decade is greater
than the entire amount of personal property in 1814; and
that if there had not been any property at all in the country
fifty years back, if we had then started from zero and could
have made it at the rate at which we are now making it,
nearly the whole of what we now possess would by this
time have been accumulated in that brief term of years.
A review, even upon paper, of these enormous changes
seems to make the head giddy, and suggests the need of
knowing something of their actual and probable effect upon

the entire, and especially upon the higher, destinies of man. And this the more gravely, because there is not the slightest reason to suppose that we have reached, or have even approached, the close of this great epoch of industrial and material development. It has been owing to two grand causes. The first of them has been the removal of fetters from human thought and human action by the repeal of unwise laws, which hampered and restrained at every point the interchange among men both of mental and material products. The other has been the progress of the natural sciences and the inventive arts. The first of these causes is negative; it is, speaking generally, not the doing of good so much as the undoing of mischief; and it has among other effects provided enormous scope and field for the positive action of the second cause. At this moment it can hardly be said to be an enlarging operation, for while its work in this country has very nearly been accomplished, the rest of the world is tending for the time to retrogression rather than to advance. When this folly shall have passed away, there will remain in other lands a great work to be done, a noble harvest to be reaped. To the operation of the second cause, the progress of science and inventive arts, whether here or elsewhere, it seems hard to set any limit whatever.

Material and mental growth. Let us now, therefore, attempt a more general survey from a somewhat higher point of view. The great salient feature of the age is, on a first view, the constant discovery of the secrets of nature, and the progressive subjugation of her forces to the purposes and will of man. This, however, is a view taken from the material side. If we plant ourselves at an elevation sufficient to command the prospects of the moral world, we then perceive that, as in war so in peace, the victor often succumbs inwardly to the vanquished. So Rome to Greece—

'Græcia capta ferum victorem cepit.'

So Hercules was reproached by Dejanira—

'Victorem victa succubuisse queror.'

These conquests over nature have enormously multiplied the means of enjoyment. Had that multiplication been so distributed as, either wholly or principally, to sweeten the cup of those for whom this life is habitually a life of care and labour and daily pressure in a thousand forms, it might have seemed rather to redress a painful inequality than create an excess or threaten a disturbance. We may contemplate with unmixed satisfaction that rise of wages, and that increased command of the necessaries and conveniences of life for the many which has marked our time. But this has not been the only, perhaps not the principal result of the conquests I have described. If they have done much for industry, they have done more for capital; if much for labour, more for luxury. They have enormously extended the numbers—they have, I believe, extended even the relative numbers of the leisured and wealthy classes; they have variously and vastly multiplied the incitements to gain, the avenues of excitement, the solicitations to pleasure, among those for whom all these had been, at the very least, sufficient in the more quiet and stationary times that went before. These tendencies to excess, these activities beyond the mean, have acted upon the classes that mainly govern affairs, and, what is more, that mainly form and propagate the current opinion of the day. Among them, the pursuit of material enjoyment, and of wealth as the means of it, has made a progress wholly out of proportion to any advancement they may have effected during the last quarter of a century in mental resources or pursuits. Disproportioned growth, if large in degree, is in the physical world deformity; in the moral and social world it is derangement that answers to deformity, and partakes of its nature.

Among the signs of this derangement has been the growth *A hybrid class.*

of a new class—a class unknown to the past, and one whose existence the future will have cause to deplore. It is the class of hybrid or bastard men of business, men of family, men of rank, men of titles, men gallant by courtesy and, perhaps, by nature, county gentlemen, members of both Houses of Parliament, members of various professions, generally alike in being unsuited for apprenticeship to commercial enterprise. It is made up from the scattered and less considerate members of all classes. The bond that unites them is the bond of gain; not the legitimate produce of toil by hand or brain—in most cases not fenced off from rashness, as in former times, by liability to ruinous loss in the event of failure, but to be had without the conditions which alone make pecuniary profit truly honourable. It may be said that in giving their names to speculations which they neither understand nor examine, as directors or trustees, or in other like responsible positions, these spurious representatives of British enterprise give the best of what they have. They continue not to see that this is simply true, that they are merely wanted as decoys to allure the unwary and entrap them into the subscription list. For it is a serious truth that there is a proportion of the free people inhabiting these islands who are ever ready to accept merely decorative names as guarantees for the soundness of a project, without the presence or the presumption of knowledge, or skill, or judgment, or proved and hardy integrity. I do not enter into the question whether and how this social and economic nuisance, with all the loss, discredit, and demoralization it entails, may be abated, but I note its existence as a salient proof that we live in a time when, among the objects offered to the desire of a man, wealth and the direct accompaniments and fruits of wealth have of late years augmented their always dangerous preponderance.

The pursuit of wealth and of knowledge. In all times, and all places, and all stages of its existence, it is the office of the University, as such, to embody a protest and to work a comprehensive and powerful machinery, in rebuke and in abatement of this preponderance. In all times,—ancient, mediæval, modern; in all places,—in Athens and Alexandria, in the Padua and Bologna, the Paris and Oxford of the Middle Ages, and in the German, Scottish, English, and all other Universities of to-day; in all stages of their existence,—for the ancients do not seem to have had more than the rudiment of our University, which it was reserved for the Christian period to bring up to its full maturity and development. It is not from this source that the age has derived its tendencies to excess in wealth-making pursuits and in material enjoyment. This is the home of hard labour, and of modest emoluments. Here, undoubtedly, it is that many a Scottish youth obtains the means of advancement in life; but the improvement in his condition, to which they lead him, flows from the improvement of his mind, from the exercise and expansion of his powers to perceive and to reflect, from the formation of habits of attention and application, from a bias given to character in favour of cultivating intelligence for its own sake, as well as for the sake of the direct advantages it brings. These advantages lie in the far future, and do not administer to the feverish excitement which are of necessity, in the various degrees, incidental to the pursuits of the modern commercial world. The habits of mind formed by Universities are founded in sobriety and tranquillity. They help to settle the spirit of a man firmly upon the centre of gravity; they tend to self-command, self-government, and that genuine self-respect which has in it nothing of mere self-worship, for it is the reverence that each man ought to feel for the nature that God has given him, and for the laws of that nature. It is one thing to plough and sow with the expectation of the harvest in due season when the year shall have come round; it is another to ransack the ground in a gold-field with the heated hope and craving for vast returns to-morrow or to-day. All honour, then, to the University, because, while it prepares young men in the most useful manner for the practical purposes of life, it embodies a protest against the excessive

dominion of worldly appetites, and supplies a powerful agency
for neutralizing the specific dangers of this age.

*Legal studies
and their
tendencies.*

How, then, gentlemen, studying at Glasgow, how are you
best to turn to account your opportunities ?   Many of you are
preparing yourselves with defined intentions for one or other of
the three great professions best known to our fathers,—I mean
medicine, the law, and the ministry of religion.   Others have
other views, already fixed, or have not yet fixed their views.
But let me say a few words on these.   The medical and legal
professions are not likely to be displaced or menaced by any of
the mutations of this or a future century.   The demand for
their services lies deep, if not in the order of nature,
yet in the actual constitution of things, as the one is
founded upon dissension and the other on disease.   Nay, this
demand is likely to be a growing demand, for with material
and economic progress, the relations of property become
more complex and diversified ; and as the pressure and unrest of
life increase with accelerated movement of mind and body, the
nervous system which connects mind and body acquires greater
intensity ; and new susceptibilities of disorder and suffering,
giving occasion for new problems and new methods of treatment, are continually developed.   As the god Terminus was
an early symbol of the first form of property, so the word law
is the venerable emblem of the union of mankind in society.
Its personal agents are hardly less important to the general
welfare than its written or customary prescriptions ; for neither
statute, nor Parliament, nor press is more essential to liberty
than an absolutely free-spoken bar.   Considered as a mental
training, the profession of the bar is probably in its kind
the most perfect and thorough of all professions.   For this
very reason, perhaps, it has something like an intellectual
mannerism of its own, and admits of being tempered with
advantage by other pursuits lying beyond its own precincts, as
well as by large intercourse with the world,—by studies not only
such as those of art and poetry, which have beauty for their

objects, but such as history, which opens the whole field of human motive as well as act, which is not tied in the same degree to position and immediate issues, and which, introducing wider laws of evidence, gives far more scope for suspense of judgment, or, in other words, more exact conformity or more close approximation between the mind and the truth which is in all things its proper object. We all appreciate that atmosphere of freedom which within the legal precinct is constantly diffused by a healthy competition. The non-legal world, indeed, is sometimes sceptical as to limitations which prevail within the profession itself. It is sometimes inclined also to think that of all professions its action is in these modern times most shrouded in something of technicality and mystery, which seriously encumber the transaction of affairs, and in some cases tend to exclude especially the less wealthy classes from the benefits which it is the glory of law to secure for civilised man in the easy establishment and full security of rights.

But these are questions which, in more tranquil times, will *The medical* find their own adjustment; and while I have hinted to youths *profession.* intending to follow this noble profession the expediency of tempering it with collateral studies, I congratulate them on the solidity of the position they are to hold. No change, practical or speculative, social or political or economic, has any terrors for the profession of the law. The medical profession offers at the present time, even to the uninstructed eye, an object of perhaps yet livelier interest. Here, indeed, much is changing, but all in the direction of advance. The dominant activity of the age, addressed to conquests over nature, continually enlarges the knowledge and the apparatus lying at the command of the physician and the surgeon. There was a time when the writer of *Gil Blas* could represent his hero, who had been accidentally taken ill in an insignificant town, as having easily and rapidly recovered, because by good fortune there was no doctor in the place. Such a jest, good at the time, such a weapon, if any novelist could now think of using it, would slay nothing but his own reputation.　The medical art is now universally recognised as having learned much for the benefit of mankind, and as honestly and resolutely set on learning more.　While becoming more learned, it has also grown more intelligible; for the physician, falling back more and more on the duty of interpreting and assisting nature, more and more (so far as I know) assumes a ground common to him and to his patient, and obtains in consequence more and more an intelligent and sympathetic obedience.　It is no wonder if, simultaneously with all this, the social standing of the profession has come to be more worthy of its character and object; and that equality with the other cultivated or leisured classes, which was only granted a century and a half or two centuries ago to the chiefs of the profession, and that in one only of its branches, may now be said to be in the enjoyment of its members generally and as of right.　It is not, however, only on the physical side that the great medical profession for which Glasgow is rearing five hundred, and the sister University of Edinburgh over twelve hundred students, has gained, and is gaining ground.　The constantly growing complexity of life appears to bring with it a constantly growing complexity of disease.　The pace at which we live is quickened; the demands, both on thought and on emotion, are heightened without any corresponding increase of natural force in the organs or faculties which are to meet these demands.　While the mind asks so much more of the frail flesh, its halting partner, and when so many infirm lives are through skill preserved, which would formerly have lapsed in early death, immense as is the advantage of a more widely diffused sufficiency of food, it has, I believe, been matter of argument whether on the whole the physical structure of our race is in course of improvement or of decline; but, however that may be, it can hardly be matter of doubt that the enhancement of interaction between the body and the mind both enlarges and elevates the province of the medical man, brings him more and more into the inner sanctuary of our nature, quickens their search for expedients by which he may even

> ' Minister to a mind diseased,'

and gives to his art more and more frequently the character of a joint process operating on the seen and the unseen parts of our compound nature. If this be so, medicine must more and more come to be not an art only, but also a philosophy; and in this nursery of its future sages I give hearty utterance to the wish that the medical students of this University may render themselves worthy of the growing influence and widened scope of their profession, not alone by their technical accomplishments, but by the strength of their characters and the elevation of their aims.

I turn, gentlemen, to the case of another great profession. *The Christian ministry.* Still availing myself of the information which has been supplied to me by the Principal and by Professor Ramsay, I estimate that more than an eighth part of the students of Glasgow, and possibly even a larger proportion of the aggregate numbers in the four Scottish Universities, are preparing themselves for the Christian ministry. The total number of this section may perhaps safely be taken at seven hundred, intended to supply recruits for a body which, in Scotland, consists of between three and four thousand, and which has also missionary ramifications abroad. The University of Glasgow is, I believe, strictly a Christian University. It is no part of my business in this place to take account of differences which lie within the compass of that venerable and imperishable name. But it is, I think, in every way appropriate to an occasion when we are considering the great interests and purposes of the institution, to have some regard to that which is the highest interest and purpose of them all, and to include this profession in my cursory review. I am glad, then, to infer with confidence from the figures that have been before me, that in Scotland there is no lack of youths who take the business of a Christian ministry for their vocation in life. This is not so in all lands at the present time. In two great countries, Germany and France, there is a great decline in the body of young men candidates for ordination, either in numbers, or in intellectual standard, or in both. I do not speak inclusively of any one communion, but I refer to both Roman and Protestant. The latest intimation I have seen on the subject has regard to Holland; and in that country I find, on what appears to be excellent authority, that one-seventh of the Protestant cures are vacant for want of persons to fill them. There were, some time back, similar apprehensions on this score in England, at least in the Established Church of England, amidst the desolating convulsions which it has undergone; but I think these have diminished or passed away.

Christianity and scepticism.

There are, however, traces of a latent feeling there and elsewhere, either that Divine interests are secondary or unreal, in comparison with those of the visible and experimental world, or that the difficulties belonging to subjects of religion are such that to handle them effectually, and with a sound conscience, is hopeless. Gentlemen, at my years, as one who has seen much of the age, both in its practical and in its speculative contentions, I am desirous to bear my testimony in the face of this young assembly, full of the 'promise and potency' of the future, on behalf of the intellectual dignity of the Christian ministry. No doubt it is a time of trial, but this is the very feature by which that dignity is most enhanced. No doubt it is a time when you have not only to contend against assailants from without, respectable alike by talents and research, and on the yet higher ground of character, but have also to discharge the still more arduous duty of humbly but steadily reconsidering from within the forms of the great Christian tradition in which you have respectively been bred. It is a time in which we have many things to learn, and some things to unlearn. All this means difficulty, toil, misgiving, the hesitation of many, the falling back of some. But depend upon it, gentlemen, those who boast or think that the intellectual battle against Christianity has been fought and won are reckoning without their host. If it had, then I for one should be disposed to agree with them in the further proposition that no permanent reliance could be placed upon the multitude of uninstructed numerical adhesions, or upon integrity of institutions and unbroken continuity of rite. Thought is the citadel. But in my belief human thought is not yet divorced either from the vital essence of Christianity or from the cardinal facts and truths which are to that essence as the body to the soul; and if and when that divorce arrives, with it will come the commencement and the pledge of radical decay in the civilisation of the world. Christianity, gentlemen, even in its sadly imperfect development, is as matter of fact at the head of the world. As the first existing power, it rules the world; and of all the more or less noisy pretenders who, as if it were an Ottoman despotism, are prematurely disputing for the succession, there is not one which has given evidence either of being capable or of being accepted for the place it has so long held. The work, indeed, of defence, under the conditions to which I have referred, is truly a grave one, for it involves something of what is called in common contentions a change of front in face of the enemy. But as the difficulties, so the aids and the resources are more than meet the eye. A deliberate survey of the field convinces me that at no time have richer and more fruitful opportunities been offered to the best minds among us for the investigation and maintenance of truth in that transcendent region which determines the relation between this material life and the unseen, between this transitory life and the imperishable.

I am tempted, gentlemen, further to offer you, with a daring which I hope may be thought excusable, a general observation on the frame of mind in which we all—and, most of all, those specially engaged—should meet that conflict or contact with opposing forces, which in this day no thoughtfully educated *A cross-examination of doubt.*

man can hope wholly to escape. No defence is to be found in timidity, but much defence is to be found in circumspection. What we have perhaps most to complain of is a perceptible rapidity of question trial, and summary condemnation, which is perhaps as far removed from reason as is the grossest of the superstitions it condemns. There is a kind of steeplechase philosophy in vogue; sometimes it is specialism that assumes the honours of universal knowledge, and makes short cuts to its conclusion. Sometimes it is that the knowledge of external nature is, by one of the strangest of solecisms, thought to convey a supreme capacity for judging questions which belong entirely to the sphere of moral action and of moral needs. All this suggests that abnormal causes are in some degree at work; that besides research and the great modern art of literary criticism, and a useful reaction against usurping traditions, there is, so to speak, something of an epidemic in the air. We have need to examine whether there does not creep about among us a predisposition to disturbance, a preference for negation, and something of a mental levity, which are more or less included in the term scepticism—a temper to be discouraged, a frame of mind broadly distinguished from what Dante has sanctioned and Tennyson has called 'honest doubt,' as well as from a hearty allegiance to truth essential to us all, and a determination, so to speak, even to hate father and mother for its sake. If this be so, what I suggest, gentlemen, is, in a manner, to meet scepticism with scepticism, a wanton scepticism with a scepticism more legitimate. Put it on its trial; allow none of its assumptions; compel it to expound its formulæ; do not let it move a step except with proof in its hand; bring it front to front with history; even demand that it shall show the positive elements with which it proposes to replace the mainstays it seems bent on withdrawing from the fabric of modern society. When it alleges that our advanced morality (such as it is) is really the work, not of Christianity, but of civilisation, require it to show cause why this advanced morality has never grown up except under the ægis of the Gospel—why the old civilisations were one and all smitten with decay, and degenerated in moral tissue even before they lost their intellectual vigour. When you are assured that marriage and the laws of purity are safe, whatever happens, ask how it was that the ancients in these capital respects marched continually downwards, and that only in Christian times and lands have these laws come to and maintained authority. If we are told that morality does not require the artificial supports of belief in God and in a future life, since it can be shown to be founded in the dictates of our nature, may we not reasonably inquire whether it is, indeed, now endowed with strength in such superabundance that it can afford to part with the most operative portion, or with any portion whatever of its supports ? If we are taught that it is vain to think of knowing God, since such a conception is beyond our grasp, inquire of the teachers how much there is of our knowledge which is more than an account of probabilities, or a contact with isolated parts and mere exteriors, and whether, if we will accept nothing as knowledge but what is absolute and perfect knowledge, we shall not bring the catalogue of what we know dangerously near to zero. Again, it is urged, with great plausibility, that a religion built upon or expressed in a book, or creed, or formula of written doctrine, cannot be a permanent religion, since all the forms of human language must vary with the advancing thought of man. I think we may ask, in reply, whether that is not by far too large a generalization. No doubt there are branches of knowledge which have undergone, and may undergo, total revolution. But there are others which do not, and among these are the great constructive elements of the moral law. Nor can it be shown that the very phrases in which moral and religious wisdom found its highest expression thousands of years ago, have ceased in any degree to fit the thoughts which they convey. Our inheritance from former times would be but meagre if our condition were such that at every point, before we could be sure of the substance, we must re-cast or re-try the form. No doubt there is much in our thought and more in our language which, like the butterfly, is 'born to flutter and decay.' But that no part even of our applied speech is permanently adequate to our prospective needs has yet to be shown. Proverbs do not grow old, but seem as a rule to keep their freshness through an unbounded period. Without touching the domain of Scripture, and the words of our Lord, I take leave to say that the oldest of the creeds and hymns of Christendom have lost no part of their hold upon the Christian mind and heart as to the forms of their expression, and are rarely, if ever, challenged except by those whose objection is not limited to the form, but pierces into the substance. In this rapid and slight enumeration I purposely have avoided other important formulæ of what, in a phrase of the sixteenth century, I may call the 'new learning.' They are those which belong to the domain of external nature; and I have no acquaintance with that domain which would warrant my touching upon it before this assembly. Earlier in this address I spoke, gentlemen, of the great conflict between material and mental interests which marks our time. I have now made bold to touch upon the twin controversy which it has for a second distinguishing characteristic — that great controversy of belief as to which there are those who think that the present assault, far from being destined to final triumph, is in large measure a sign of a mental movement, unsteady through extreme rapidity, but destined perhaps in the wise counsels of Providence to elevate and strengthen by severely testing processes the religion which it seeks to over-throw. In the meantime, I would commend to you as guides in this controversy, truth, charity, diligence, and reverence, which indeed may be called the four cardinal virtues of all controversies, be they what they may.

The teaching profession.   In dealing with professions, gentlemen, I have not particu-larly referred to the new profession, as it may well be called, of the teacher. In other times, our fathers were content to leave this important office, like some other great social functions, to be learned, not by apprenticeship or theory, but by practice. In the results of the old method there was much imperfection, and I am afraid no small brutality. What we awkwardly call social science is a great growth of the day we live in; and the first place among its achievements appears to be due to the organization of teaching. We must rejoice that, long unduly depressed, this weighty avocation has now, at least as regards male teachers, and in principle, if not in detail, found its level. And I congratulate the teacher upon this, that though his office is laborious, yet, in Scotland at least, he works upon a willing subject. And if he is strong enough to have some energies yet available after his heavy duties of routine have been discharged, he is happy in his opportunities of knowledge and experience, for he is always in contact with human nature and the human mind. This brings me, gentlemen, to a single remark which, parting from the subject of professions, I will offer upon studies. I will offer it in the generally perilous form of a general proposition. I submit to you, gentlemen, that man is the crown of the visible creation, and that studies upon man—studies in the largest sense of humanity, studies conversant with his nature, his works, his duties, and his destinies—are the highest of all studies. That as the human form is the groundwork of the highest training in art, so those mental pursuits are the highest which have man, considered at large, for their object.

There is one among the pursuits of what I have termed *The study of history.* humanity upon which, before I close, I would particularly remark, because it is a branch which is only now beginning in England to assume its proper place in education and in letters, and as to which I am under the impression that Scotland also may have been backward, notwithstanding its loyal care for all the records of its own olden time. Excuse me, then, gentlemen, if I return for a few moments to the subject of historical studies. These studies do not, it is true, directly subserve the purposes of any particular profession. To be a good historian does not make a man a good lawyer, or a good physician, or a good divine. They must, therefore, when they are put upon their trial, or when the question lies between them and some other study, be judged not according to their immediate effect in enlarging the apparatus of professional knowledge, but by their immediate effect upon the man himself in his general aptitudes, and by their mediate effect through these upon his professional competency. They can only then be recommended, gentlemen, subject to conditions. The law of necessity, the limitation of time, may not allow us to widen our course of application so far as to include them. Again, they can only be recommended in the sense of a large, not of a narrow utility. But in so far as a happy lot may give you liberty of choice, I would urge and entreat you, gentlemen, to give a place, and that no mean place, in the scheme of your pursuits, to the study of human history. The several kinds of knowledge need to be balanced one with another, somewhat as the several limbs of the body need a proportioned exercise in order to secure a healthy and equable development. The knowledge of the heavenly bodies, the knowledge of the planet on which we live, of the qualities of its material elements, and of all its living orders, valuable, nay, invaluable as it may be shown to be, is nevertheless knowledge wholly inferior in rank to the knowledge of the one living order that beyond measure transcends all the rest, and that has, for perhaps its most distinctive characteristic, this, that it possesses a history.

History is among the most potent instruments of human education.

This history is among the most potent and effective of all the instruments of human education. It introduces us to forms of thought and action which are infinitely diversified. It gives us far larger materials of judgment upon human conduct, and upon the very springs of action, than any present experience can confer. Allow me to observe to you, gentlemen, that judgment upon human conduct is perhaps the most arduous among all the tasks to which the mind of man can be addressed. It is a work the perfect performance of which, I apprehend, surpasses all our powers. To some it may sound like a paradox, but I believe it to be the simple truth, that no man, and no combination of men, is capable of weighing action in the scales of absolute justice, any more than the greatest artists that ever lived in Greece were competent to express absolute beauty by the force of their imaginations and the labour of their hands. But as in the case of the artist the constant effort to reach an unattainable perfection availed to produce approximations at least to ideal excellence, so in the case of the historian the steady and loyal endeavour to be absolutely just and true in the lofty task of passing judgment will keep the head steady and the foot sure in many a danger-ous path by bog and precipice, and will give mighty aid in raising the mind of man to its best capacity for the noblest of all its operations, the search and discernment of the truth. But there is one peculiar note of the consummate historic student, nay the historic reader, which deserves beyond all others to be pressed upon your attention, and in which he partakes of the highest quality of the historian himself. Let us ask ourselves what is that highest quality ? Of him who betakes himself to the writing of history, to the telling us what man and the world have been in other times, much indeed is required. He must, for example, be learned, upright, exact, methodical, and clear. This is much, but it is not enough. The question remains behind—By what standard is the child of the present to judge the children of the past ? Our mental habits are shaped according to the age in which we live, our thought is saturated with its colour. But, in like manner, those who went before us in the long procession of our race, took the form and pressure of their own time. Therefore, they must not be judged according to the form and pressure of ours. Those who in other days denounced death against idolators, or those who inflicted it upon heretics, must not be sentenced without taking into view the enormous difference in mental habits produced by two opposed religious atmospheres,—the one, in which dogma was never questioned; the other, in which doubt, denial, and diverse apprehension so prevail as greatly to bewilder and unsettle the ordinary mind. Charles the First must not be tried by the rules of a constitutional monarchy, now so familiar to our thoughts and language. Queen Elizabeth, working under the terrible conditions of her epoch and her position, must not be judged by the standards which will be applicable to Queen Victoria. The great Popes of the Middle Ages, especially the two greatest of them all, Gregory the Seventh and Innocent the Third, must not be denounced as aggressors upon civil authority, without bearing in mind that in those days the guardians of law and right were oftentimes the glaring examples of violence, lawlessness, and fraud. The historian, and in his measure the reader of the historian, must lift himself out of what is now called his own environment, and by effort of mind assume the point of view and think under the entire conditions which belonged to the person he is calling to account. In so far as he fails to do this, he perverts judgment by taking his seat on the tribunal loaded with irrelevant and with misleading matter. But in so far as he succeeds, he not only discharges a duty of equity, but he acquires by degrees a suppleness and elasticity of mental discernment which enable him to separate, even in complicated subject-matter, between the wine and the lees, between the grain and the chaff, between the relevant matter in a controversy—which, when once ascertained and set in order, easily leads up to a right judgment—and the by-paths of prejudice, ignorance, and passion, which lead away from it. The historical mind is the judicial mind in the exactness of its balance; it is the philosophic mind in the comprehensiveness and refinement of its view. Nor is there

any toiler in the wide field of thought who more than the
historian requires to eschew what is known in trade by the
homely but expressive phrase of 'scamping' his work. He
must, if only for his own sake, and to give himself a chance
of holding a place in the kindly memory of men, bestow upon
his work that ample expenditure of labour of which Macaulay,
independently of all his other brilliant gifts, has given to this
age a superlative and rare example. In him we have an
illustration of a vital truth; in mental work the substance
and the form are so allied that they cannot be severed. The
form is the vehicle through which the work of the substance
is to pass; if the point of the arrow be too blunt, the strength
of the arm is vain; and every student, in whatever branch,
should carry with him the simple specific of recollecting the
well-known saying of Dr. Johnson, who, when he was asked
how he had attained to his extraordinary excellence in con-
versation, replied that, whatever he had had to say, he had
constantly taken pains to say it in the best manner that he
could.

Yet once more, gentlemen, in a recent lecture on Galileo, *The dangers of*
Professor Jack has said with great truth and force, ' that *an exclusive*
pursuit.
greatness is scarcely compatible with a narrow concentration
of intellect to one family of subjects.' I remember when the
late Sir James Simpson, conversing on some extremely small
human skulls, which had then recently been uncovered in the
Orkneys, and which had been treated as belonging to some
pre-Celtic and inferior race, observed that exclusive devotion
to one pursuit and one narrow round of ideas is known to
give contracted skulls in many cases. It is difficult, perhaps,
for those to whom one pursuit and one set of subjects are to
be their daily bread, to know how far they may with safety
indulge in collateral studies. But there can hardly be a
doubt as to the benefit of these, if they can be had. An
absolute singleness of pursuit almost means a mind always in

one attitude, an eye that regards every object, however many-sided, from one point of view — an intellectual dietary beginning and ending with one article. Good sense and modesty obviate a multitude of mischiefs, but the exclusiveness of which I now speak is in itself prone to serious evils. It loses the benefit of the side-lights which each of the kingdoms of knowledge cast upon every other. It disposes each man to exaggerate the force and value of his own particular attainment, and perhaps therewith his own importance. It deprives the mind of the refreshment which is healthfully offered by alternation of labour, and of the strength as well as the activity to be gained by allowing varied subjects to evoke and put in action its wonderfully varied powers.

Conclusion.   So much, gentlemen, for your future callings and your actual studies. As to the temper in which you should set about them, you have little need of exhortation, and my closing words under this head shall be few. Be assured that every one of you, without exception, has his place and vocation on this earth, and that it rests with himself to find it. Do not believe those who too lightly say that nothing succeeds like success; effort, gentlemen, honest, manful, humble effort, succeeds by its reflected action upon character, especially in youth, better than success. Success, indeed, too easily and too early gained, not seldom serves, like winning the first throw of the dice, to blind and stupefy. Get knowledge all you can; and the more you get, the more you breathe upon its nearer heights their invigorating air and enjoy the widening prospect, the more you will know and feel how small is the elevation you have reached in comparison with the immeasurable altitudes that yet remain unscaled. Be thorough in all you do, and remember that, though ignorance often may be innocent, pretension is always despicable. Quit you like men, be strong, and the exercise of your strength to-day will give you more strength to-morrow. Work onwards, and work upwards ; and may the blessing of the Most High soothe your cares, clear your vision, and crown your labours with reward.

Loud cheers, again and again renewed, crowned the conclusion of the address, the Lord Rector repeatedly bowing his acknowledgments.

Sections I and II of Appendix to
POLITICAL SPEECHES IN SCOTLAND
March and April 1880

W. E. GLADSTONE

APPENDIX.

———

I

ADDRESS ISSUED BY MR. GLADSTONE TO THE ELECTORS OF MIDLOTHIAN.

GENTLEMEN,—I heartily rejoice that the time has at length arrived when you will be called upon to declare by your votes whether you approve or whether you condemn the manner in which the Government of this great Empire has during these last years been carried on. This, gentlemen, is well; although by a striking departure from established practice, which must cause great inconvenience, a session opened by Her Majesty, with the regular announcement of its annual work, is, without the occurrence of any Parliamentary difficulty, for the first time in our history to be interrupted after a few weeks by a dissolution.

In the electioneering address which the Prime Minister has issued, an attempt is made to work upon your fears by dark allusions to the repeal of the Union and the abandonment of the Colonies. Gentlemen, those who endangered the Union with Ireland were the party that maintained there an alien Church, an unjust land law, and franchises inferior to our own ; and the true supporters of the Union are those who firmly uphold the supreme authority of Parliament, but exercise that authority to bind the three nations by the indissoluble tie of liberal and equal laws.

As to the Colonies, Liberal Administrations set free their

trade with all the world, gave them popular and responsible government, undertook to defend Canada with the whole strength of the Empire, and organized the great scheme for uniting the several settlements of British North America into one Dominion, to which, when we quitted office in 1866, it only remained for our successors to ask the ready assent of Parliament. It is by these measures that the Colonies have been bound in affection to the Empire, and the authors of them can afford to smile at baseless insinuations.

Gentlemen, the true purpose of these terrifying insinuations is to hide from view the acts of the Ministry, and their effect upon the character and condition of the country. To these I will now begin to draw your attention. With threescore years and ten upon my head, I feel the irksomeness of the task. But in such a crisis no man should shrink from calls which his duty may make and his strength allow. At home, the Ministers have neglected legislation, aggravated the public distress by continual shocks to confidence, which is the life of enterprise, augmented the public expenditure and taxation for purposes not merely unnecessary but mischievous, and plunged the finances, which were handed over to them in a state of singular prosperity, into a series of deficits unexampled in modern times. Of these deficits it is now proposed to meet only a portion, and to meet it partly by a new tax on personal property, and partly by the sacrifice of the whole Sinking Fund, to which, five years ago, we were taught to look for the systematic reduction, with increased energy and certainty, of the National Debt.

Abroad they have strained, if they have not endangered, the prerogative, by gross misuse, and have weakened the Empire by needless wars, unprofitable extensions, and unwise engagements, and have dishonoured it in the eyes of Europe by filching the island of Cyprus from the Porte under a treaty clandestinely concluded in violation of the Treaty of Paris, which formed part of the international law of Christendom.

If we turn from considerations of principle to material results, they have aggrandized Russia, lured Turkey on to her dismemberment, if not her ruin, replaced the Christian population of Macedonia under a debasing yoke, and loaded India with the cost and danger of a prolonged and unjustifiable war, while they have at the same time augmented her taxation and curtailed her liberties.

At this moment we are told of other secret negotiations with Persia, entailing further liabilities without further strength; and from day to day, under a Ministry called as if in mockery Conservative, the nation is perplexed with fear of change.

As to the domestic legislation of the future, it is in the election address of the Prime Minister a perfect blank. No prospect is opened to us of effectual alteration in the Land Laws, of better security for occupiers, of the reform and extension of local government throughout the three kingdoms, of a more equal distribution of political franchises, or of progress in questions deeply affecting our social and moral condition.

It seems, then, that as in the past, so in the future, you will look with more confidence to the Liberal party for the work of domestic improvement, although the inheritance which the present Administration will leave to its successors threatens to be one of difficulty and embarrassment without parallel. It is true that you are promised the advantage of ' presence, not to say ascendency,' in the councils of Europe. The word ascendency, gentlemen, is best known to us by its baneful connection with the history of Ireland.

I must assert the co-equal rights of independent and allied Powers. But in the mouth of the present Ministry the claim is little less than ridiculous. You may judge of our present ascendency in Europe from our ascendency in the councils of Turkey, where we recently demanded the dismissal of a Minister, who has not only been retained in office, but selected for special honours.

There is, indeed, an ascendency in European councils to which Great Britain might reasonably aspire, by steadily sustaining the character of a Power no less just than strong; attached to liberty and law; jealous of peace, and therefore opposed to intrigue and aggrandizement, from whatever quarter they may come; jealous of honour, and therefore averse to the clandestine engagements which have marked our two latest years. To attain a moral and envied ascendency such as this, is indeed a noble object for any Minister or any Empire.

You have, then, gentlemen, great issues before you. The majority of the House of Commons, and all the members of that majority, have, by their unqualified support of the Government, fully taken over upon themselves the responsibility of its acts. If the constituencies are well pleased with the results which after six years have been attained, they have only to return again a similar majority, which will do its best to secure to them the like for six years more. But let no individual voter who supports at the election a member of that majority conceal from himself the fact that he is taking on himself both what has been done already, and what may be done by the same agency hereafter.

I have not a doubt that the County of Midlothian will nobly discharge its share of the general duty, and I have the honour to remain, gentlemen, your most obedient and faithful servant,   W. E. GLADSTONE.

LONDON, *March* 11, 1880.

II

MR. GLADSTONE'S ADDRESSES ON ELECTION
AND RE-ELECTION.

THE following address was issued by Mr. Gladstone upon his election :—

TO THE ELECTORS OF MIDLOTHIAN.

GENTLEMEN,—Contending against many influences which we think misguided, and against the illegitimate influence of spurious votes, you have, by your spontaneous efforts, more than fulfilled all the expectations with which you invited me to come among you, and have achieved a victory which had already told by anticipation, and which will now further tell by direct example, upon the course of the elections.

That course, however, has from the first day of the contests been unambiguous ; and the party, which termed itself the Constitutional party, the patriotic party, the country party, and the national party, has now seen the NATION rise up and shatter at a stroke the fabric of its power.

There is yet, indeed, much to complete. The constituencies generally, and those of Scotland in particular, will, I am persuaded, end in the same spirit as that in which they have begun.

On the whole, however, gentlemen, and as to the main issue, the country at large has already spoken ; the fight is fought and won.

Since this is so, I gladly, and as far as depends on me, once for all desist from any further reference to that indictment against the policy of the existing Administration which, encouraged by your patience, I have laboriously endeavoured to place before you. To arrest mischief has been my only object. We can well dispense with exultation in the hour of victory. Personally long engaged in the hottest of the conflict, I rejoice not only in the prospect of good to be accomplished by the accession of the Liberal leaders to power, but in the cessation of a controversy always on the verge of bitterness.

The efforts of the party, which now seems likely to attain the full measure of its predominance, will, I trust, be steadily and temperately addressed towards establishing the external policy of this country upon the lines of peace, justice, equal right, and sympathy with freedom; and towards the direction of its internal Government and legislation in the methods and the spirit which, during the last half-century, have done so much to relieve the people, to gain respect for the laws, to strengthen the foundations of the Throne, and to consolidate the structure of this great and noble Empire.

To assist in this work to the utmost of my limited power will be, gentlemen, the best and only return that I can make for the confidence which you have given me with a generosity I never can forget, and amidst tokens of enthusiasm which have made this election memorable even in the annals of Scotland.—I have the honour to be, gentlemen, your faithful and grateful servant,

W. E. GLADSTONE.

EDINBURGH, *April* 5, 1880.

MR. GLADSTONE issued the following address of thanks for his re-election :—

TO THE ELECTORS OF MIDLOTHIAN.

GENTLEMEN, — I offer you my grateful thanks for that renewal of your confidence which you have been pleased to signify by my re-election to Parliament.

Your electoral victory is now completed by the accomplishment of that change of Ministry which has been consequent upon the General Election. Looking back upon the means by which the triumph was achieved in the metropolitan county of Scotland, I desire to render an emphatic testimony alike to their purity, their efficiency, and their completeness. The Parochial Committees, themselves the result of spontaneous and energetic conviction, and taking account of the known opinions of the electors in preference to building upon supposed promises, the doubtful fruit of importunity, ascertained the ground with an extraordinary accuracy, and made clear to us from the first what our opponents only discovered when too late. I have therefore great pleasure in interweaving with my thanks to the constituency at large my special and warm acknowledgments for the generous and confiding address which has been presented to me by the Executive Committee. The members of that committee will agree with me that the time for words has gone by, and the time for the beginnings of action is now come.

Of the political professions which I made among you before the General Election, I have only to say that they have now become, in their general sense and spirit, honourable engagements, which I shall do my best, as occasion offers, to redeem.

I have the honour to be, gentlemen, your obedient and grateful servant,

W. E. GLADSTONE.

10 DOWNING STREET, WHITEHALL,
May 8, 1880.